War and Post-war Environmental Impact

WAR AND POST-WAR ENVIRONMENTAL IMPACT

Dr. Bimal Chandra Kumar

PRASHANT PUBLISHING HOUSE
DELHI-110094

Published by :
Prashant Publishing House
C-34, 28 Foota Road, Gali-3,
West Karwal Nagar, Delhi-110094
Phone : 011-22963970, Mob. : 9810396373
e-mail.: prashantpublishinghouse@gmail.com

War and Post-war Environmental Impact

First Published 2015

ISBN 978-93-80565-51-4

PRINTED IN INDIA
Published by Mr. R.K. Jha M/s Prashant Publishing House and Published at H.S. Offset House Press, Delhi.

Preface

The environmental impact of war focuses on the modernization of warfare and its increasing effects on the environment. Scorched earth methods have been used for much of recorded history. However, methods of modern warfare cause far greater devastation on theenvironment. The progression of warfare from chemical weapons to nuclear weapons has increasingly created stress on ecosystems and the environment. Specific examples of the environmental impact of war include: World War I, World War II, the Vietnam War, the Rwandan Civil War, and the Gulf War.

Flooding can be used as scorched earth policy through using water to render land unusable. It can also be used to prevent the movement of enemy combatants. During theSecond Sino-Japanese War, dykes on the Yellow and the Yangtze Rivers were breached to halt the advance of Japanese forces. Also during the Siege of Leiden in 1573 the dykes were breached to halt the advance of Spanish forces. During Operation Chastise in Germany during WW2 the Eder and Sorpe river dams were bombed flooding a large area and halting industrial manufacture used by the Germans in the war effort.

The nuclear bomb exploded over Hiroshima had an explosive power of about 13 kilotonnes, denoted 13kt. One kt is the equivalent of one thousand tonnes (of one thousand kilogrammes each) of chemical explosives. The Hiroshima bomb was an enriched uranium fission bomb and the Nagasaki bomb of 21kt was a plutonium fission bomb. Much greater explosive power can be obtained by using an enriched uranium fission explosion as a trigger to cause nuclear fusion in a mixture of lithium and deuterium (heavy hydrogen). This is the thermonuclear, fusion, hydrogen or H-bomb. Unenriched uranium is often put around the fusion bomb to absorb emitted neutrons and cause further fissions and thus increase explosive power. This is the standard fission-fusion-fission bomb, whose explosive power is usually measured in megatonnes (denoted Mt), with 1Mt equal to 1000kt. The largest atmospheric nuclear explosion was one by the Soviet Union in 1961, of about 60Mt yield.

War and military activities have obvious detrimental impacts on the environment. Weaponry, troop movements, land mines, creation and destruction of buildings, destruction of forests by defoliation or general military usage, poisoning of water sources, target-shooting of animals for practice, consumption of endangered species out of desperation etc., are just some of the examples of how both war and peacetime military activities (such as training, base construction, and transportation of weaponry) harm the environment.

The text has been modified and accumulated with the views from environmental policies of various countries and developing agencies.

—Editor

Contents

1

Environmental Impact of War

INTRODUCTION

The environmental impact of war focuses on the modernization of warfare and its increasing effects on the environment. Scorched earth methods have been used for much of recorded history. However, methods of modern warfare cause far greater devastation on theenvironment. The progression of warfare from chemical weapons to nuclear weapons has increasingly created stress on ecosystems and the environment. Specific examples of the environmental impact of war include: World War I, World War II, the Vietnam War, the Rwandan Civil War, and the Gulf War.

HISTORICAL EVENTS

World War I

During World War I, all major belligerents employed the use of weapons of mass destruction (*i.e.*, chemical weapons) against each other throughout the conflict in defiance of theHague Declaration of 1899 and Hague Convention of 1907 which outlawed the use of chemical weapons in warfare. By the time of war's end, an estimated 1.3 million casualties, including 100,000-260,000 civilians, and unknown numbers of soil erosion, deforestation, and water contamination in areas were caused by chemical weapons. Many people who were affected by chemical weapons and not having full-protective gas masks during World War I were exposed to blistering agents, cytotoxins, neurotoxins, and other chemical effects, and suffered lung cancer and serious side effects and among other things. This resulted in the deaths of tens of thousands of more people from such effects decades after World War I ended.

Atomic Bombing of Japan

The atomic bombings of Hiroshima and Nagasaki was the first use of an atomic weapon and it had a devastating effect on the built environment and on human life.

The bombs killed as many as 140,000 people in Hiroshima and 80,000 in Nagasaki by the end of 1945, roughly half on the days of the bombings. Amongst these, 15 to 20% died from injuries or illness attributed to radiation poisoning. Since then, more have died from leukemia (231 observed) and solid cancers (334 observed) attributed to exposure to radiation released by the bombs.

Vietnam, Rwanda, and the Environment

The Vietnam War had significant environmental implications by the use of chemical agents to destroy military significant vegetation. Enemies who found an advantage in remaining invisible by blending into a civilian population or by taking cover in dense vegetation forced opposing armies to target natural ecosystems. The US military used "more than 20 million gallons of herbicides, were sprayed by the US to defoliate forests, clear growth along the borders of military sites and eliminate enemy crops." The chemical agents gave the US an advantage in wartime efforts. However, the vegetation was unable to regenerate and left behind bare mudflats even years after spraying. Not only was the vegetation effected, but also the wildlife: "a mid-1980s study by Vietnamese ecologists documented just 24 species of birds and 5 species of mammals present in sprayed forests and converted areas, compared to 145-170 bird species and 30-55 kinds of mammals in intact forest." The uncertain long term effects of these herbicides are now being discovered by looking at modified species distribution patterns through habitat degradation and loss in wetland systems, which absorbed the runoff from the mainland. The Rwandan genocide led to the killing of roughly 800,000 Tutsis and moderate Hutus. The war created a massive migration of nearly 2 million Hutus fleeingRwanda over the course of just a few weeks to refugee camps in Tanzania and now modern day Democratic Republic of the Congo. This large displacement of people in refugee camps put pressure on the surrounding ecosystem. Forests were cleared in order to provide wood for building shelters and creating cooking fires: "these people suffered from harsh conditions and constituted an important threat impact to natural resources." Consequences from the conflict also included the degradation of National Parks and Reserves. The population crash in Rwanda shifted personnel and capital to other parts of the country, making it hard to protect wildlife. The loss of conservationist efforts has made it harder to educate the people of Rwanda and explain the importance of conservation for the future. In order to build a solid foundation for conservation programs, according to ecologists, social and political problems need to be solved first.

Gulf War

During the 1991 Gulf War, the Kuwaiti oil fires were a result of the scorched earth policy of Iraqi military forces retreating from Kuwait in 1991 after conquering the country but being driven out by Coalition military forces. The Gulf War oil spill, regarded as the worst oil spill in history, was caused when Iraqi forces opened valves at the Sea Island oil terminal and dumped oil from several tankers into the Persian Gulf.

Some American military personnel complained of Gulf War syndrome, typified by symptoms including immune system disorders and birth defects in their children. Whether it is due to time spent in active service during the war or for other reasons remains controversial.

ENVIRONMENTAL HAZARDS

Resources are a key source of conflict between nations: "after the end of the Cold War in particular, many have suggested that environmental degradation will exacerbate scarcities and become an additional source of armed conflict." A nation's survival depends on resources from the environment. Resources that are a source of armed conflict include territory, strategic raw materials, sources of energy, water, and food. In order to maintain resource stability, chemical and nuclear warfare have been used by nations in order to protect or extract resources, and during conflict. These agents of war have been used frequently: "about 125,000 tons of chemical agent were employed during World War I, and about 96,000 tons during the Viet-Nam conflict." Nerve gas, also known as organophosphorous anticholinesterases, was used at lethal levels against human beings and destroyed a high number of nonhuman vertebrate and invertebrate populations. However, contaminated vegetation would mostly be spared, and would only pose a threat to herbivores. The result of innovations in chemical warfare led to a broad range of different chemicals for war and domestic use, but also resulted in unforeseen environmental damage.

The progression of warfare and its effects on the environment continued with the invention of weapons of mass destruction. While today, weapons of mass destruction act as deterrents and the use of weapons of mass destruction during World War II created significant environmental destruction. On top of the great loss in human life, "natural resources are usually the first to suffer: forests and wild life animals are wiped out." Nuclear warfare imposes both direct and indirect effects on the environment. The physical destruction due to the blast or by the biospheric damage due to ionizing radiation or radiotoxicity directly effect ecosystems within the blast radius. Also, the atmospheric or geospheric disturbances caused by the weapons can lead to weather and climate changes.

Agent Orange

Agent Orange is one of the herbicides and defoliants used by the British military during the Malayan Emergency and the U.S. military in its herbicidal warfare program, Operation Ranch Hand, during the Vietnam War. An estimated 21,136,000 gal. (80 000 m^3) of Agent Orange were sprayed across South

Vietnam, exposing 4.8 million Vietnamese people to Agent Orange, and resulting in 400,000 deaths and disabilities, and 500,000 children born with birth defects. Many Commonwealth personnel who handled and/or used Agent Orange during and decades after the 1948-1960 Malayan conflict suffered from serious exposure of dioxin and Agent Orange also caused major soil erosion to areas in Malaya. An estimated 10,000 civilians and possibly insurgents in Malaya also suffered heavily from defoliant effects, though many historians likely agreed it was more than 10,000 given that Agent Orange was used on a large scale in the Malayan conflict and unlike the U.S., the British government manipulated the numbers and kept its secret very tight in fear of negative world public opinion.

Testing of Nuclear Armaments

Testing of nuclear armaments has been carried out at various places including Bikini Atoll, the Marshall Islands, New Mexico in the US, Mururoa Atoll and Maralinga in Australia.

Downwinders are individuals and communities who are exposed to radioactive contamination and/or nuclear fallout from atmospheric and/or underground nuclear weapons testing, and nuclear accidents.

Strontium 90

World War II was the deadliest conflict in human history resulting in an estimated 50 million to 85 million civilian and military casualties. The strategic bombings, the invasions, and the first use of nuclear weapons in combat had severe impacts on both the human populations and environment. The United State government studied the post-war effects of a radioactive isotope found in nuclear fallout called Strontium 90. The Atomic Energy Commission discovered that "Sr-90, which is chemically similar to calcium, can accumulate in bones and possibly lead to cancer" Sr-90 found its way into humans through the ecological food chain as fallout in the soil, was picked up by plants, further concentrated in herbivorous animals, and eventually consumed by humans.

Depleted Uranium Munitions

The use of depleted uranium in munitions is controversial because of numerous questions about potential long-term health effects. Normal functioning of the kidney, brain,liver, heart, and numerous other systems can be affected by uranium exposure, because in addition to being weakly radioactive, uranium is a toxic metal. It remains weakly radioactive because of its long half-life. The aerosol produced during impact and combustion of depleted uranium munitions can potentially contaminate wide areas around the impact sites or can be inhaled by civilians and military personnel. In a three-week period of conflict in Iraq during 2003, it was estimated over 1000 tons of depleted uranium munitions were used mostly in cities. The U.S. Department of Defense claims that no human cancer of any type has been seen as a result of exposure to either natural or depleted uranium. Yet, U.S. DoD studies using cultured cells and laboratory rodents continue to suggest the possibility of leukemogenic, genetic, reproductive, andneurological effects from chronic exposure. In addition, the UK Pensions Appeal Tribunal Service in early 2004 attributed birth defect claims from a February 1991 Gulf Warcombat veteran to depleted uranium poisoning. Also, a 2005 epidemiology review concluded: "In aggregate the human epidemiological evidence is consistent with increased risk of birth defects in offspring of persons exposed to DU."

Fossil Fuel Use

With the high degree of mechanization of the military large amounts of fossil fuels are used. Fossil fuels are a major contributor to global warming and climate change, issues of increasing concern. Access to oil resources is also a factor for instigating a war.

The United States Department of Defense (DoD) is a government body with the highest use of fossil fuel in the world. According to the 2005 *CIA World Factbook*, when compared with the consumption per country the DoD would rank 34th in the world in average daily oil use, coming in just behind Iraq and just ahead of Sweden.

Intentional Flooding

Flooding can be used as scorched earth policy through using water to render land unusable. It can also be used to prevent the movement of enemy combatants.

During theSecond Sino-Japanese War, dykes on the Yellow and the Yangtze Rivers were breached to halt the advance of Japanese forces. Also during the Siege of Leiden in 1573 the dykes were breached to halt the advance of Spanish forces. During Operation Chastise in Germany during WW2 the Eder and Sorpe river dams were bombed flooding a large area and halting industrial manufacture used by the Germans in the war effort.

SPECIFIC CASES

- 1938 Yellow River flood, created by the Nationalist Government in central China during the early stage of the Second Sino-Japanese War in an attempt to halt the rapid advance of the Japanese forces. It has been called the "largest act of environmental warfare in history".
- Beaufort's Dyke, used as a dumping ground for bombs
- Jiyeh Power Station oil spill, bombed by the Israeli Air force during the 2006 Israel-Lebanon conflict.
- Formerly Used Defense Sites, a U.S. military program which is responsible for environmental restoration
- K5 Plan, an attempt between 1985 and 1989 by the government of the People's Republic of Kampuchea to seal Khmer Rouge guerrilla infiltration routes into Cambodia, resulted in environmental degradation.

WAR AND ENVIRONMENTAL LAW

From a legal standpoint, environmental protection during times of war and military activities is addressed partially by international environmental law.

Further sources are also found in areas of law such as general international law, the laws of war, human rights law and local laws of each affected country.

ENVIRONMENTAL ISSUE

Environmental issues are harmful aspects of human activity on the biophysical environment. Environmentalism, a social andenvironmental movement that started in the 1960s, addresses environmental issues through advocacy, education and activism.

The carbon dioxide equivalent of greenhouse gases (GHG) in the atmosphere has already exceeded 400 parts per million (NOAA) (with total "long-term" GHG exceeding 455 parts per million). (Intergovernmental Panel on Climate Change Report) This level is considered a tipping point. "The amount of greenhouse gas in the atmosphere is already above the threshold that can potentially cause dangerous climate change. We are already at risk...It's not next year or next decade, it's now." Report from the UN Office for the Coordination of Humanitarian Affairs (OCHA): "Climate disasters are on the rise. Around 70 percent of disasters are now climate related – up from around 50 percent from two decades ago.

These disasters take a heavier human toll and come with a higher price tag. In the last decade, 2.4 billion people were affected by climate related disasters, compared to 1.7 billion in the previous decade. The cost of responding to disasters has risen tenfold between 1992 and 2008. Destructive sudden heavy rains, intense tropical storms, repeated flooding and droughts are likely to increase, as will the vulnerability of local communities in the absence of strong concerted action." (OCHA) "Climate change is not just a distant future threat. It is the main driver behind rising humanitarian needs and we are seeing its impact. The number of people affected and the damages inflicted by extreme weather has been unprecedented."

Types

Major current environmental issues may include climate change, pollution, environmental degradation, and resource depletion etc. The conservation movement lobbies for protection of endangered species and protection of any ecologically valuable natural areas.

Scientific Grounding

The level of understanding of Earth has increased markedly in recent times through science especially with the application of the scientific method. Environmental science is now a multi-disciplinary academic study taught and researched at many universities. This is used as a basis for addressing environmental issues.

Large amounts of data have been gathered and these are collated into reports, of which a common type is the State of the Environment publications. A recent major report was the Millennium Ecosystem Assessment, with input from 1200 scientists and released in 2005, which showed the high level of impact that humans are having on ecosystem services.

Organizations

Environmental issues are addressed at a regional, national or international level by government organizations.

The largest international agency, set up in 1972, is the United Nations Environment Programme. The International Union for Conservation of Nature brings together 83 states, 108 government agencies, 766 Non-governmental organizations and 81 international organizations and about 10,000 experts and scientists from countries around the world. International non-governmental organizations include Greenpeace, Friends of the Earth and World Wide Fund for Nature. Governments enact environmental policy and enforceenvironmental law and this is done to differing degrees around the world.

Solutions

Sustainability is the key to prevent or reduce the effect of environmental issues. There is now clear scientific evidence that humanity is living unsustainably, and that an unprecedented collective effort is needed to return human use of natural resources to within sustainable limits. For humans to live sustainably, the Earth's resources must be used at a rate at which they can be replenished.

Concerns for the environment have prompted the formation of Green parties, political parties that seek to address environmental issues. Initially these were formed in Australia, New Zealand and Germany but are now present in many other countries.

Film and Television

There are an increasing number of films being produced on environmental issues, especially on climate change and global warming. Al Gore's 2006 film *An Inconvenient Truth*gained commercial success and a high media profile.

WAR AND ENVIRONMENTAL LAW

War can heavily damage the environment, and warring countries often place operational requirements ahead of environmental concerns for the duration of the war. Some international law is designed to limit this environmental harm.

Environmental Impact of War

War and military activities have obvious detrimental impacts on the environment. Weaponry, troop movements, land mines, creation and destruction of buildings, destruction of forests by defoliation or general military usage, poisoning of water sources, target-shooting of animals for practice, consumption of endangered species out of desperation etc., are just some of the examples of how both war and peacetime military activities (such as training, base construction, and transportation of weaponry) harm the environment.

Law

From a legal standpoint, environmental protection during times of war and military activities is addressed partially by international environmental law. Further sources are also found in areas of law such as general international law, the laws of war, human rights law and local laws of each affected country. However, this article is chiefly focused on the environment and as soon as two countries are battling it out, the issue becomes one of international concern. Thus, international environmental law is the appropriate focus here. The law of armed conflict is not very well developed in comparison to other areas of international law. This is because there are no international institutions in place to deal with its development and implementation, or to monitor its observance. Relying on the parties to implement it during the most heated time of a country's history is a little like asking the thief to guard a jewellery store - the temptation to ignore the obligation and to overstep the mark is enormous. Military restraint is often theoretical rather than real and the promise of punishment for environmental damage does not appear to weigh heavily on the minds of military commanders.

National laws dealing with environmental degradation caused by military activities during peacetime are also not very strong. Many countries regard military activities as sacrosanct, permitting environmental destruction in the name of country protection. However, there are indications in some countries that national governments are taking their environmental responsibilities more seriously in relation to military activities and it is perhaps from these national experiences in controlling excesses that future international controls may be better modelled and implemented.

UN Treaties

Several United Nations treaties, including the Fourth Geneva Convention, the 1972 World Heritage Convention and the 1977 Environmental Modification Convention have provisions to limit the environmental impacts of war or military activities.

1977 Environmental Modification Convention

This treaty makes explicit reference to the environment. It prohibits the hostile use of environmental modification techniques having "widespread, long-lasting or severe effects."

This treaty is in force and has been ratified (accepted as binding) by leading military powers.

Additional Protocol I & Protocol II

Additional Protocols I and II are amendments to the Fourth Geneva Convention. It prohibits methods of warfare intended to or expected to cause "widespread, long-term and severe damage to the natural environment", or to prejudice the health or survival of the civilian population.

The understanding behind this obligation is that this is aimed directly at those capable of unleashing the use of unconventional weapons that cause biological and chemical warfare (e.g. herbicides, fungicides, chemical agents etc.).

Under this Protocol, parties must take care to protect the natural environment. In addition, the Protocol provides for limits on the situations during which a warring side can make use of "works or installations containing dangerous forces" as an object of attack. This is aimed squarely at such potentially devastating sites as nuclear power plants, power plants and large dams or waterworks.

Protocol II has the same limitations but in relation only to non-international armed conflict. Although both Protocols have been ratified widely, there are many major Western military powers missing from the ratification.

1972 World Heritage Convention

Although not related to armed conflict, the obligations under this convention to protect cultural or ecologically significant sites is of potential usefulness. This is especially important in relation to military activities during peacetime but may also become relevant during armed conflict to deter direct attacks on such sites. Partly this will depend on raising the awareness of soldiers during both peace and war times that there are some sites in our world of such significance that their destruction is absolutely forbidden ethically, culturally and morally.

Proposed Fifth Geneva Convention

Attempts have been made to get a specific Geneva convention dealing with protection of the environment during times of armed conflict but so far this has not been successful.

Customary International Law

Customary international law also has something to say about protection of the environment during times of armed conflict and military activities.

- Under the Rio Declaration, Principle 24 provides: "States shall... respect international law providing protection for the environment in times of armed conflict and cooperate in its further development, as necessary."
- UN General Assembly Resolution 47/37 (1992) provides: "[D]estruction of the environment not justified by military necessity and carried out wantonly is clearly contrary to existing international law."

Other Sources

- The ILC has a Code of Offences Against the Peace and Security of Mankind.
- The International Criminal Court treats certain acts of serious and intentional harm to the environment as war crimes. In this instance, there is a possibility for holding an individual responsible for committing such acts against the environment.

Case Law

In the case of the Nuclear Weapons Advisory Opinion, the ICJ found that as a matter of general international law that States must take the environment into account when deciding on what is necessary and proportionate in pursuing legitimate military objectives. The ICJ stated that there must be a respect for the environment and that this will be a factor that is weighed when considering the legitimacy or otherwise of the military actions.

Organisations

The international organisations with environmental mandates may be called upon during times of armed conflict to assist with mediating or remedying damage caused by armed conflict. Such agencies as the UN Environment Programme, the World Health Organization and the IMO will be of relevance here. The UN Security Council has also demonstrated environmental concern in deliberations on recent conflicts, for example, during the 1991 Gulf War. UNEP and IMO were also involved in this conflict, attempting to remedy the most serious of the environmental impacts.

- UNEP
- IMO
- ICAO
- WHO
- International Committee of the Red Cross.

2

Environmental Impact of Gulf Wars

INTRODUCTION

Persian Gulf countries especially Kuwait and Iraq faced the most destroy able environmental disaster because of the behavior of the Iraqi government at that time, which was the main reason of the Gulf wars. Because of the previous, the environment is in poor condition and civilians were not spared of the effect of the wars. It brings many Physical andmental disorder for civilians. The purpose of writing this report is to demonstrate the effect of the gulf wars on local citizen. Therefore, there are many local citizens wondering about the reasons of these impacts.

WARS

- The Iran–Iraq War from September 1980 to August 1988 killed hundreds of thousands.
- In 1991 Iraq invaded Kuwait claiming that Kuwait was a part of Iraq. and that Kuwait stole oil from it. This Gulf war resulted in operation Desert Storm in which Saddam Husseinwas defeated. This was a much smaller war.
- In April 2003, allies conquered Iraq. This again was a much smaller war than the first one, but security deteriorated afterwards.

The Effects

The first victim of the wars always is the environment and human health. Wars make environmental disaster, kill people, and make them suffer from disease.

Environment

According to Elaph report the gulf war is one possible reason of the bad weather in gulf countries.

After the first Gulf war the absorption of air pollutant has increased by 705 percent in Baghdad which is more by 887 percent than recommended by the World Health Organization. In addition, In the Gulf war II oil fire wells caused a global problem and a hazard to humans.

The smoke rose one to four kilometers high and blocked sun shine in Kuwait. The smoke reached United Arab Emirates and Iran. Some countries such as Turkey, Syria and Afghanistan reported black rain.

On January 21, 1991, Iraqi troops opened valves at the Persian Gulf releasing between four and eleven million oil barrels into the sea. Kuwaiti experts estimate the oil leaks about 200 lakes.

The oil in these pools evaporating, which will result of a thick sediment of oil. These residues will be absorbed by the desert causing unseen damage. Regarding these, the human health and the underground water will be at fatal situation. What is more, the number of aquatic animals and birds deficiency dramatically 100,000 -230,000waterbirds and 100 mammals were killed.

The behavior of the Iraqi army has a destructive effect on the soil of the Persian Gulf region. Oil leak from fire wells mixed with gravel result in a new layer on the surface of the desert called "tarcrete" with depth of nine feet. All the plant life under these layers died and it is impossible for flora to grow there. However, scientists suggest to do not eliminate these layers because if they remove it, the dunes under the tarcrete will cause huge traveling dunes which will sabotage everything in their way.

Health

Gulf wars caused serious health problems in Persian Gulf countries. These are the most common health problems here.

Cancer

According to Jamail article the main reason of the rising number of Cancer and birth defects is Depleted Uranium and military weapons inIraq. The present age of cancer cases in Iraq. Even with this statistic the actual number is much higher and it could be double because of leaking of research and the private hospital. Also, Many people did not report on their case. After Gulf War I, many doctors think that the war pollution is probably the reason for the sharp increasing at the rate of cancer in Kuwait .

Psychological

In 1995, Post-traumatic stress disorder was shockingly spread in Kuwait.27 percent of Kuwaiti and 86 percent of them are adult has this psychiatric disorder . 66 percent of those who diagnosable post-traumatic disorder were still dreaming nightmares about some war events. In addition, many boys were dreaming different dreams about Saddam trying to kill them or hurt their families. A client documentary movie meets some affected families.A boy saw his father tortures then killed by the Iraqi soldiers . After this the boy loses the ability to speak. Another affected victim has difficulty of speech because the Iraqi soldiers forced her to watch her two son's killed by them.

Congenital Defects

Dr. Haddad and his colleagues noticed a sharp increase in congenital defects and infertility in Fallujah after it had been bombed by the Americans. Fallujah now has the highest rate of genetic damage in a population at all.Many children now born with two heads, one eye or problems in the nervous system. Scientists said that the rate is fourteen times worse than Hiroshima .

Other Disease

Many scientists believe that Depleted Uranium is the main reason of appearing new disease like new illnesses in the kidney, lungs, liver, and total immune system collapse. In addition, it has been noticed that the number of abortions higher in the busy area of military operations. Families are afraid to have babies. Moreover, because of the second Gulf War many new diseases spread in the region. Also, respiratory diseases increased horribly.

PREVENTION AND TREATMENT

Persian Gulf countries cooperate to clean up the ruin and prevent future havoc. This section of the report will mention what has been cleaned up and the future prevention.

Treatment

Over the last decade volunteer Kuwaiti divers were busy cleaning the benthos. We had extracted two cannons and seven shell partners with ministry of defining Walid Al-Shatti the leader of the Kuwaiti Divers Association said. In addition, it is common to find a turtle caught in fishing nets. What is more, Saudi Aramco was one of the largest contributors to the cleaning process.

It provides support to other Oil-response teams. It distributes protection equipment and materials. Moreover, many Saudi Aramco employees are involved in volunteer teams to clean up marine life.

Prevention

Royal commission in Jubail has established a new program to monitor oil spill or any other chemical materials.In addition, it study the possibility of oil leakage and how can be stopped in an emergency situation. Also, Aramco makes a plan by storage additional antipollution equipment's and ships. Moreover, Aramco always takes care about training their employees to face similar problems by using same machines that will be used in case of oil spill.

Conclusion

Saving and taking care of the environment is a duty for all human being. Unfortunately, people around the world destroy the environment and do not know that they are destroying and fighting themselves by doing that. Contamination of the Persian Gulf, that has elapsed several years ago, killed many people and destroyed many towns and cities. All what I hope in the end of this report that Persian Gulf countries take care about this issue it has been two decades and the problem has not been solved.

GULF WAR

The Gulf War (2 August 1990 – 28 February 1991), codenamed Operation Desert Shield (2 August 1990 - 17 January 1991), for operations leading to the buildup of troops and defense of Saudi Arabia and Operation Desert Storm (17 January 1991 – 28 February 1991) was a war waged by coalition forces from 34 nations led by the United States against Iraq in response to Iraq's invasion and annexation of Kuwait.

The war is also known under other names, such as the Persian Gulf War, First Gulf War, Gulf War I, Kuwait War,First Iraq War, or Iraq War before the term "Iraq War" became identified instead with the 2003 Iraq War(also referred to in the U.S. as "Operation Iraqi Freedom"). Kuwait's invasion by Iraqi troops that began 2 August 1990 was met with international condemnation, and brought immediate economic sanctions against Iraq by members of the U.N. Security Council. U.S. President George H. W. Bush deployed U.S. forces into Saudi Arabia, and urged other countries to send their own forces to the scene. An array of nations joined the Coalition, the largest military alliance since World War II. The great majority of the Coalition's military forces were from the U.S., with Saudi Arabia, the United Kingdom and Egypt as leading contributors, in that order. Saudi Arabia paid around US$36 billion of the US$60 billion cost.

The war was marked by the introduction of live news broadcasts from the front lines of the battle, principally by the

U.S. network CNN. The war has also earned the nickname *Video Game War* after the daily broadcast images on board the U.S. bombers during Operation Desert Storm.

The initial conflict to expel Iraqi troops from Kuwait began with an aerial bombardment on 17 January 1991. This was followed by a ground assault on 24 February. This was a decisive victory for the Coalition forces, who liberated Kuwait and advanced into Iraqi territory. The Coalition ceased its advance, and declared a cease-fire 100 hours after the ground campaign started. Aerial and ground combat was confined to Iraq, Kuwait, and areas on Saudi Arabia's border. Iraq launched Scud missiles against Coalition military targets in Saudi Arabia and against Israel.

United Nations Security Council Resolution 687 passed in April 1991 established formal cease-fire terms. The controversies over enforcing this and subsequent resolutions would lead to the outbreak of another war 12 years later.

Etymology

The following names have been used to describe the conflict itself:

- *Gulf War* and *Persian Gulf War* have been the most common terms for the conflict used within western countries. These names have been used by the overwhelming majority of popular historians and journalists in the United States. The major problem with these terms is that the usage is ambiguous, having now been applied to at least three conflicts: see Gulf War (disambiguation). With no consensus of naming, various publications have attempted to refine the name. Some variants include:
- *War in the Gulf*
- *1990 Gulf War*
- *Gulf War (1990–1991)*
- *First Gulf War*: to distinguish it from the 2003 invasion of Iraq and the subsequent war.

- *Second Gulf War*: to distinguish it from the Iran–Iraq War.
- *Liberation of Kuwait* is the term used by Kuwait and most of the Coalition's Arab states including Saudi Arabia, Bahrain, Egypt and the United Arab Emirates.
- In addition to "Gulf War", the names *War of Kuwait* and *Second Gulf War* are commonly used in France and Germany.
- *Mother of Battles* is the term used by Iraq.
- Other names sometimes used include *Iraq-Kuwait conflict* and *U.N.-Iraq conflict*.

Operational Names

Most of the Coalition states used various names for their operations and the war's operational phases. These are sometimes incorrectly used as the conflict's overall name, especially the U.S. *Desert Storm*:

- *Operation Desert Shield* was the U.S. operational name for the U.S. buildup of forces and Saudi Arabia's defense from 2 August 1990, to 16 January 1991.
- *Operation Desert Storm* was the U.S. name of the airland conflict from 17 January 1991, through 11 April 1991.
- *Operation Desert Sabre* (early name *Operation Desert Sword*) was the U.S. name for the airland offensive against the Iraqi Army in the Kuwaiti Theater of Operations (the "100-hour war") from 24–28 February 1991, in itself, part of *Operation Desert Storm*.
- *Operation Desert Farewell* was the name given to the return of U.S. units and equipment to the U.S. in 1991 after Kuwait's liberation, sometimes referred to as *Operation Desert Calm*.
- *Operation Granby* was the British name for British military activities during the operations and conflict.
- *Opération Daguet* was the French name for French military activities in the conflict.
- *Operation FRICTION* was the name of the Canadian operations

- *Operazione Locusta* (Italian for Locust) was the Italian name for the operations and conflict.

In addition, various phases of each operation may have a unique operational name.

Campaign Names

The U.S. divided the conflict into three major campaigns:

- *Defense of Saudi Arabian country* for the period 2 August 1990, through 16 January 1991.
- *Liberation and Defense of Kuwait* for the period 17 January 1991, through 11 April 1991.
- *Southwest Asia Cease-Fire* for the period 12 April 1991, through 30 November 1995, including *Operation Provide Comfort.*

BACKGROUND

Throughout the Cold War, Iraq had been an ally of the Soviet Union, and there was a history of friction between it and the United States. The U.S. was concerned with Iraq's position on Israeli–Palestinian politics, and its disapproval of the nature of the peace between Israel and Egypt . The U.S. also disliked Iraqi support for many Araband Palestinian militant groups such as Abu Nidal, which led to Iraq's inclusion on the developing U.S. list of State Sponsors of Terrorism on 29 December 1979. The U.S. remained officially neutral after Iraq's invasion of Iran in 1980, which became the Iran–Iraq War, although it provided resources, political support, and some "non-military" aircraft to Iraq. In March 1982, Iran began a successful counteroffensive (Operation Undeniable Victory), and the U.S. increased its support for Iraq to prevent Iran from forcing a surrender. In a U.S. bid to open full diplomatic relations with Iraq, the country was removed from the U.S. list of State Sponsors of Terrorism. Ostensibly this was because of improvement in the regime's record, although former U.S. Assistant Defense Secretary Noel Koch later stated, "No one had any doubts about [the Iraqis'] continued involvement in terrorism ... The real reason was to help them succeed in the war against Iran." With Iraq's newfound success in the war, and the Iranian rebuff of a peace offer in July, arms sales to Iraq reached a record spike in 1982. When Iraqi President Saddam Hussein expelled Abu Nidal to Syria at the U.S.' request in November 1983, the Reagan administrationsent Donald Rumsfeld to meet Saddam as a special envoy and to cultivate ties. By the time the ceasefire with Iran was signed in August 1988, Iraq was heavily debt-ridden and tensions within society were rising. Most of its debt was owed to Saudi Arabia and Kuwait. Iraq pressured both nations to forgive the debts, but they refused.

The Iraq–Kuwait dispute also involved Iraqi claims to Kuwait as Iraqi territory. Kuwait had been a part of the Ottoman Empire's province of Basra, something that Iraq claimed made it rightful Iraq territory. Its ruling dynasty, the al-Sabah family, had concluded aprotectorate agreement in 1899 that assigned responsibility for its foreign affairs to the United Kingdom. The UK drew the border between the two countries in 1922, making Iraq virtually landlocked. Kuwait rejected Iraqi attempts to secure further provisions in the region.

Iraq also accused Kuwait of exceeding its OPEC quotas for oil production. In order for the cartel to maintain its desired price of $18 a barrel, discipline was required. The United Arab Emirates and Kuwait were consistently overproducing; the latter at least in part to repair losses caused by Iranian attacks in the Iran–Iraq War and to pay for the losses of an economic scandal. The result was a slump in the oil price – as low as $10 a barrel – with a resulting loss of $7 billion a year to Iraq, equal to its 1989 balance of payments deficit. Resulting revenues struggled to support the government's basic costs, let alone repair Iraq's damaged infrastructure. Jordan and Iraq both looked for more discipline, with little success. The Iraqi government described it as a form of economic warfare, which it claimed was aggravated by Kuwait slant-drilling across the border into Iraq's Rumaila oil field. At the same time, Saddam looked for closer ties with those Arab states that had supported Iraq in the war. This was supported by the U.S., who believed that Iraqi ties with pro-Western Gulf states would help bring and maintain Iraq inside the U.S.' sphere of influence.

In 1989, it appeared that Saudi-Iraqi relations, strong during the war, would be maintained. A pact of non-interference and non-aggression was signed between the countries, followed by a Kuwaiti-Iraqi deal for Iraq to supply Kuwait with water for drinking and irrigation, although a request for Kuwait to lease Iraq Umm Qasr was rejected. Saudi-backed development projects were hampered by Iraq's large debts, even with the demobilization of 200,000 soldiers. Iraq also looked to increase arms production so as to become an exporter, although the success of these projects was also restrained by Iraq's obligations; in Iraq, resentment to OPEC's controls mounted.

Iraq's relations with its Arab neighbors – in particular Egypt – were degraded by mounting violence in Iraq against expatriate groups, well-employed during the war, by Iraqi unemployed, among them demobilized soldiers. These events drew little notice outside the Arab world because of fast-moving events in Eastern Europe. The U.S. did, however, begin to condemn Iraq's human rights record, including the well-known use of torture. The UK also condemned the execution of Farzad Bazoft, a journalist working for the British newspaper *The Observer*. Following Saddam's declaration that "binary chemical weapons" would be used on Israel if it used military force against Iraq, Washington halted part of its funding. A U.N. mission to the Israeli-occupied territories, where riots had resulted in Palestinian deaths, was vetoed by the U.S., making Iraq deeply skeptical of U.S. foreign policy aims in the region, combined with the U.S.' reliance on Middle Eastern energy reserves.

In early July 1990, Iraq complained about Kuwait's behavior, such as not respecting their quota, and openly threatened to take military action. On the 23rd, the CIA reported that Iraq had moved 30,000 troops to the Iraq-Kuwait border, and the U.S. naval fleet in the Persian Gulf was placed on alert. Saddam believed an anti-Iraq conspiracy was developing– Kuwait had begun talks with Iran, and Iraq's rival Syria had arranged a visit to Egypt. On 15 July 1990, Saddam's government laid out its combined objections to the Arab League, including that policy moves were costing Iraq $1 billion a year, that Kuwait was still using the Rumaila oil field, that loans made by the UAE and Kuwait could not be considered debts to its "Arab brothers". He threatened force against Kuwait and the UAE saying "The policies of some Arab rulers are American ... They are inspired by America to undermine Arab interests and security." The U.S. sent aerial refuelling planes and combat ships to the Persian Gulf in response to these threats. Discussions in Jeddah, Saudi Arabia, mediated on the Arab League's behalf by Egyptian President Hosni Mubarak, were held on 31 July and led Mubarak to believe that a peaceful course could be established.

On the 25th, Saddam met with April Glaspie, the U.S. Ambassador to Iraq, in Baghdad. the Iraqi leader attacked American policy with regards to Kuwait and the United Arab Emirates:

"So what can it mean when America says it will now protect its friends? It can only mean prejudice against Iraq. This stance plus maneuvers and statements which have been made has encouraged the UAE and Kuwait to disregard Iraqi rights ... If you use pressure, we will deploy pressure and force. We know that you can harm us although we do not threaten you. But we too can harm you. Everyone can cause harm according to their ability and their size. We cannot come all the way to you in the United States, but individual Arabs may reach you ... We do not place America among the enemies. We place it where we want our friends to be and we try to be friends. But repeated American statements last year made it apparent that America did not regard us as friends."

Glaspie replied: "I know you need funds. We understand that and our opinion is that you should have the opportunity to rebuild your country. But we have no opinion on the Arab-Arab conflicts, like your border disagreement with Kuwait ... Frankly, we can only see that you have deployed massive troops in the south. Normally that would not be any of our business. But when this happens in the context of what you said on your national day, then when we read the details in the two letters of the Foreign Minister, then when we see the Iraqi point of view that the measures taken by the UAE and Kuwait is, in the final analysis, parallel to military aggression against Iraq, then it would be reasonable for me to be concerned."

Saddam stated that he would attempt last-ditch negotiations with the Kuwaitis but Iraq "would not accept death".

According to Glaspie's own account, she stated in reference to the precise border between Kuwait and Iraq, "... that she had served in Kuwait 20 years before; 'then, as now, we took no position on these Arab affairs'." Glaspie similarly believed that war was not imminent.

Invasion of Kuwait

The result of the Jeddah talks was an Iraqi demand for $10 billion to cover the lost revenues from Rumaila; the Kuwaiti response was to offer $9 billion. The Iraqi response was to immediately order the invasion. On 2 August 1990, Iraq launched the invasion by bombing Kuwait's capital,Kuwait City.

At the time of the invasion, the Kuwaiti military was believed to have numbered 16,000 men, arranged into three armored, one mechanised infantry and one under-strength artillery brigade. The pre-war strength of the Kuwait Air Force was around 2,200 Kuwaiti personnel, with 80 aircraft and forty helicopters. In spite of Iraqi saber-rattling, Kuwait didn't have its forces on alert; the army had been stood down on 19 July.

By 1988, at the Iran–Iraq War's end, the Iraqi Army was the world's fourth largest army; it consisted of 955,000 standing soldiers and 650,000 paramilitary forces in the Popular Army. According to John Childs and André Corvisier, a low estimate shows the Iraqi Army capable of fielding 4,500 tanks, 484 combat aircraft and 232 combat helicopters. According to Michael Knights, a high estimate shows the Iraqi Army capable of fielding one million men and 850,000 reservists, 5,500 tanks,

3,000 artillery pieces, 700 combat aircraft and helicopters; and held 53 divisions, 20 special-forces brigades, and several regional militias, and had a strong air defense.

Iraqi commandos infiltrated the Kuwaiti border first to prepare for the major units which began the attack at midnight. The Iraqi attack had two prongs, with the primary attack force driving south straight for Kuwait City down the main highway, and a supporting attack force entering Kuwait farther west, but then turning and driving east, cutting off Kuwait City from the country's southern half. The commander of a Kuwaiti armored battalion, 35th Armoured Brigade, deployed them against the Iraqi attack and was able to conduct a robust defense (Battle of the Bridges), near Al Jahra, west of Kuwait City.

Kuwaiti aircraft scrambled to meet the invading force, but approximately 20% were lost or captured. A few combat sorties were flown against Iraqi ground forces.

The main Iraqi thrust into Kuwait City was conducted by commandos deployed by helicopters and boats to attack the city from the sea, while other divisions seized the airports and two airbases. The Iraqis attacked the Dasman Palace, the Royal Residence of Kuwait's Emir, Jaber Al-Ahmad Al-Jaber Al-Sabah, which was defended by the Emiri Guard supported with M-84 tanks. In the process, the Iraqis killed Fahad Al-Ahmed Al-Jaber Al-Sabah, the Emir's youngest brother.

Within 12 hours, most resistance had ended within Kuwait and the royal family had fled, leaving Iraq in control of most of Kuwait. After two days of intense combat, most of theKuwaiti military were either overrun by the Iraqi Republican Guard, or had escaped to Saudi Arabia. The Emir and key ministers were able to get out and head south along the highway for refuge in Saudi Arabia. Iraqi ground forces consolidated their control of Kuwait City, then headed south and redeployed along the Saudi border. After the decisive Iraqi victory, Saddam initially installed a puppet regime known as the "Provisional Government of Free Kuwait" before installing his cousin Ali Hassan al-Majid as Kuwait's governor on 8 August.

Kuwaiti Resistance Movement

Kuwaitis founded a local armed resistance movement following the Iraqi occupation of Kuwait. The Kuwaiti resistance's casualty rate far exceeded that of the coalition military forces and Western hostages. The resistance predominantly consisted of ordinary citizens who lacked any form of training and supervision. The majority of Kuwaitis who stayed in Kuwait during the Gulf War were Shias.

RUN-UP TO THE WAR

Diplomatic Means

A key element of U.S. political-military and energy economic planning occurred in early 1984. The Iran-Iraq war had been going on for five years and there were significant casualties on both sides, reaching hundreds of thousands. Within President Ronald Reagan's National Security Council concern was growing that the war could spread beyond the boundaries of the two belligerents. A National Security Planning Group meeting was formed, chaired by then Vice President George H. W. Bush to review U.S. options. It was determined that there was a high likelihood that the conflict would spread into Saudi Arabia and other Gulf states, but that the United States had little capability to defend the region. Furthermore it was determined that a prolonged war in the region would induce much higher oil prices and threaten the fragile recovery of the world economy which was just beginning to gain momentum. On 22 May 1984, President Reagan was briefed on the project conclusions in the Oval Office by William Flynn Martin who had served as the head of the NSC staff that organized the study. The full declassified presentation can be seen here. The conclusions were threefold: first oil stocks needed to be increased among members of the International Energy Agency and, if necessary, released early in the event of oil market disruption; second the United States needed to beef up the security of friendly Arab states in the region and thirdly an embargo should be placed on sales of military equipment to Iran and Iraq. The Plan was approved by the President Reagan and later affirmed by the G-7 leaders headed by Great Britain's Prime Minister Margaret Thatcher in the London Summit of 1984. The plan was implemented and became the basis for U.S. preparedness to respond to the Iraqi occupation of Kuwait in 1991.

Within hours of the invasion, Kuwait and U.S. delegations requested a meeting of the United Nations Security Council, which passed Resolution 660, condemning the invasion and demanding a withdrawal of Iraqi troops. On 3 August, the Arab League passed its own resolution, which called for a solution to the conflict from within the League, and warned against outside intervention; Iraq and Libya were the only two Arab League states which opposed a resolution for Iraq to withdraw from Kuwait. The PLO opposed it as well. The Arab states of Yemen and Jordan – a Western ally which bordered Iraq and relied on the country for economic support – opposed military intervention from non-Arab states. The Arab state of Sudan aligned itself with Saddam.

On 6 August, Resolution 661 placed economic sanctions on Iraq. Resolution 665 followed soon after, which authorized a naval blockade to enforce the sanctions. It said the "use of measures commensurate to the specific circumstances as may be necessary ... to halt all inward and outward maritime shipping in order to inspect and verify their cargoes and destinations and to ensure strict implementation of resolution 661."

From the beginning, U.S. officials insisted on a total Iraqi pullout from Kuwait, without any linkage to other Middle Eastern problems, fearing any concessions would strengthen Iraqi influence in the region for years to come.

On 12 August 1990, Saddam "propose[d] that all cases of occupation, and those cases that have been portrayed as occupation, in the region, be resolved simultaneously". Specifically, he called for Israel to withdraw from occupied territories in Palestine, Syria, and Lebanon, Syria to withdraw from Lebanon, and "mutual withdrawals by Iraq and Iran and arrangement for the situation in Kuwait." He also called for a replacement of U.S. troops that mobilized in Saudi Arabia in response to Kuwait's invasion with "an Arab force", as long as that force did not involve Egypt. Additionally, he requested an "immediate freeze of all boycott and siege decisions" and a general normalization of relations with Iraq. From the beginning of the crisis, President Bush was strongly opposed to any "linkage" between Iraq's occupation of Kuwait and the Palestinian issue.

On 23 August, Saddam appeared on state television with Western hostages to whom he had refused exit visas. In the video, he asks a young British boy, Stuart Lockwood, whether he is getting his milk, and goes on to say, through his interpreter, "We hope your presence as guests here will not be for too long. Your presence here, and in other places, is meant to prevent the scourge of war."

Another Iraqi proposal communicated in August 1990 was delivered to U.S. National Security Advisor Brent Scowcroft by an unidentified Iraqi official. The official communicated to the White House that Iraq would "withdraw from Kuwait and allow foreigners to leave" provided that the U.N. lifted sanctions, allowed "guaranteed access to the Persian Gulf through the Kuwaiti islands of Bubiyan and Warbah", and allowed Iraq to "gain full control of the Rumaila oil field that extends slightly into Kuwaiti territory".

The proposal also "include[d] offers to negotiate an oil agreement with the United States 'satisfactory to both nations' national security interests,' develop a joint plan 'to alleviate Iraq's economical and financial problems' and 'jointly work on the stability of the gulf.'"

In December 1990, Iraq made a proposal to withdraw from Kuwait provided that foreign troops left the region and that an agreement was reached regarding the Palestinian problem and the dismantlement of both Israel's and Iraq's weapons of mass destruction. The White House rejected the proposal. The PLO's Yasser Arafat expressed that neither he nor Saddam insisted that solving the Israel-Palestine issues should be a precondition to solving the issues in Kuwait, though he did acknowledge a "strong link" between these problems.

Ultimately, the U.S. stuck to its position that there would be no negotiations until Iraq withdrew from Kuwait and that they should not grant Iraq concessions, lest they give the impression that Iraq benefited from its military campaign. Also, when U.S. Secretary of State James Baker met withTariq Aziz in Geneva, Switzerland, for last minute peace talks in early 1991, Aziz reportedly made no concrete proposals and did not outline any hypothetical Iraqi moves.

On 29 November 1990, the Security Council passed Resolution 678 which gave Iraq until 15 January 1991 to withdraw from Kuwait and empowered states to use "all necessary means" to force Iraq out of Kuwait after the deadline.

On 14 January 1991, France proposed that the U.N. Security Council call for "a rapid and massive withdrawal" from Kuwait along with a statement to Iraq that Council members would bring their "active contribution" to a settlement of the region's other problems, "in particular, of the Arab-Israeli conflict and in particular to the Palestinian problem by convening, at an appropriate moment, an international conference" to assure "the security, stability and development of this region of the world." The French proposal was supported by Belgium (at the moment one of the rotating Council members), Germany, Spain, Italy, Algeria, Morocco, Tunisia, and several non-aligned nations. The U.S., the UK, and the Soviet Union rejected it; U.S. Ambassador to the U.N. Thomas Pickering stated that the French proposal was unacceptable, because it went beyond previous Council resolutions on the Iraqi invasion. France dropped this proposal when it found "no tangible sign of interest" from Baghdad.

Military Means

One of the West's main concerns was the significant threat Iraq posed to Saudi Arabia. Following Kuwait's conquest, the Iraqi Army was within easy striking distance of Saudi oil fields. Control of these fields, along with Kuwaiti and Iraqi reserves, would have given Saddam control over the majority of the world's oil reserves. Iraq also had a number of grievances with Saudi Arabia. The Saudis had lent Iraq some 26 billion dollars during its war with Iran. The Saudis had backed Iraq in that war, as they feared the influence of Shia Iran's Islamic revolution on its own Shia minority. After the war, Saddam felt he shouldn't have to repay the loans due to the help he had given the Saudis by fighting Iran.

Soon after his conquest of Kuwait, Saddam began verbally attacking the Saudis. He argued that the U.S.-supported Saudi state was an illegitimate and unworthy guardian of the holy cities of Mecca and Medina. He combined the language of the Islamist groups that had recently fought in Afghanistan with the rhetoric Iran had long used to attack the Saudis.

Acting on the Carter Doctrine's policy, and out of fear the Iraqi Army could launch an invasion of Saudi Arabia, U.S. President George H. W. Bush quickly announced that the U.S. would launch a "wholly defensive" mission to prevent Iraq from invading Saudi Arabia under the codename Operation Desert Shield. Operation Desert Shield began on 7 August 1990 when U.S. troops were sent to Saudi Arabia due also to the request of its monarch, King Fahd, who had earlier called for U.S. military assistance. This "wholly defensive" doctrine was quickly abandoned when, on 8 August, Iraq declared Kuwait to be Iraq's 19th province and Saddam named his cousin, Ali Hassan Al-Majid, as its military-governor.

The U.S. Navy dispatched two naval battle groups built around the aircraft carriers USS *Dwight D. Eisenhower* and USS *Independence* to the Gulf, where they were ready by 8 August. The U.S. also sent the battleships USS *Missouri* and USS *Wisconsin* to the region. A total of 48 U.S. Air Force F-15s from the 1st Fighter Wing at Langley Air Force Base, Virginia, landed in Saudi Arabia, and immediately commenced round the clock air patrols of the Saudi–Kuwait–Iraq border to discourage further Iraqi military advances. They were joined by 36 F-15 A-Ds from the 36th Tactical Fighter Wing at Bitburg, Germany. The Bitburg contingent was based at Al Kharj Air Base, approximately 1-hour southeast of Riyadh. The 36th TFW would be responsible for 11 confirmed Iraqi Air Force aircraft shot down during the war. There were also two Air

National Guard units stationed at Al Kharj Air Base, the South Carolina Air National Guard's 169th Fighter Wing flew bombing missions with 24 F-16s flying 2,000 combat missions and dropping 4 million pounds of munitions, and the New York Air National Guard's 174th Fighter Wing from Syracuse flew 24 F-16s on bombing missions. Military buildup continued from there, eventually reaching 543,000 troops, twice the number used in the 2003 invasion of Iraq. Much of the material was airlifted or carried to the staging areas viafast sealift ships, allowing a quick buildup.

Creating a Coalition

A series of U.N. Security Council resolutions and Arab League resolutions were passed regarding Iraq's invasion of Kuwait. One of the most important was Resolution 678, passed on 29 November 1990, which gave Iraq a withdrawal deadline until 15 January 1991, and authorized "all necessary means to uphold and implement Resolution 660", and a diplomatic formulation authorizing the use of force if Iraq failed to comply.

To ensure that economic backing, Baker went on an eleven day journey to nine countries that the press dubbed "The Tin Cup Trip". The first stop was Saudi Arabia, who a month before had already granted permission to the United States to use its facilities. However, Baker believed that Saudi Arabia, an immensely wealthy nation, should assume some of the cost of the military efforts, since one of the most decisive military objectives was defending Saudi Arabia. When Baker asked King Fahd for 15 billion dollars, the King readily agreed, with the promise that Baker ask Kuwait for the same amount.

The next day, 7 September, he did just that, and the Emir of Kuwait, displaced in a Sheraton hotel outside his invaded country, easily agreed. Baker then moved to enter talks with Egypt, whose leadership he considered to be "the moderate voice of the middle east". President Mubarak of Egypt was furious with Saddam for his invasion of Kuwait, for the fact that Saddam had assured Mubarak that an invasion was not his intention. Therefore, he was willing to commit troops to the coalition forces to quell Saddam, as well as relieved the United States was willing to forgive his country's 7.1 billion dollar debt.

After stops in Helsinki and Moscow to smooth out Iraqi demands for a middle-eastern peace conference with Russia, Baker traveled to Syria to discuss its role in the crisis with its President Hafez Assad. Assad had a deep personal enmity towards Saddam, which was defined by the fact that "Saddam had been trying to kill him [Assad] for years". Harboring this animosity and being impressed with Baker's diplomatic initiative to visit Damascus (relations had been severed since the 1983 bombing of U.S. Marine barracks in Beirut), Assad agreed to pledge up to 100,000 Syrian troops to the coalition effort. This was a vital step in ensuring Arab states were represented in the coalition.

Baker flew to Rome for a brief visit with the Italians in which he was promised the use of some military equipment, before journeying to Germany to meet with American ally Chancellor Kohl. Although Germany's constitution (which was brokered essentially by the United States) prohibited military involvement in outside nations, Kohl was willing to repay his gratitude for the United States with a two billion dollar contribution to the coalition's war effort, as well as further economic and military support of coalition ally Turkey, and the execution of the transport of Egyptian soldiers and ships to the Persian Gulf.

A coalition of forces opposing Iraq's aggression was formed, consisting of forces from 34 countries: Argentina, Australia, Bahrain, Bangladesh, Belgium, Canada, Denmark, Egypt, France, Greece, Italy, Kuwait, Morocco, Netherlands, New Zealand, Niger, Norway, Oman, Pakistan, Portugal, Qatar, South Korea, Saudi Arabia, Senegal, Sierra Leone, Singapore, Spain, Syria, the United Arab Emirates, the United Kingdom and the U.S. itself. It was the largest coalition since World War II. U.S. Army General Norman Schwarzkopf, Jr. was designated to be the commander of the Coalition forces in the Persian Gulf area. The Soviet Union also supported United States intervention.

Although they didn't contribute any forces, Japan and Germany made financial contributions totaling $10 billion and $6.6 billion respectively. U.S. troops represented 73% of the Coalition's 956,600 troops in Iraq.

Many of the Coalition's forces were reluctant to join. Some felt that the war was an internal Arab affair, or didn't want to increase U.S. influence in the Middle East. In the end, however, many nations were persuaded by Iraq's belligerence towards other Arab states, offers of economic aid or debt forgiveness, and threats to withhold aid.

Justification for Intervention

The U.S. and the U.N. gave several public justifications for involvement in the conflict, the most prominent being the Iraqi violation of Kuwaiti territorial integrity. In addition, the U.S. moved to support its ally Saudi Arabia, whose importance in the region, and as a key supplier of oil, made it of considerable geopolitical importance. Shortly after the Iraqi invasion, U.S. Defense Secretary Dick Cheney made the first of several visits to Saudi Arabia where King Fahd requested U.S. military assistance. During a speech in a special joint session of the U.S. Congress given on 11 September 1990, U.S. President George H. W. Bush summed up the reasons with the following remarks: "Within three days, 120,000 Iraqi troops with 850 tanks had poured into Kuwait and moved south to threaten Saudi Arabia. It was then that I decided to act to check that aggression."

The Pentagon stated that satellite photos showing a buildup of Iraqi forces along the border were this information's source, but this was later alleged to be false. A reporter for the *St. Petersburg Times* acquired two commercial Soviet satellite images made at the time in question, which showed nothing but empty desert.

Other justifications for foreign involvement included Iraq's history of human rights abuses under Saddam. Iraq was also known to possess biological weapons and chemical weapons, which Saddam had used against Iranian troops during the Iran–Iraq War and against his own country's Kurdish population in the Al-Anfal Campaign. Iraq was also known to have anuclear weapons program, but the report about it from January 1991 was partially declassified by the CIA on 26 May 2001.

Although there were human rights abuses committed in Kuwait by the invading Iraqi military, the alleged incidents which received most publicity in the U.S. were inventions of the public relations firm hired by the government of Kuwait to influence U.S. opinion in favor of military intervention. Shortly after Iraq's invasion of Kuwait, the organization *Citizens for a Free Kuwait* was formed in the U.S. It hired the public relations firm Hill & Knowlton for about $11 million, paid by Kuwait's government.

Among many other means of influencing U.S. opinion (distributing books on Iraqi atrocities to U.S. soldiers deployed in the region, 'Free Kuwait' T-shirts and speakers to college campuses, and dozens of video news releases to television stations), the firm arranged for an appearance before a group of members of the U.S. Congress in which a woman identifying herself as a nurse working in the Kuwait City hospital described Iraqi soldiers pulling babies out of incubators and letting them die on the floor.

The story was an influence in tipping both the public and Congress towards a war with Iraq: six Congressmen said the testimony was enough for them to support military action against Iraq and seven Senators referenced the testimony in debate. The Senate supported the military actions in a 52–47 vote. A year after the war, however, this allegation was revealed to be a fabrication. The woman who had testified was found to be a member of Kuwait's Royal Family, in fact the daughter of Kuwait's ambassador to the U.S. She hadn't lived in Kuwait during the Iraqi invasion.

The Hill & Knowlton public relations campaign, including the incubator testimony, were published in John R. MacArthur's *Second Front: Censorship and Propaganda in the Gulf War* (Berkeley, CA: University of CA Press, 1992), and came to wide public attention when an Op-ed by MacArthur was published in *The New York Times*. This prompted a reexamination by Amnesty International, which had originally promoted an account alleging even greater numbers of babies torn from incubators than the original fake testimony. After finding no evidence to support it, the organization issued a retraction. President Bush then repeated the incubator allegations on television.

At the same time, the Iraqi Army committed several well-documented crimes during its occupation of Kuwait, such as the summary execution without trial of three brothers after which their bodies were stacked in a pile and left to decay in a public street. Iraqi troops also ransacked and looted private Kuwaiti homes; one residence was repeatedly defecated in. A resident later commented, "The whole thing was violence for the sake of violence, destruction for the sake of destruction ... Imagine a surrealistic painting bySalvador Dalí".

EARLY BATTLES

Air Campaign

The Gulf War began with an extensive aerial bombing campaign on 17 January 1991. The Coalition flew over 100,000 sorties, dropping 88,500 tons of bombs, and widely destroying military and civilian infrastructure. The air campaign was commanded by USAF Lieutenant GeneralChuck Horner, who briefly served as U.S. Central Command's Commander-in-Chief – Forward while General Schwarzkopf was still in the U.S.

A day after the deadline set in Resolution 678, the Coalition launched a massive air campaign, which began the general offensive codenamedOperation Desert Storm. The first priority for Coalition forces was the destruction of Iraq's Air Force and anti-aircraft facilities. The sorties were launched mostly from Saudi Arabia and the six Coalition carrier battle groups (CVBG) in the Persian Gulf and Red Sea.

The next Coalition targets were command and communication facilities. Saddam Hussein had closelymicromanaged Iraqi forces in the Iran–Iraq War, and initiative at lower levels was discouraged. Coalition planners hoped that Iraqi resistance would quickly collapse if deprived of command and control. The air campaign's third and largest phase targeted military targets throughout Iraq and Kuwait: Scud missile launchers, weapons research facilities, and naval forces. About one-third of the Coalition's air power was devoted to attacking Scuds, some of which were on trucks and therefore difficult to locate. U.S. and British special operations forces had been covertly inserted into western Iraq to aid in the search for and destruction of Scuds.

Iraqi anti-aircraft defenses, including Man-portable air-defense systems, were surprisingly ineffective against Coalition aircraft and the Coalition suffered only 75 aircraft losses in over 100,000 sorties, 44 of which were the result of Iraqi action. Two of these losses are the result of aircraft colliding with the ground while evading Iraqi ground fired weapons. One of these losses is a confirmed air-air victory.

Iraqi Missile Strikes on Israel and Saudi Arabia

Iraq's government made no secret that it would attack if invaded. Prior to the war's start, Tariq Aziz, Iraq's English-speaking Foreign Minister and Deputy Prime Minister, was asked in the aftermath of the failed U.S.-Iraq peace talks in Geneva, Switzerland, by a reporter. "Mr. Foreign Minister, if war starts ... will you attack?" His response was, "Yes, absolutely, yes."

Five hours after the first attacks, Iraq's state radio broadcast declaring that "The dawn of victory nears as this great showdown begins." Iraq fired eight missiles the next day. These missile attacks were to continue throughout the war. A total of 88 Scud missiles were fired by Iraq during the war's seven weeks.

Iraq hoped to provoke a military response from Israel. The Iraqi government hoped that many Arab states would withdraw from the Coalition, as they would be reluctant to fight alongside Israel. Following the first attacks, Israeli Air Force jets were deployed to patrol the northern airspace with Iraq. Israel prepared to militarily retaliate, as its policy for the previous forty years had always been retaliation. However, President Bush pressured Israeli Prime Minister Yitzhak Shamir not to retaliate and withdraw Israeli jets, fearing that if Israel attacked Iraq, the other Arab nations would either desert the Coalition or join Iraq. It was also feared that if Israel used Syrian or Jordanian airspace to attack Iraq, they would intervene in the war on Iraq's side or attack Israel. The Coalition promised to deploy Patriot missiles to defend Israel if it refrained from responding to the Scud attacks.

The Scud missiles targeting Israel were relatively ineffective, as firing at extreme range resulted in a dramatic reduction in accuracy and payload. According to the Jewish Virtual Library, a total of 74 Israelis died as a result of the Iraqi attacks: two directly and the rest from suffocation and heart attacks. Approximately 230 Israelis were injured. Extensive property damage was also caused, and according to Israel Ministry of Foreign Affairs, "Damage to general property consisted of 1,302 houses, 6142 apartments, 23 public buildings, 200 shops and 50 cars." It was feared that Iraq would fire missiles filled with nerve agents such as sarin. As a result, Israel's government issued gas masks to its citizens. When the first Iraqi missiles hit Israel, some people injected themselves with an antidote for nerve gas. It has been suggested that the sturdy construction techniques used in Israeli cities, coupled with the fact that Scuds were only launched at night, played an important role in limiting the number of casualties from Scud attacks.

In response to the threat of Scuds on Israel, the U.S. rapidly sent a Patriot missile air defense artillery battalion to Israel along with two batteries of MIM-104 Patriot missiles for the protection of civilians. The Royal Netherlands Air Force also deployed a Patriot missile squadron to Israel. The Dutch Defense Ministry later stated that the military use of the Patriot missile system was largely ineffective, but its psychological value was high, even though the Patriot missiles caused far more casualties and property damage than the Scuds themselves did.

Coalition air forces were also extensively exercised in "Scud hunts" in the Iraqi desert, trying to locate the camouflaged trucks before they fired their missiles at Israel or Saudi Arabia. On the ground, special operations forces also infiltrated Iraq, tasked with locating and destroying Scuds. Once special operations were combined with air patrols, the number of attacks fell sharply, then increased slightly as Iraqi forces adjusted to Coalition tactics.

As the Scud attacks continued, the Israelis grew increasingly impatient, and considered taking unilateral military action against Iraq. On 22 January 1991, a Scud missile and two Coalition Patriots that had been fired to intercept it but missed hit the Israeli city of Ramat Gan. The incident caused three elderly people to suffer fatal heart attacks. Another 96 people were injured, and 20 apartment buildings were damaged. After this attack, the Israelis warned that if the US failed to stop the attacks, they would. At one point, Israeli commandos were loaded onto helicopters prepared to fly into Iraq, but the mission was called off after a phone call from U.S. Defense Secretary Dick Cheney, reporting on the extent of Coalition efforts to destroy Scuds and emphasizing that Israeli intervention could endanger U.S. forces.

In addition to the attacks on Israel, 47 Scud missiles were fired into Saudi Arabia, and one missile was fired at Bahrain and another at Qatar. The missiles were fired at both military and civilian targets. One Saudi civilian was killed, and 78 others were injured. No casualties were reported in Bahrain or Qatar. The Saudi government issued all its citizens and expatriates with gas masks in the event of Iraq using missiles with chemical or biological warheads. The government broadcast alerts and 'all clear' messages over television to warn citizens during Scud attacks.

On 25 February 1991, a Scud missile hit a U.S. Army barracks of the 14th Quartermaster Detachment, out of Greensburg, Pennsylvania, stationed in Dhahran, Saudi Arabia, killing 28 soldiers and injuring over 100.

Iraqi invasion of Saudi Arabia (Battle of Khafji)

On 29 January, Iraqi forces attacked and occupied the lightly defended Saudi city of Khafji with tanks and infantry.

The Battle of Khafji ended two days later when the Iraqis were driven back by the Saudi Arabian National Guard, supported by Qatari forces and U.S. Marines. The allied forces used extensive artillery fire.

Both sides suffered casualties, although Iraqi forces sustained substantially more dead and captured than the allied forces. Eleven Americans were killed in two separate friendly fire incidents, an additional 14 U.S. airmen were killed when their AC-130 gunship was shot down by an Iraqi surface-to-air missile, and two U.S. soldiers were captured during the battle. Saudi and Qatari forces had a total of 18 dead. Iraqi forces in Khafji had 60–300 dead and 400 captured.

The Battle of Khafji was an example of how air power could single-handedly hinder the advance of enemy ground forces. Upon learning of Iraqi troop movements, 140 coalition aircraft were diverted to attack an advancing column consisting of two armored divisions in battalion-sized units. Precision stand-off attacks were conducted during the night and through to the next day. Iraqi vehicle losses included 357 tanks, 147 armored personnel carriers, and 89 mobile artillery pieces. Some crews simply abandoned their vehicles upon realizing that they could be destroyed by guided bombs without warning, stopping the divisions from massing for an organized attack on the town. One Iraqi soldier, who had fought in the Iran-Iraq War, remarked that his brigade "had sustained more punishment from allied airpower in 30 minutes at Khafji than in eight years of fighting against Iran."

Ground Campaign

The Coalition forces dominated the air with their technological advantages. Coalition forces had the significant advantage of being able to operate under the protection of air supremacy that had been achieved by their air forces before the start of the main ground offensive. Coalition forces also had two key technological advantages:

1. The Coalition main battle tanks, such as the U.S. M1 Abrams, British Challenger 1, and Kuwaiti M-84AB were vastly superior to the Chinese Type 69 and T-72

tanks used by the Iraqis, with crews better trained and armored doctrine better developed.

2. The use of GPS made it possible for Coalition forces to navigate without reference to roads or other fixed landmarks. This, along with aerial reconnaissance, allowed them to fight a battle of maneuver rather than abattle of encounter: they knew where they were and where the enemy was, so they could attack a specific target rather than searching on the ground for enemy forces.

Kuwait's Liberation

U.S. decoy attacks by air attacks and naval gunfire the night before Kuwait's liberation were designed to make the Iraqis believe the main Coalition ground attack would focus on central Kuwait.

For months, American units in Saudi Arabia had been under almost constant Iraqi artillery fire, as well as threats from Scud missile or chemical attacks. On 24 February 1991, the 1st and 2nd Marine Divisions, and the 1st Light Armored Infantry Battalion crossed into Kuwait and headed toward Kuwait City. They encountered trenches, barbed wire, and minefields. However, these positions were poorly defended, and were overrun in the first few hours. Several tank battles took place, but apart from that, Coalition troops encountered minimal resistance, as most Iraqi troops surrendered. The general pattern was that the Iraqis would put up a short fight before surrendering. However, Iraqi air defenses shot down nine U.S. aircraft. Meanwhile, forces from Arab states advanced into Kuwait from the east, encountering little resistance and suffering few casualties.

Despite the successes of Coalition forces, it was feared that the Iraqi Republican Guard would escape into Iraq before it could be destroyed. It was decided to send British armored forces into Kuwait fifteen hours ahead of schedule, and to send U.S. forces after the Republican Guard. The Coalition advance was preceded by a heavy artillery and rocket barrage, after which 150,000 troops and 1,500 tanks began their advance. Iraqi forces in Kuwait counterattacked against U.S. troops, acting on a direct order from Saddam himself. Despite the intense combat, the Americans repulsed the Iraqis and continued to advance towards Kuwait City.

Kuwaiti forces were tasked with liberating the city. Iraqi troops offered only light resistance. The Kuwaitis lost one soldier killed and one plane shot down, and quickly liberated the city. On 27 February, Saddam ordered a retreat from Kuwait, and President Bush declared it liberated. However, an Iraqi unit at Kuwait International Airport appeared not to have gotten the message, and fiercely resisted. U.S. Marines had to fight for hours before securing the airport, after which Kuwait was declared secure. After four days of fighting, Iraqi forces were expelled from Kuwait. As part of a scorched earth policy, they set fire to nearly 700 oil wells, and placed land mines around the wells to make extinguishing the fires more difficult.

Initial Moves into Iraq

The war's ground phase was officially designated Operation Desert Saber.

The first units to move into Iraq were three patrols of the British Special Air Service's B squadron, call signs Bravo One Zero, Bravo Two Zero, and Bravo Three Zero, in late January. These eight-man patrols landed behind Iraqi lines to gather intelligence on the movements of Scud mobile missile launchers, which couldn't be detected from the air, as they were hidden under bridges and camouflage netting during the day. Other objectives included the destruction of the launchers and their fiber-optic communications arrays that lay in pipelines and relayed coordinates to the TEL operators that were launching attacks against Israel. The operations were designed to prevent any possible Israeli intervention. Due to lack of sufficient ground cover to carry out their assignment, One Zero and Three Zero abandoned their operations, while Two Zero remained, and was later compromised, with only Sergeant Chris Ryan escaping to Syria.

Elements of the 2nd Brigade, 1st Battalion 5th Cavalry of the 1st Cavalry Division of the U.S. Army performed a direct attack into Iraq on 15 February 1991, followed by one in force on 20 February that led directly through 7 Iraqi divisions which were caught off guard. From 15–20 February, the Battle of Wadi Al-Batin took place inside Iraq; this was the first of two attacks by 1 Battalion 5th Cavalry of the 1st Cavalry Division. It was a feint attack, designed to make the Iraqis think that a Coalition invasion would take place from the south. The Iraqis fiercely resisted, and the Americans eventually withdrew as planned back into the Wadi Al-Batin. Three U.S. soldiers were killed and nine wounded as well with only 1 M-2 IFV turret destroyed, but they had taken 40 prisoners and destroyed five tanks, and successfully deceived the Iraqis. This attack led the way for the XVIII Airborne Corps to sweep around behind the 1st Cav and attack Iraqi forces to the west. On 22 February 1991, Iraq agreed to a Soviet-proposed ceasefire agreement. The agreement called for Iraq to withdraw troops to pre-invasion positions within six weeks following a total cease-fire, and called for monitoring of the cease-fire and withdrawal to be overseen by the U.N. Security Council.

The Coalition rejected the proposal, but said that retreating Iraqi forces wouldn't be attacked, and gave twenty-four hours for Iraq to begin withdrawing forces. On 23 February, fighting resulted in the capture of 500 Iraqi soldiers. On 24 February, British and American armored forces crossed the Iraq-Kuwait border and entered Iraq in large numbers, taking hundreds of prisoners. Iraqi resistance was light, and 4 Americans were killed.

Coalition Forces enter Iraq

Shortly afterwards, the U.S. VII Corps, in full strength and spearheaded by the 2nd Armored Cavalry Regiment, launched an armored attack into Iraq early on 24 February, just to the west of Kuwait, taking Iraqi forces by surprise. Simultaneously, the U.S. XVIII Airborne Corps launched a sweeping "left-hook" attack across southern Iraq's largely undefended desert, led by the U.S. 3rd Armored Cavalry Regiment and the 24th Infantry Division (Mechanized). This movement's left flank was protected by France's 6th Light Armoured Division Daguet.

The French force quickly overcame Iraq's 45th Infantry Division, suffering light casualties and taking a large number of prisoners, and took up blocking positions to prevent an Iraqi counter-attack on the Coalition's flank. The movement's right flank was protected by theUnited Kingdom's 1st Armoured Division. Once the allies had penetrated deep into Iraqi territory, they turned eastward, launching a flank attack against the elite Republican Guard before it could escape. The Iraqis resisted fiercely from dug-in positions and stationary vehicles, and even mounted armored charges.

Unlike many previous engagements, the destruction of the first Iraqi tanks did not result in a mass surrender. The Iraqis suffered massive losses and lost dozens of tanks and vehicles, while U.S. casualties were comparatively low, with a single Bradley knocked out. Coalition forces pressed another ten kilometers into Iraqi territory, and captured their objective within three hours. They took 500 prisoners and inflicted heavy losses, defeating Iraq's 26th Infantry Division. A U.S. soldier was killed by an Iraqi land mine, another five by friendly fire, and thirty wounded during the battle. Meanwhile, British forces attacked Iraq's Medina Division and a major Republican Guard logistics base. In nearly two days of some of the war's most intense fighting, the British destroyed 40 enemy tanks and captured a division commander.

Meanwhile, U.S. forces attacked the village of Al Busayyah, meeting fierce resistance. They suffered no casualties, but destroyed a considerable amount of military hardware and took prisoners.

On 25 February 1991, Iraqi forces fired a Scud missile at an American barracks in Dhahran, Saudi Arabia. The missile attack killed 28 U.S. military personnel.

The Coalition's advance was much swifter than U.S. generals had expected. On 26 February, Iraqi troops began retreating from Kuwait, after they had set its oil fields on fire (737 oil wells were set on fire). A long convoy of retreating Iraqi troops formed along the main Iraq-Kuwait highway. Although they were retreating, this convoy was bombed so extensively by Coalition air forces that it came to be known as the Highway of Death. Hundreds of Iraqi troops were killed. American, British, and French forces continued to pursue retreating Iraqi forces over the border and back into Iraq, eventually moving to within 150 miles (240 km) of Baghdad before withdrawing back to Iraq's border with Kuwait and Saudi Arabia.

One hundred hours after the ground campaign started, on 28 February, President Bush declared a ceasefire, and he also declared that Kuwait had been liberated.

THE END OF ACTIVE HOSTILITIES

In Coalition-occupied Iraqi territory, a peace conference was held where a ceasefire agreement was negotiated and signed by both sides. At the conference, Iraq was approved to fly armed helicopters on their side of the temporary border, ostensibly for government transit due to the damage done to civilian infrastructure. Soon after, these helicopters and much of Iraq's military were used to fight an uprising in the south. The rebellions were encouraged by an airing of "The Voice of Free Iraq" on 2 February 1991, which was broadcast from a CIA-run radio station out of Saudi Arabia. The Arabic service of the Voice of America supported the uprising by stating that the rebellion was large, and that they soon would be liberated from Saddam.

In the North, Kurdish leaders took American statements that they would support an uprising to heart, and began fighting, hoping to trigger a coup d'état. However, when no U.S. support came, Iraqi generals remained loyal to Saddam and brutally crushed the Kurdish uprising. Millions of Kurds fled across the mountains to Turkey and Kurdish areas of Iran. These events later resulted in no-fly zones being established in northern and southern Iraq. In Kuwait, the Emir was restored, and suspected Iraqi collaborators were repressed. Eventually, over 400,000 people were expelled from the country, including a large number of Palestinians, due to PLO support of Saddam. Yasser Arafat didn't apologize for his support of Iraq, but after his death, the Fatah under Mahmoud Abbas' authority formally apologized in 2004.

There was some criticism of the Bush administration, as they chose to allow Saddam to remain in power instead of pushing on to capture Baghdad and overthrowing his government. In their co-written 1998 book, *A World Transformed*, Bush and Brent Scowcroft argued that such a course would have fractured the alliance, and would have had many unnecessary political and human costs associated with it.

In 1992, the U.S. Defense Secretary during the war, Dick Cheney, made the same point: I would guess if we had gone in there, we would still have forces in Baghdad today. We'd be running the country. We would not have been able to get everybody out and bring everybody home.

And the final point that I think needs to be made is this question of casualties. I don't think you could have done all of that without significant additional U.S. casualties, and while everybody was tremendously impressed with the low cost of the (1991) conflict, for the 146 Americans who were killed in action and for their families, it wasn't a cheap war.

And the question in my mind is, how many additional American casualties is Saddam (Hussein) worth? And the answer is, not that damned many. So, I think we got it right, both when we decided to expel him from Kuwait, but also when the President made the decision that we'd achieved our objectives and we were not going to go get bogged down in the problems of trying to take over and govern Iraq. — Dick Cheney

Instead of a greater involvement of its own military, the U.S. hoped that Saddam would be overthrown in an internal *coup d'état*. The CIA used its assets in Iraq to organize a revolt, but the Iraqi government defeated the effort.

On 10 March 1991, 540,000 U.S. troops began moving out of the Persian Gulf.

Coalition Involvement

Coalition members included Argentina, Australia, Bahrain, Bangladesh, Belgium, Canada, Czechoslovakia, Denmark, Egypt, France, Greece, Honduras, Hungary, Italy, Kuwait, Malaysia, Morocco, Netherlands, New Zealand, Niger, Norway, Oman, Pakistan, Philippines, Poland, Portugal, Qatar, Romania, Saudi Arabia, Senegal, South Korea, Spain, Sweden, Syria, Turkey, United Arab Emirates, United Kingdom of Great Britain and Northern Ireland, and the United States of America.

Germany and Japan provided financial assistance and donated military hardware, but didn't send direct military assistance. This later became known as *checkbook diplomacy*.

United Kingdom

The United Kingdom committed the largest contingent of any European state that participated in the war's combat operations. Operation Granby was the code name for the operations in the Persian Gulf. British Army regiments (mainly with the 1st Armoured Division), Royal Air Force squadrons and Royal Navy vessels were mobilized in the Gulf. The Royal Air Force, using various aircraft, operated from airbases in Saudi Arabia. Almost 2,500 armored vehicles and 53,462 troops were shipped for action.

Chief Royal Navy vessels deployed to the Gulf included *Broadsword*-class frigates, and *Sheffield*-class destroyers, other R.N. and R.F.A.ships were also deployed. The light aircraft carrier HMS *Ark Royal* was deployed to the Mediterranean Sea.

Special operations forces were deployed in the form of several SAS squadrons.

France

The second largest European contingent was from France, which committed 18,000 troops. Operating on the left flank of the U.S. XVIII Airborne Corps, the main French Army force was the 6th Light Armoured Division, including troops from the French Foreign Legion. Initially, the French operated independently under national command and control, but coordinated closely with the Americans (viaCENTCOM) and Saudis. In January, the Division was placed under the tactical control of the XVIII Airborne Corps. France also deployed several combat aircraft and naval units. The French called their contribution Opération Daguet.

Canada

Canada was one of the first countries to condemn Iraq's invasion of Kuwait, and it quickly agreed to join the U.S.-led coalition. In August 1990, Prime Minister Brian Mulroney committed theCanadian Forces to deploy a Naval Task Group. The destroyers HMCS *Terra Nova* andHMCS *Athabaskan* joined the maritime interdiction force supported by the supply shipHMCS *Protecteur* in Operation Friction. The Canadian Task Group led the Coalition's maritime logistics forces in the Persian Gulf. A fourth ship, HMCS *Huron*, arrived in-theater after hostilities had ceased and was the first allied ship to visit Kuwait.

Following the U.N.-authorized use of force against Iraq, the Canadian Forces deployed a CF-18 Hornet and CH-124 Sea King squadron with support personnel, as well as a field hospital to deal with casualties from the ground war. When the air war began, the CF-18s were integrated into the Coalition force and were tasked with providing air cover and attacking ground targets. This was the first time since theKorean War that Canada's military had participated in offensive combat operations. The only CF-18 Hornet to record an official victory during the conflict was an aircraft involved in the beginning of the Battle of Bubiyan against the Iraqi Navy.

The Canadian Commander in the Middle East was Commodore Kenneth J. Summers.

Australia

Australia contributed a Naval Task Group, which formed part of the multi-national fleet in the Persian Gulf and Gulf of Oman, underOperation Damask. In addition, medical teams were deployed aboard a U.S. hospital ship, and a naval clearance diving team took part in de-mining Kuwait's port facilities following the end of combat operations.

While the Australian forces didn't see combat, they did play a significant role in enforcing the sanctions put in place against Iraq following Kuwait's invasion, as well as other small support contributions to Operation Desert Storm. Following the war's end, Australia deployed a medical unit on Operation Habitat to northern Iraq as part of Operation Provide Comfort.

Argentina

Argentina was the only Latin American country to participate in the 1991 Gulf War sending a destroyer, ARA Almirante Brown (D-10). a corvette, ARA Spiro (P-43) (later replaced by another corvette, ARA Rosales (P-42)) and a supply ship (ARA *Bahía San Blas* (B-4)) to participate on the United Nations blockade and sea control effort of the gulf. The success of Operación Alfil ("English: Operation Bishop") as it was known, with more than 700 interceptions and 25,000 miles sailed on the operations theatre helped to overcome the so-called "Malvinas syndrome".

Argentina was later classified as major non-NATO ally due to its contributions during the war.

CASUALTIES

Civilian

Over 1,000 Kuwaiti civilians were killed in the conflict. More than 600 Kuwaitis went missing during Iraq's occupation, and approximately 375 remains were found in mass graves in Iraq. The increased importance of air attacks from both Coalition warplanes andcruise missiles led to controversy over the number of civilian deaths caused during Desert Storm's initial stages. Within Desert Storm's first 24 hours, more than 1,000 sorties were flown, many against targets in Baghdad. The city was the target of heavy bombing, as it was the seat of power for Saddam and the Iraqi forces' command and control. This ultimately led to civilian casualties.

In one noted incident, two USAF stealth planes bombed a bunker in Amiriyah, causing the deaths of 408 Iraqi civilians who were in the shelter. Scenes of burned and mutilated bodies were subsequently broadcast, and controversy arose over the bunker's status, with some stating that it was a civilian shelter, while others contended that it was a center of Iraqi military operations, and that the civilians had been deliberately moved there to act as human shields.

Saddam's government gave high civilian casualty figures, in order to draw support from Islamic countries. The Iraqi government claimed that 2,300 civilians died during the air campaign. According to the Project on Defense Alternatives study, 3,664 Iraqi civilians were killed in the conflict. An investigation by Beth Osborne Daponte estimated total civilian fatalities at about 3,500 from bombing, and some 100,000 from the war's other effects.

Iraqi

The exact number of Iraqi combat casualties is unknown, but is believed to have been heavy. Some estimate that Iraq sustained between 20,000 and 35,000 fatalities. A report commissioned by the U.S. Air Force, estimated 10,000–12,000 Iraqi combat deaths in the air campaign, and as many as 10,000 casualties in the ground war. This analysis is based on Iraqi prisoner of war reports.

According to the Project on Defense Alternatives study, between 20,000 and 26,000 Iraqi military personnel were killed in the conflict while 75,000 others were wounded.

Coalition

The DoD reports that U.S. forces suffered 148 battle-related deaths (35 to friendly fire), with one pilot listed as MIA (his remains were found and identified in August 2009). A further 145 Americans died in non-combat accidents. The U.K. suffered 47 deaths (9 to friendly fire, all by U.S. forces), France 2, and the other countries, not including Kuwait, suffered 37 deaths (18 Saudis, 1 Egyptian, 6 UAE, and 3 Qataris). At least 605 Kuwaiti soldiers were still missing 10 years after their capture.

The largest single loss of life among Coalition forces happened on 25 February 1991, when an Iraqi Al Hussein missile hit a U.S. military barrack in Dhahran, Saudi Arabia, killing 28 U.S. Army Reservists from Pennsylvania. In all, 190 Coalition troops were killed by Iraqi fire during the war, 113 of whom were American, out of a total of 358 Coalition deaths. Another 44 soldiers were killed, and 57 wounded, by friendly fire. 145 soldiers died of exploding munitions, or non-combat accidents.

The largest accident among Coalition forces happened on 21 March 1991, a Royal Saudi Air Force C-130H crashed in heavy smoke on approach to Ras Al-Mishab Airport, Saudi Arabia. 92 Senegalese soldiers and 6 Saudi crew members were killed.

The number of Coalition wounded in combat seems to have been 776, including 458 Americans.

190 Coalition troops were killed by Iraqi combatants, the rest of the 379 Coalition deaths being from friendly fire or accidents. This number was much lower than expected. Among the American dead were three female soldiers.

Friendly Fire

While the death toll among Coalition forces engaging Iraqi combatants was very low, a substantial number of deaths were caused by accidental attacks from other Allied units. Of the 148 U.S. troops who died in battle, 24% were killed by friendly fire, a total of 35 service personnel. A further 11 died in detonations of coalition munitions. Nine British military personnel were killed in a friendly fire incident when a USAF A-10 Thunderbolt II destroyed a group of two Warrior IFVs.

CONTROVERSIES

Gulf War Illness

Many returning Coalition soldiers reported illnesses following their action in the war, a phenomenon known as Gulf War syndrome or Gulf War illness. Common symptoms that were reported are chronic fatigue, Fibromyalgia, and

Gastrointestinal disorder. There has been widespread speculation and disagreement about the causes of the illness and the reported birth defects. Researchers found that infants born to male veterans of the 1991 war had higher rates of two types of heart valve defects. Gulf War veterans' children born after the war had a certain kidney defect that was not found in Gulf War veterans' children born before the war. Researchers have said that they did not have enough information to link birth defects with exposure to toxic substances. Some factors considered as possibilities include exposure to depleted uranium, chemical weapons,anthrax vaccines given to deploying soldiers, and/or infectious diseases. Major Michael Donnelly, a USAF officer during the War, helped publicize the syndrome and advocated for veterans' rights in this regard.

Effects of Depleted Uranium

Depleted uranium was used in the war in tank kinetic energy penetrators and 20–30 mm cannon ordnance. DU is a pyrophoric,genotoxic, and teratogenic heavy metal. Many have cited its use during the war as a contributing factor to a number of instances of health issues in the conflict's veterans and surrounding civilian populations. However, scientific opinion on the risk is mixed.

Some say that Depleted uranium is not a significant health hazard unless it is taken into the body. External exposure to radiation from depleted uranium is generally not a major concern because the alpha particles emitted by its isotopes travel only a few centimeters in air or can be stopped by a sheet of paper. Also, the uranium-235 that remains in depleted uranium emits only a small amount of low-energy gamma radiation. However, if allowed to enter the body, depleted uranium, like natural uranium, has the potential for both chemical and radiological toxicity with the two important target organs being the kidneys and the lungs

Highway of Death

On the night of 26–27 February 1991, some Iraqi forces began leaving Kuwait on the main highway north of Al Jahra in a column of some 1,400 vehicles. A patrolling E-8 Joint STARS aircraft observed the retreating forces and relayed the information to the DDM-8 air operations center in Riyadh, Saudi Arabia. These vehicles and the retreating soldiers were subsequently attacked, resulting in a 60 km stretch of highway strewn with debris—the Highway of Death. *New York Times* reporter Maureen Dowd wrote, "With the Iraqi leader facing military defeat, Mr. Bush decided that he would rather gamble on a violent and potentially unpopular ground war than risk the alternative: an imperfect settlement hammered out by the Soviets and Iraqis that world opinion might accept as tolerable."

Chuck Horner, Commander of U.S. and allied air operations has written:

[By February 26], the Iraqis totally lost heart and started to evacuate occupied Kuwait, but airpower halted the caravan of Iraqi Army and plunderers fleeing toward Basra. This event was later called by the media "The Highway of Death." There were certainly a lot of dead vehicles, but not so many dead Iraqis. They'd already learned to scamper off into the desert when our aircraft started to attack. Nevertheless, some people back home wrongly chose to believe we were cruelly and unusually punishing our already whipped foes.

[...]

By February 27, talk had turned toward terminating the hostilities. Kuwait was free. We were not interested in governing Iraq. So the question became "How do we stop the killing."

Bulldozer Assault

Another incident during the war highlighted the question of large-scale Iraqi combat deaths. This was the "bulldozer assault", wherein two brigades from the U.S. 1st Infantry Division (Mechanized) were faced with a large and complex trench network, as part of the heavily fortified "Saddam Hussein Line". After some deliberation, they opted to use anti-mine plows mounted on tanks and combat earthmovers to simply plow over and bury alive the defending Iraqi soldiers. Not a single American was killed during the attack. Reporters were banned from witnessing the attack, near the neutral zone that touches the border between Saudi Arabia and Iraq. Every American in the assault was inside an armored vehicle. One newspaper story reported that U.S. commanders estimated thousands of Iraqi soldiers surrendered, escaping live burial during the two-day assault 24–26 February 1991. Patrick Day Sloyan of *Newsday* reported, "Bradley Fighting Vehicles and Vulcan armored carriers straddled the trench lines and fired into the Iraqi soldiers as the tanks covered them with mounds of sand. 'I came through right after the lead company,' [Col. Anthony] Moreno said. 'What you saw was a bunch of buried trenches with peoples' arms and things sticking out of them ... '" However, after the war, the Iraqi government said that only 44 bodies were found. In his book *The Wars Against Saddam*, John Simpson alleges that U.S. forces attempted to cover up the incident. After the incident, the commander of the 1st Brigade said: "I know burying people like that sounds pretty nasty, but it would be even nastier if we had to put our troops in the trenches and clean them out with bayonets." Secretary of Defense Dick Cheney did not mention the First Division's tactics in an interim report to Congress on Operation Desert Storm. In the report, Cheney acknowledged that 457 enemy soldiers were buried during the ground war.

Palestinian Exodus from Kuwait

A Palestinian exodus from Kuwait took place during and after the Gulf War. During the Gulf War, more than 200,000 Palestinians voluntarily fled Kuwait during the Iraqi occupation of Kuwait due to harassment and intimidation by Iraqi security forces, in addition to getting fired from work by Iraqi authority figures in Kuwait. After the Gulf War, the Kuwaiti authorities forcibly pressured nearly 200,000 Palestinians to leave Kuwait in 1991. Kuwait's policy, which led to this exodus, was a response to alignment of Palestinian leader Yasser Arafat and the PLO with the dictator Saddam Hussein, who had earlier invaded Kuwait.

The Palestinians who fled Kuwait were Jordanian citizens. In 2013, there were 280,000 Jordanian citizens of Palestinian origin in Kuwait. In 2012, 80,000 Palestinians (without Jordanian citizenship) lived in Kuwait.

Saudi Arabia expelled Yemeni workers after Yemen supported Saddam during the Gulf War.

Coalition Bombing of Iraq's Civilian Infrastructure

In the 23 June 1991 edition of *The Washington Post*, reporter Bart Gellman wrote: "Many of the targets were chosen only secondarily to contribute to the military defeat of [Iraq] ... Military planners hoped the bombing would amplify the economic and psychological impact of international sanctions on Iraqi society ... They deliberately did great harm to Iraq's ability to support itself as an industrial society ..." In the Jan/Feb 1995 edition of *Foreign Affairs*, French diplomat Eric Rouleau wrote: "[T]he Iraqi people, who were not consulted about the invasion, have paid the price for their government's madness ... Iraqis understood the legitimacy of a military action to drive their army from Kuwait, but they have had difficulty comprehending the Allied rationale for using air power to systematically destroy or cripple Iraqi infrastructure and industry: electric power stations (92 percent of installed capacity destroyed), refineries (80 percent of production capacity), petrochemical complexes, telecommunications centers (including 135 telephone networks), bridges (more than 100), roads, highways, railroads, hundreds of locomotives and boxcars full of goods, radio and television broadcasting stations, cement plants, and factories producing aluminum, textiles, electric cables, and medical supplies." However, the U.N. subsequently spent billions rebuilding hospitals, schools, and water purificationfacilities throughout the country.

Abuse of Coalition POWs

During the conflict, Coalition aircrew shot down over Iraq were displayed as prisoners of war on TV, most with visible signs of abuse. Amongst several testimonies to poor treatment, Air Force Captain, Richard Storr was allegededly tortured by Iraqis during the Persian Gulf War. Iraqi secret police broke his nose, dislocated his shoulder and punctured his eardrum.

Royal Air Force Tornado crew John Nichol and John Peters have both alleged that they were tortured during this time. Nichol and Peters were forced to make statements against the war in front of television cameras. Members of British Special Air Service Bravo Two Zero were captured while providing information about an Iraqi supply line of Scud missiles to Coalition forces. Only one, Chris Ryan, evaded capture while the group's other surviving members were violently tortured. Flight surgeon (later General) Rhonda Cornum was raped by one of her captors after the Black Hawk she was riding in was shot down while searching for a downed F-16 pilot.

Operation Southern Watch

Since the war, the U.S. has had a continued presence of 5,000 troops stationed in Saudi Arabia – a figure that rose to 10,000 during the 2003 conflict in Iraq. Operation Southern Watch enforced the no-fly zones over southern Iraq set up after 1991; oil exports through the Persian Gulf's shipping lanes were protected by the Bahrain-based U.S. Fifth Fleet.

Since Saudi Arabia houses Mecca and Medina, Islam's holiest sites, many Muslims were upset at the permanent military presence. The continued presence of U.S. troops in Saudi Arabia after the war was one of the stated motivations behind the 11 September terrorist attacks, the Khobar Towers bombing, and the date chosen for the 1998 U.S. embassy bombings (7 August), which was eight years to the day that U.S. troops were sent to Saudi Arabia. Osama bin Laden interpreted the Islamic prophet Muhammad as banning the "permanent presence of infidels in Arabia". In 1996, bin Laden issued a fatwa, calling for U.S. troops to leave Saudi Arabia. In a December 1999 interview withRahimullah Yusufzai, bin Laden said he felt that Americans were "too near to Mecca" and considered this a provocation to the entire Islamic world.

Sanctions

On 6 August 1990, after Iraq's invasion of Kuwait, the U.N. Security Council adopted Resolution 661 which imposed economic sanctions on Iraq, providing for a full trade embargo, excluding medical supplies, food and other items of humanitarian necessity, these to be determined by the Council's sanctions committee. From 1991 until 2003, the effects of government policy and sanctions regime led tohyperinflation, widespread poverty and malnutrition.

During the late 1990s, the U.N. considered relaxing the sanctions imposed because of the hardships suffered by ordinary Iraqis. Studies dispute the number of people who died in south and central Iraq during the years of the sanctions.

Draining of the Qurna Marshes

The draining of the Qurna Marshes was an irrigation project in Iraq during and immediately after the war, to drain a large area of marshes in the Tigris–Euphrates river system. Formerly covering an area of around 3,000 square kilometers, the large complex of wetlands were almost completely emptied of water, and the local Shi'ite population relocated, following the war and 1991 uprisings. By 2000, United Nations Environment Programme estimated that 90% of the marshlands had disappeared, causing desertification of over 7,500 square miles (19,000 km^2).

The draining of the Qurna Marshes also called The Draining of the Mesopotamian Marshes occurred in Iraq and to a smaller degree in Iran between the 1950s and 1990s to clear large areas of the marshes in the Tigris-Euphrates river system. Formerly covering an area of around 20,000 km^2 (7,700 sq mi), the large complex ofwetlands was 90% drained prior to the 2003 Invasion of Iraq. The marshes are typically divided into three main sub-marshes, the Hawizeh, Central, and Hammar Marshes and all three were drained at different times for different reasons. Initial draining of the Central Marshes was intended to reclaim land for agriculture but later all three marshes would become a tool of war and revenge.

Many international organizations such as the U.N. Human Rights Commission, the Islamic Supreme Council of Iraq, the Wetlands International, and Middle East Watch have described the project as a political attempt to force the Marsh Arabs out of the area through water diversion tactics.

Oil Spill

On 23 January, Iraq dumped 400 million US gallons (1,500,000 m^3) of crude oil into the Persian Gulf , causing the largest offshore oil spill in history at that time. It was reported as a deliberate natural resources attack to keep U.S. Marines from coming ashore (*Missouri* and *Wisconsin* had shelled Failaka Island during the war to reinforce the idea that there would be an amphibious assault attempt). About 30–40% of this came from allied raids on Iraqi coastal targets.

Kuwaiti Oil Fires

The Kuwaiti oil fires were caused by the Iraqi military setting fire to 700 oil wells as part of a scorched earth policy while retreating from Kuwait in 1991 after conquering the country but being driven out by Coalition forces. The fires started in January and February 1991 and the last one was extinguished by November 1991.

The resulting fires burned out of control because of the dangers of sending in firefighting crews. Land mines had been placed in areas around the oil wells, and a military cleaning of the areas was necessary before the fires could be put out. Somewhere around 6 million barrels (950,000 m^3) of oil were lost each day. Eventually, privately contracted crews extinguished the fires, at a total cost of US$1.5 billion to Kuwait. By that time, however, the fires had burned for approximately ten months, causing widespread pollution.

Cost

The cost of the war to the United States was calculated by the U.S. Congress to be $61.1 billion. About $52 billion of that amount was paid by other countries: $36 billion by Kuwait, Saudi Arabia and other Arab states of the Persian Gulf; $16 billion by Germany and Japan (which sent no combat forces due to their constitutions). About 25% of Saudi Arabia's contribution was paid in the form of in-kind services to the troops, such as food and transportation. U.S. troops represented about 74% of the combined force, and the global cost was therefore higher.

Effect on Developing Countries

Apart from the impact on the Gulf states themselves, the resulting economic disruptions after the crisis affected many states. The Overseas Development Institute (ODI) undertook a study in 1991 to assess the effects on developing states and the international community's response. A briefing paper finalized on the day that the conflict ended draws on their findings which had two main conclusions: Many developing states were severely affected and while there has been a considerable response to the crisis, the distribution of assistance was highly selective.

The ODI factored in elements of "cost" which included oil imports, remittance flows, re-settlement costs, loss of export earnings and tourism. For Egypt, the cost totaled $1 billion, 3% of GDP. Yemen had a cost of $830 million, 10% of GDP, while it cost Jordan $1.8 billion, 32% of GDP.

International response to the crisis on developing states came with the channeling of aid through The Gulf Crisis Financial Co-ordination Group. They were 24 states, comprising most of the OECD countries plus some Gulf states: Saudi Arabia, United Arab Emirates, Qatar and Kuwait. The members of this group agreed to disperse $14 billion in development assistance.

The World Bank responded by speeding up the disbursement of existing project and adjustment loans. The International Monetary Fund adopted two lending facilities – the Enhanced Structural Adjustment Facility (ESAF) and the Compensatory & Contingency Financing Facility (CCFF). The European Community offered $2 billion in assistance.

MEDIA COVERAGE

The war was heavily televised. For the first time, people all over the world were able to watch live pictures of missiles hitting their targets and fighters departing from aircraft carriers. Allied forces were keen to demonstrate their weapons' accuracy.

In the United States, the "big three" network anchors led the war's network news coverage: ABC's Peter Jennings, CBS's

Dan Rather, and NBC's Tom Brokaw were anchoring their evening newscasts when air strikes began on 16 January 1991. ABC News correspondent Gary Shepard, reporting live from Baghdad, told Jennings of the city's quietness. But, moments later, Shepard was back on the air as flashes of light were seen on the horizon and tracer fire was heard on the ground.

On CBS, viewers were watching a report from correspondent Allen Pizzey, who was also reporting from Baghdad, when the war began. Rather, after the report was finished, announced that there were unconfirmed reports of flashes in Baghdad and heavy air traffic at bases in Saudi Arabia. On the "NBC Nightly News", correspondent Mike Boettcherreported unusual air activity in Dhahran, Saudi Arabia. Moments later, Brokaw announced to his viewers that the air attack had begun.

Still, it was CNN whose coverage gained the most popularity and indeed its wartime coverage is often cited as one of the landmark events in the network's history (ultimately leading to the establishment of CNN International). CNN correspondents John Holliman and Peter Arnett and CNN anchor Bernard Shaw relayed audio reports from Baghdad's Al-Rashid Hotel as the air strikes began. The network had previously convinced the Iraqi government to allow installation of a permanent audio circuit in their makeshift bureau. When the telephones of all of the other Western TV correspondents went dead during the bombing, CNN was the only service able to provide live reporting. After the initial bombing, Arnett remained behind and was, for a time, the only American TV correspondent reporting from Iraq.

In the United Kingdom, the BBC devoted the FM portion of its national speech radio station BBC Radio 4 to an eighteen-hour rolling news format creating Radio 4 News FM. The station was short lived, ending shortly after President Bush declared the ceasefire and Kuwait's liberation. However, it paved the way for the later introduction of Radio Five Live.

Two BBC journalists, John Simpson and Bob Simpson (no relation), defied their editors and remained in Baghdad to report on the war's progress. They were responsible for a report which included an "infamous cruise missile that travelled down a street and turned left at a traffic light."

Newspapers all over the world also covered the war and *Time* magazine published a special issue dated 28 January 1991, the headline "WAR IN THE GULF" emblazoned on the cover over a picture of Baghdad taken as the war began.

U.S. policy regarding media freedom was much more restrictive than in the Vietnam War. The policy had been spelled out in a Pentagon document entitled *Annex Foxtrot*. Most of the press information came from briefings organized by the military. Only selected journalists were allowed to visit the front lines or conduct interviews with soldiers. Those visits were always conducted in the presence of officers, and were subject to both prior approval by the military and censorship afterward. This was ostensibly to protect sensitive information from being revealed to Iraq. This policy was heavily influenced by the military's experience with the Vietnam War, in which public opposition within the U.S. grew throughout the war's course. It was not only the limitation of information in the Middle East; media were also restricting what was shown about the war with more graphic depictions like Ken Jarecke's image of a burnt Iraqi soldier being pulled from the American AP wire whereas in Europe it was given extensive coverage.

At the same time, the war's coverage was new in its instantaneousness. About halfway through the war, Iraq's government decided to allow live satellite transmissions from the country by Western news organizations, and U.S. journalists returned en masse to Baghdad. NBC's Tom Aspell, ABC's Bill Blakemore, and CBS News' Betsy Aaronfiled filed reports, subject to acknowledged Iraqi censorship. Throughout the war, footage of incoming missiles was broadcast almost immediately.

A British crew from CBS News (David Green and Andy Thompson), equipped with satellite transmission equipment traveled with the front line forces and, having transmitted live TV pictures of the fighting en route, arrived the day before the forces in Kuwait City, broadcasting live television from the city and covering the entrance of the Arab forces the next day.

Alternative media outlets provided views in opposition to the war. Deep Dish Television compiled segments from independent producers in the U.S. and abroad, and produced a ten-hour series that was distributed internationally, called The Gulf Crisis TV Project . The series' first program War, Oil and Power was compiled and released in 1990, before the war broke out. News World Order was the title of another program in the series; it focused on the media's complicity in promoting the war, as well as Americans' reactions to the media coverage. In San Francisco, as a local example, Paper Tiger Television West produced a weekly cable television show with highlights of mass demonstrations, artists' actions, lectures, and protests against mainstream media coverage at newspaper offices and television stations. Local media outlets in cities across the country screened similar oppositional media.

The organization Fairness and Accuracy in Reporting (FAIR) critically analyzed media coverage during the war in various articles and books, such as the 1991 *Gulf War Coverage: The Worst Censorship was at Home*.

Technology

Precision-guided munitions, such as the U.S. Air Force's AGM-130 guided missile, were heralded as key in allowing military strikes to be made with a minimum of civilian casualties compared to previous wars, although they were not used as often as more traditional, less accurate bombs. Specific buildings in downtown Baghdad could be bombed while journalists in their hotels watched cruise missiles fly by.

Precision-guided munitions amounted to approximately 7.4% of all bombs dropped by the Coalition. Other bombs included cluster bombs, which disperse numerous submunitions, and daisy cutters, 15,000-pound bombs which can disintegrate everything within hundreds of yards.

Global Positioning System units were important in enabling Coalition units to easily navigate across the desert. Since military GPS receivers were not available for most troops, many used commercially available units. To permit these to be used to best effect, the "selective availability" feature of the GPS system was turned off for the duration of Desert Storm, allowing these commercial receivers to provide the same precision as the military equipment.

Airborne Warning and Control System (AWACS) and satellite communication systems were also important. Two examples of this are the U.S. Navy's Grumman E-2 Hawkeye and the U.S. Air Force's Boeing E-3 Sentry. Both were used in command and control area of operations. These systems provided essential communications links between air, ground, and naval forces. It is one of several reasons why Coalition forces dominated the air war.

American-made color photocopiers were used to produce some of Iraq's battle plans. Some of the copiers contained concealed high-tech transmitters that revealed their positions to American electronic warfare aircraft, leading to more precise bombings.

3

The Prevention of War

THE NATURE OF STRATEGIC DECISIONS

Military calculations must take into account numerous objective factors such as force levels, weapons performance, defense systems, and the like. A strategist's advice will thus be based in part on his predictions of the material factors of battle. Success in war, however, is dependent on the competence of generals and commanders as well as on their equipment. Bad generals can lose wars even though they have the best armies, as witness the performance of the "finest army in Europe" (that of France in 1940), while good generalship can more than make up for numerical and even technical inferiority. The strategist calculates his chances of success not from statistics but from an operational plan.

His plan must take into account the quantitative factors, but it will also seek to create and exploit opportunities. War is a matter of will as well as equipment, and paralysis of the enemy's will through surprise is one of the most successful of all techniques. In war, there are real uncertainties as well as statistical probabilities. Many factors can never be quantified. The strategist is dealing with the enemy's creative force, and will counter it with his own. The calculation of destruction by means of slide rule and computer can only be a part of this process. If this appears vague and uncertain to those more used to scientific calculation, it is because war is uncertain. War is after all an operation primarily against the will of the opponent,

In some few cases, of course, the opponent is so reduced in capability that his will is no longer an important factor, but most wars have ended long before the loser's capability to damage the victor was destroyed. The great losses have occurred after surrender, in pursuit or by deliberate execution of prisoners, rather than before the decisive moment of battle. But once a combatant has lost the will to fight, his means are unimportant; and often this failure of will has been caused by surprise, by the opponent doing the unthinkable, and by so doing producing overwhelming paralysis.

It is generalship, not a calculus of forces, that decides the outcome of wars. A good general identifies opportunities to paralyze the will of his opponent and exploits them. Indeed a good strategist creates such opportunities. Generalship operates against the enemy's forces as well, of course, but even then the war is primarily against the will. When the enemy ceases to fight, the war is over, no matter that the vanquished may actually be stronger than the victor—as Darius was at Arbela. Success in war is above all dependent on generalship; it is not that objective factors such as force relationships do not count, but that generalship is far more significant. And generalship means optimal utilization of available strengths and out-thinking the enemy. Bad generalship is a repeat performance, whereas good generalship is an act of creation, hence unpredictable by either side.

Historical experience is explicit on the crucial impact of generalship: a bad general can lose despite superiority in material force and a good general can win despite considerable inferiority. Given reasonable means, and sufficient strike and reserve forces, so that the aggressive side would not be crushed even if mistakes were committed, the aggressor will calculate his chances of success not on the basis of statistics, but an operational plan, as we have pointed out. If he is a sound planner, his plan will take into account all the qualitative factors, but go beyond them to employ surprise in all elements such as strategy, technology, tactics, training, direction, concentration, and phasing. If the would-be aggressor estimates that the defender will be unable to anticipate his plan and will not have ready countersurprise operations to upset the implementation of the operation plan, he will conclude that his chances of success are high.

It is very important to understand that in these matters the calculus of generalship is far more important than the calculus of force relations. A homely example would be an investor who plays the stock market through mutual funds and thus essentially benefits by or loses from the overall movements of the market. Such an investor can calculate his probable successes on the basis of curves depicting the performance of the market in the past. However, the most successful investors operate both with and against the market. In like manner, a good strategist can identify special situations or opportunities and work out a scheme to take advantage of the openings. Naturally, in a war where there are many opportunities there are only a few that hold great promise of massive success, even if they are exploited with the greatest skill. Furthermore, good opportunities may be fleeting and there may not be enough time to exploit them properly. On the other hand, the strategist who possesses large resources, like the market operator controlling large funds, can create suitable opportunities.

These observations apply to both the offensive and the defensive strategist. Success always depends on more than the resources in hand. It results from a clear knowledge of the objectives to be gained by the particular strategy and from seizing the initiative in carrying out the strategy.

Whether planning aggression or defense against aggression, the strategist must calculate the results of the clashes of forces. He must always remember that he is dealing with human action, the essence of which is creativity. As a consequence, he knows he is grappling with uncertainties, with the basic uncertainties that result from the creativeness of the adversary.

OFFENSE AND DEFENSE

In this interplay of creativities, the aggressor has certain advantages that come from his position. The decision to attack is his. Thus, he knows when hostilities will begin. The defender cannot have this certainty. Every moment can be the moment of the attack. To heighten the effects of his blow, the attacker strives for surprise in as many elements of his strategy as possible. One of the problems of the defender is to prevent his being the surprised. This increases his needs for information about the intent of the enemy and requires him to expend resources on being constantly ready.

The attacker can build his plan for aggression around the availability of a decisive weapon. This can take the form of a technical surprise for the defender, but it need not. If the aggressor calculates that the defender cannot counter his new advance in time, he can make his decision on the basis of this crucial superiority.

In the present age of total conflict, the aggressor can manipulate the many facets of his strategy to produce a wide variety of threats and opportunities. Political warfare, economic warfare, propaganda, the struggle for technological supremacy, diplomatic maneuverings, subversion, and military operations, taken together or individually, give the aggressor many opportunities. The defender, for his part, must provide a total defense against all these forms of conflict. Most important, he must avoid being second in technical advances that can lead to a decisive military advantage.

The defensive strategist is not without advantages on his side, provided that he does not passively wait for the blow. he can take initiatives to gain and maintain a position of superiority in the various forms of conflict. By having such superiority, he prevents the aggressor from finding the moment for the attack. The defender can plan and execute his own surprises against the would-be aggressor. The combination of initiative and surprise on the part of the defensive strategist produces the creative uncertainty that negates the advantages of the attacker. It is a military truism that strategic offensive and tactical defensive is often a superior position. Sun Tzu says, "Take what the enemy holds dear and await attack."

It is axiomatic that the objectives of the attacker and defender are asymmetric. Thus, the initiatives they take and the advances they make need not and probably should not be of the same kind. They should be chosen for their potential ability to reach the objectives of the strategy.

THE MODERN STRATEGIC WAR

The strategy of the United States, and indeed free world strategy, is defensive. We seek no political, economic, or territorial aggrandizement. We do seek to prevent war. These objectives are clearly in direct opposition to those of the Communist bloc. They seek world domination. They create opportunities to use warfare to attain it.

We should recognize clearly that our defensive strategy must include initiatives and surprises. Ours need not be a reactive strategy. In fact, the struggle for technological supremacy makes a reactive strategy a most dangerous one.

Waiting for clear indications of Soviet initiatives can prevent us from acting in time. We must be constantly on the initiative to anticipate their moves and to create situations to which they must react.

In the past, we used technology to overcome the advantages of the Soviets both in the resources they control and in the initiatives we conceded them. We succeeded in negating their quantitative superiority by the qualitative advantages we acquired through a superior technology.

The circumstances today are radically different. The Soviets have challenged us in technology. They have enlarged the spectrum of conflict, taking advantage of the inevitable new struggle, the Technological War. No longer are we free to follow an independent course in implementing our strategy. We must meet the technological threat as well as the threats in other forms of conflict.

This form of warfare has become crucial. A technical advance can lead to a decisive military advantage. It is not enough for us to continue past approaches to our total strategy. The strategist must recast his thinking if he is to make his defensive strategy effective.

He must find avenues for the initiative in technology. He must prevent the would-be aggressor from attaining a clear advantage in any aspect of technology that could be translated into a decisive military advantage.

Broader horizons are needed in another aspect of the problem of the defensive strategist. Planning methodology and decision processes reflect the past situation. They are no longer adequate. The time has come to break the shackles of science on planning methodology.

We need to rehumanize planning and strategy. This process will have a direct impact on decision making. Decision makers can no longer find refuge in the alleged certainties and probabilities that past planning provided them. We are now in an era of creative, dynamic uncertainty. We must have a strong defensive position. But we must also create strategic diversions, feints, deceptions, and surprises.

Only in this way can the defensive strategist ensure that the attacker will choose not to strike. A viable strategy poses insurmountable problems for the aggressor.

The Effect of Nuclear Weapons

Nuclear weapons have not changed the nature of strategy; however, they have introduced new complications, just as they have introduced new opportunities. The major new opportunity is that the strategist, once he decides to strike, can apply far more power, over larger areas, than could any of his predecessors who fought with low-energy weapon systems.

The main new complication is that the defender, even though deprived of a large portion of his initial strength in the course of the first battle, would still retain enormous firepower to hurt the attacker far more dangerously than it was ever before possible for a defensive force to do.

This residual force can be used against the attacker's population, industry, urban areas, government control centers, and armed forces, provided that the defender has not acquired active and passive defenses, and the defender's will to retaliate has not failed. The scope of war has grown to include entire undefended populations, not merely military forces. Also, it is easily conceivable that under some circumstances the attacker, although he may defeat the defender, may achieve only Pyrrhic victory. Or, even if he achieves an unqualified victory, he would not enjoy the fruits because he has paid an excessive price. In fact, he may have lost his country to the blows that his defeated adversary was still able to inflict. Nuclear weapons have not worked totally to the advantage of the attacker.

It would be a grave mistake to assume that this particular strategic problem is new. Even if it were new, the significant aspect is whether the danger of devastating retaliation would prevent war.

To put it in different terms, the question is whether such a hazard would prevent the aggressive strategist from planning for war in a rational manner. Obviously a great deal of the strategist's mental effort must be devoted to the security of the aggressor's homeland. If the defender can be induced to leave his weapons unused, the aggressor can still achieve decisive victory.

In order to prevent aggression, the defender must seek safety in strength. He must seek superior technology, modern weapons that can survive attack, and engage actively in the Technological War. He cannot rely on agreements, planned weaknesses, or minimum strength.

In the last analysis, superior strength remains the most reliable insurance for survival of the defender. The strategist of the superior power has some chance of predicting what his enemy might do; the strategist of a greatly inferior power can only hope. A defensive strategy aiming at superiority in power offers the only dependable hedge against errors in planning.

Force Levels in the Nuclear Era

It is clear that as the armaments race takes place on high force levels the aggressor will be hard-put to achieve decisive superiority. The conclusion to draw from this is that relatively low levels of nuclear power are a chief prerequisite for nuclear attack. This is especially true in a period when cities have not been fully dispersed and populations have not been cannot be effectively protected by a program of active and civil defense.

Low levels of forces in being are more of a danger to the United States than high levels—fears of genocide and the arms race notwithstanding. This is an important finding, which casts a very disturbing light on the recent history of U.S. armaments and armament negotiations.

Of the two belligerents, the one who is able to continue the war beyond the initial strike will have an enormous advantage because the side that does not have this capability will cave in morally and will be unable to reconstitute its force. Such a capability can only be provided by vigorous pursuit of technology, including the design and the deployment of weapons.

The survival force is one key to security. As long as the U.S. has secure weapon systems that can ride out the initial and follow-on strikes, the U.S. will be able to deter any rationally planned attack. The in-being power that is still effective after the battles are over will determine the final outcome.

Our defensive strategy requires us to have a survivable force. Hardening, dispersal, mobility, and concealment contribute to survival, but they are supporting strategic themes. The single most important element of our defensive strategy is to have in being a clear superiority in effective and reliable numbers. This is the one factor in the strategic equation that is most easily understood and the one the enemy is least likely to misunderstand. Numerical superiority on our side is necessary to convince the aggressor not to strike.

A would-be aggressor, if he were to act rationally, would realize that he cannot cope with high force levels. Therefore, he must make an attempt to bring forces down to a level where he can fight nuclear war—especially if through clandestine armaments of his own he achieves an enormous superiority. It is clear that the aggressor is not particularly perturbed by high force levels of his own, let alone by relative superiority, but is disturbed by a high force level owned by the defender. His problem, therefore, is to achieve a substantial quantitative superiority. To achieve this goal he must persuade the defender to be content with moderate strength. Another reason why the aggressor needs the low level of forces is that decisive increments in strength are difficult to conceal if they have to be produced within the framework of high force levels. This means that psycho-political strategy is an integral part of nuclear strategy, first to achieve some sort of reduction of armament levels, then to provide a cover to conceal the aggressor's armaments and third, to facilitate nuclear blackmail and prevent retaliation.

Security Through Arms Control

The unending process of armaments has often been criticized as the greatest waste of which mankind is guilty. It is true that if both sides stay in the race and run well the world situation will remain stable and no war will occur; the weapons will then be said to have been wasted.

The arms control argument is that if both sides agree not to engage in arms races, peace would be preserved effectively and at far less cost.

However, we have already seen that by lowering the levels of destruction war would bring, reductions in arms make war thinkable and more therefore likely. This, it would seem, is one major argument against arms control and disarmament. However, it is hardly the only such argument.

Since technology is dynamic, no one can agree to stand still. Force relationships change in the course of armament cycles despite the best planning possible. Sudden accretions of military power can come to a side not even expecting them. New technologies create new power.

It is true that the tempo of this eternal race can be accelerated or slowed. Aside from the technological factors that often determine this tempo, the speed of the process is largely set by political factors, including strategic intentions.

If no disturber power is at work, the tempo will slacken almost automatically. If there is a disturber power, explicit or tacit slow-down agreements are at best highly unreliable and temporary. The side that takes the risk of slowing down unilaterally will soon be punished.

The history of disarmament agreements teaches an explicit lesson: international promissory treaties are almost invariably broken and are therefore an utterly undependable instrument of national security.

The fundamental reason for the defender to stay in this expensive race, and to run hard in it, is to stay alive and not allow the would-be attacker to achieve such an advantage that he might be inclined to break the peace and impose his will on the naive and gullible defender.

So long as the defender must stay in the arms competition, he does not really have the option of running a selective race. He cannot leave open any geographical or technological flanks, or the opponent will take advantage of his opportunities. Thus, the United States does not really have the free choice of saying that it will stop communism in Europe and defend the East Coast, but ignore Communist advances in Asia.

Nor can it say that it will maintain offensive nuclear weapons but not acquire defensive ones, or that it will try to be strong in inner space but will assume that outer space is of no military relevance.

Least of all can the United States entrust its security to so-called disarmament treaties, not because it must necessarily and always presuppose bad faith on the part of other nations (although sometimes it must make preçisely such an assumption of bad faith), but for the far more elementary reasons that (a) reliable inspection of disarmament agreements is unfeasible, (b) that enforcement against treaty violations requires war, and (c) that disarmament agreements apply to weapons already in existence, but will be speedily outdated and be rendered irrelevant by new weapons, the characteristics of which were unknown at the time the treaty was written.

Security in the Modern Era

As we have seen, security cannot be guaranteed by Soviet intentions; not only do Soviet theorists predict inevitable victory by the U.S.S.R., and Soviet generals hasten to install the latest weapons, but, even were we convinced that the U.S.S.R. is ruled by men who have lost their aggressive drives, there is no guarantee that a new Stalin will never again take power.

Security cannot be guaranteed by passive measures. The most modern force purchased at enormous cost will become obsolete in only a few years. Security cannot be guaranteed by agreements to halt the Technological War; the stream of technology moves on without regard for our intentions. The only way to guarantee security is to engage in the Technological War with the intention of winning it. It is as true today as in Roman times that "If you would have peace, prepare thou then for war."

Regardless of the enormous effects of modern weapons, organized brainpower remains the strongest and ultimately decisive factor.

The experience of Vietnam, the test ban, and the Sputnik have shown that we do not excel in that department. It is not that we lack intelligent people but that we lack an effective organization through which we can optimize our brainpower and collective memory. On the contrary, the more we have overorganized, the more we reduced brainpower and the more we forgot. Secretary McNamara even organized strategic amnesia.

We must decide to engage in the Technological War, and we must create the planning staff to guide us in this decisive conflict. To do anything short of this is to risk national suicide. At the same time, we must preserve the values that make our society worth defending; we cannot contemplate ending the Technological War by destroying our enemies without warning. Our goal is the indefinite preservation of peace and order, and our hope is that in such an environment the root causes of conflict will slowly wither.

The era of Technological War has not ended conflict, and that millennium may never come. Technological War does, however, have the advantage of being relatively peaceful, so long as the stabilizer powers remain strong. Despite the greatest threat Western civilization has ever known, since 1945 the amount of blood shed to preserve the peace has been quite small—smaller than that shed on the highways. The Technological War can be kept silent and apparently peaceful so long as we continue to engage in it successfully.

Despite fashionable rhetoric, history shows that American supremacy brings relative peace and stability to the world; where the U.S.S.R. has enjoyed local superiority the results have been quite different. American success in the Technological War is the primary prerequisite for the preservation of world peace.

In 1985 Secretary of Defense Caspar Weinberger said, "To the extent that we in the United States desire true peace with freedom, peace based on individual and sovereign rights and on the principle of resolution of disputes through negotiation, we must acknowledge and follow our interests in creating conditions in which democratic forces can gain and thrive in this world. A world not of our making, but a world in which we must fight to maintain our peace and our strength. And a world in which the very best way to maintain peace is to be militarily strong and thus deter war." Of course we agree.

The dramatic benefits of that strategy became apparent in 1989. It is vital that we understand that despite the events in Eastern Europe the Technological War is not over. It has only changed fronts.

FOUNDATIONS OF THE TECHNOLOGICAL WAR

Fundamentals of Technological Strategy

There are four overall aspects to technological strategy. Enumerating them does not constitute a strategy but merely sets forth certain criteria with which to judge the conduct of the conflict. They are:

- Forces In Being
- Modernization of Weapons
- Modernization of the Technological Base
- Operational Capability to Use New Technology

A power that does not intend to end the Technological War by destroying the enemy must constantly maintain superiority and continuously modernize its forces. At all times, the defending nation in the Protracted Conflict must maintain sufficient forces in being to assure that the enemy does not end the conflict by *coup de main*, or an overwhelming surprise blow. These forces must *have* the modern weapons they require, and must know how to use them; must have operational familiarity with them.

The result is a highly dynamic process, requiring careful judgment. We certainly cannot depend on our former strategy of industrial mobilization, relying on overseas allies to bear the initial brunt of the war while we convert from a peace to a war economy. We must have a force in being which cannot be destroyed by the enemy, and which can *quickly* move to counter the enemy's aggressive actions.

Secondly, the force in being must be a modern force. It is unimportant if we surpass the enemy in capability to conduct horse-cavalry conduct, or even guerrilla war, if we do not have a force that can fight successfully with modern high-energy weapons. The situation is not symmetrical; if we possess superiority or supremacy, we need not end the conflict by destroying the enemy, and will not do so because of our essentially defensive grand strategy. However, we cannot afford to allow the enemy superiority or supremacy, because he could use it to force so many concessions — particularly from our then-unprotected allies — that the contest would be decided in his favor even if he did not employ his decisive weapons to destroy us.

Finally, we must assure that the technological base from which our forces in being are derived is truly modern and creative. We must be certain that we have missed no decisive bets in the Technological War, that we have abandoned no leads which the enemy could exploit for a decisive advantage over us. For every capability he has, we must have a counter, either through defending against the weapon or riposte against him if he uses it. More important, we must keep a sufficient technological base to allow us to generate the capability to counter any new weapons he constructs or may suddenly invent; and we must stay sufficiently current to allow us to seize the technological initiative when the enemy poses new threats.

Dimensions of the Technological War

The dimensions of the Technological War range farther than any conflict previously known in human history. They include the aerospace, from ground-level to trans-lunar space; the ground and the underground deep within the earth; and the surface of the seas and the underwater world we call inner space. The battlegrounds of the Technological War could include every conceivable area in which military conflict can occur. Yet, this is merely the endgame aspect of the Technological War. Actual military battle may never take place. The dimensions of the war also include the nonmilitary struggles, psycho-political warfare, ideological warfare, economics and trade, and the educational process. A college campus with students shrilly screaming obscenities at the police, and a quiet laboratory populated with soft-spoken men armed with chalk and blackboards are equally important battlegrounds.

Technological Warfare in its decisive phase will aim at bypassing the other forms of military conflict and striking directly at the will to resist. Military power may be used, and thermonuclear warfare may be necessary to consolidate the victory, but the true aim of the Technological War is the denial, paralysis, and negation of all forms of hostile military power. Often this may be achieved through psycho-political pressure employing tactics of demonstration, terror, despair, and surprise, conducted in concert perhaps with other forms of warfare.

An Overview of the Nature of Technology

Before we examine the strategy of Technological War, it is necessary to understand the nature of technology. Contrary to what people have often been encouraged to believe, it is not necessary to be a scientist or technologist to comprehend the general nature of technology, or to employ technology in a strategic contest. Indeed, sometimes specialization on one aspect of technology and strategy prevents understanding of technology in its broader sense.

The following discussion is a nontechnical introduction to the general nature of technology and strategy. Later sections of this book develop each of these themes more fully, but because of the interdependence of strategy and technology in modern warfare, it is not possible to organize this book into discrete sections and chapters. Modern Technological Warfare is a mixture of strategy and technology, and their interrelationships.

The primary fact about technology in the twentieth century is that it has a momentum of its own. Although the technological stream can to some extent be directed, it is impossible to dam it; the stream flows on endlessly. This leaves only three choices. You may swim with the stream, exploiting every aspect of technology to its fullest; you may attempt to crawl out on the bank and watch the rest of the world go past; or you can attempt to swim against the stream and "put the genii back in the bottle".

Since nearly every nation, and certainly both superpowers, swim in more or less the same technological stream, only the first course of action makes sense. To continue the analogy for a moment, there is a fog over the surface of the water, so that you cannot know exactly what and how your opponents — open enemies, or economic competitors — are doing. An opponent may tell you he has crawled out on the bank and is enjoying the view, while in fact he is either treading water or racing away from you. If you do not intend to lose, you have little choice but to swim with the current as long and as hard as you can.

The nature of technology makes meaningless the gunpowder era phrase 'arms race'. It is fashionable at present to speak of the action-reaction arms race, in which each power constructs weapons for fear that the other has done so. According to this theory, the primary reason nations arm themselves is that they react to others.

The newest catch phrases are "arms race stability" and "assured stability". These slogans are essentially undefined by their authors, who advocate that the U.S. simply opt out of a Technological War we can't afford. The Soviet Union, under this notion, will also see the advantages of "arms race stability" and likewise abandon the struggle. The money saved by both sides can be invested in social programs and increased consumption.

We make no doubt that there will be other such catch phrases and buzz words, and that they will also remain undefined and only loosely coupled with reality.

In fact, in the Technological War, opposing powers essentially react to the seemingly impersonal stream that carries them along. They really have no choice and never will have so long as the current flows and there is asymmetry of information between them. The technology stream *exists* independent of the will of those who create technology. The *direction and pace*, however, are more amenable to control by strategists.

To continue our analogy, the fog over the technological battlefield is made denser by confusion caused partly by deliberate deception and partly by self-deceptions. Only when the Communist states have transformed themselves into open societies and there is a complete exchange of information — that is, when the fog has lifted from the stream of technology — can meaningful efforts to arrange the contest on a more economical and less risky basis be successful. Until that time we must engage in the Technological War. It is fairly obvious that rationalization of the Technological War will not come in our lifetimes. *glasnost* may be genuinely desired by Mikhael Gorbachev and most subjects of the Soviet empire, but its permanence as a policy is not guaranteed. *glasnost* is especially fragile if the USSR is faced with the opportunity for a decisive win. Finally, we would do well to expect that even if the U.S.S.R. were to change its character, other threats might arise in its stead.

Arms races in the nuclear era differ from those in the gunpowder era in one fundamental way: they are qualitative rather than quantitative. In the gunpowder era, numbers of divisions, tanks, battleships, and aircraft gave rough estimates of the strength of the possessor and his capability to defend himself. It was possible to overcome an enemy by sheer numbers of weapons alone. In the nuclear era, numbers remain important, of course, but the primary strength lies in quality of weapons and their survivability. Nuclear weapons can destroy an enemy's entire military power in one strike if the attacker possess sufficient qualitative superiority. Space technology gives the promise of negating the ICBM as a deterrent to a first strike. This too is a result of the nature of modern technology.

One of the most easily observed phenomena of technology is that it moves by "S" curves, as illustrated in Figure One. Take for example speed; for centuries the speed of military operations increased only slightly as each side developed better horses. Then came the internal combustion engine. Speed rose sharply for a while. Eventually, though, it flattened out again, and each increase took longer and longer to achieve.

Technology is interdependent: advances in one sector of technology soon influence areas which might naively have been believed unrelated. For example, the development of molecular chemistry techniques led to the art of microminiaturization, which allows development of computer technology beyond the expectations of only a few years ago. The revolution in computer sciences has made possible the development of on-board computers for missile guidance, and thus of accuracies not previously predicted. Increased accuracy has made possible the destruction of missile silos with much greater ease and smaller warheads.

Nuclear research, meanwhile, had developed smaller and lighter warheads; this coupled with increased accuracy has led to the development of Multiple Independently Targetable Re-Entry Vehicles (MIRV), each one of which uses on-board guidance computers. The increased kill capability stimulated research into silo hardening techniques, which led directly to what were called "hard rock silo" designs. That development made it possible to conduct certain mining operations that were previously financially infeasible. Examples of interdependence can be given without limit.

Thus, technology influences nearly every aspect of national life. In particular, technology influences strategy, forcing strategic revolutions at frequent intervals. There are those who say that strategy never changes. If they mean literally what they say, they have never appreciated the effects of the airplane and the ICBM, the possibilities for surprise attack created by these radical new weapons delivery systems coupled with thermonuclear explosives, and the effect they have on ground battles.

The important fact is that technology paces strategy to a great extent, and forces the development of new military strategies which take the new technology into account. As we will show, it is dangerous to regard this relationship as one-sided. Technology and strategy are interrelated, and strategy can and should also pace technology.

This is well illustrated by the SDI program. President Reagan was convinced that the U.S. needed a new strategy. That strategy was impossible without new technology. His call for technology to make possible a strategy of 'assured survival' stimulated a dozen technology development programs. It is important to note that most of them worked, and some worked much better than we had supposed they would.

We have not always done badly in this race. Despite the opposition of a number of scientists, the feasibility and potentially decisive advantages of ballistic missiles were early recognized, and a program to develop and deploy these weapons was undertaken. The Thor IRBM was designed, developed, and ready to deploy in just over three years. Submarine launched missiles were developed in parallel. The IRBM was soon followed by the ICBM. Meanwhile, missile research led to capabilities in space technology.

Shortly before the first edition of this book was written, the major computer companies of the world decided that the United States would need no more than a dozen computers, none of them more powerful than the equipment that now sits on desktops in small businesses. The demands for further accuracy in missiles led to developments in miniaturization of components, including on-board guidance computers; the result became a full revolution in computer technology. That revolution's full extent cannot yet be measured.

Despite some spectacular successes, technology appears to many of our national leaders, and most of the Congress, to be an impersonal force. Although America is the leading technological power — perhaps because we are the leading technological power — many of our leaders do not really comprehend technology. As a consequence, technology remains largely a matter of individual initiative. Sometimes we do well. The first edition of this book contained lengthy analyses of our faults. Many have since been corrected.

Unfortunately, we still have no comprehensive strategy for winning the Technological War.

THE DECISIVE WAR

The technological contest is a war. It is not a game against an impersonal force, it is a deadly conflict with an intelligent and implacable enemy. We do not suppose that a military commander who conducted his battles as they occurred, understanding neither the terrain nor the enemy and preparing only for the battle that he had already fought, would be properly performing his task.

Yet, too often this is precisely what happens in the Technological War, which may be the most decisive engagement in the history of mankind. Technology has grown into the driving force, dictating to strategy; and strategy is conceived of as employment of systems already created by the technologists; that is, strategy is confined to operational decisions. This is akin to allowing the recruiting and supply officers to decide the conduct of a traditional land war.

The danger in the Technological War is that it is closely coupled with the Protracted Conflict, and a decisive lead in the Technological War can be converted into a decisive advantage in military weapons. Note that military power and technological power are coupled, but are not identical; military technology is not in and of itself a weapon system, but it can be used to create weapons systems. Thus a commanding lead in the Technological War can be achieved before a corresponding lead in military technology has been obtained.

As an example, the Soviet Union could, through the development of strategic nuclear defense technology, obtain a decisive lead in the Technological War at a time when the United States still possessed a clear superiority in deliverable weapons. This technology could then be used to create defense systems, and if the United States took no countermeasures during the deployment of those defensive systems, we would find ourselves in an inferior military position.

This is an especial danger if the numbers of strategic offensive weapons has been limited by arms reduction treaties and the Soviets then "break out" of the defensive and offensive limits imposed by the ABM Treaty and SALT. The closed nature of Soviet society makes planning for breakouts rather simple; the open nature of the US makes that nearly impossible. Note that the USSR used the breakout strategy following the 'gentleman's agreement' Test Ban.

During the 1970's the Soviet Union achieved (entirely predictable) spectacular gains in achievable accuracies, and also built large new missiles capable of carrying a dozen and more warheads over intercontinental distances. The United States relied on Arms Control negotiations for security; when these failed, we found ourselves facing a "window of vulnerability" — that is, a period of time during which, if we do not act promptly and intelligently, the Soviet Union could construct a first strike capability. The Soviets continued to deploy ICBM's in large numbers. The "window of vulnerability" has not entirely been overcome as of 1988, although President Reagan's strategic force modernization program took away much of the danger.

In addition, the USSR has undertaken serious research into strategic defense systems, not merely building on the single system permitted under the ABM Treaty, but also investigating entirely new concepts. When the US began its own strategic defense investigation in 1983, the Soviet Union redoubled its efforts, including construction of large components such as the radar system at Krasnyarsk. None of this was decisive. Victory in the Technological War is achieved when a finite game participant (ie, one who wishes to bring the game to an end by winning it) has a technological lead so far advanced that his opponent cannot overcome it until after the leader has converted his technology into decisive weapons systems. The loser may know that he has lost, and know it for quite a long time, yet be unable to do anything about it. To continue the above example, if the Soviet Union were able to develop the technology in time to deploy ballistic missile defense systems of his own before ours could be installed and operational, we would be beaten, even though the U.S.S.R. might spend several years in deployment of his own system. Our only choices would be the development of a penetration system that his defenses could not counter (such as manned bombers of very high capabilities), surrender, or preventive war.

Now, in the late 1980's, many believe that development of space laser battle stations will be a decisive move in the technological war. The laser battle station could, at least in theory, destroy an entire ICBM force in flight, then burn down the enemy's bomber fleet for encore. Such a station once in place could give a decisive lead to its owner.

In practice a space laser battle station would require auxiliary equipment for its own defense, since there are many ways to attack such a system; on the other hand, it is likely that such escort systems would be deployed by any power constructing a large space laser battle station.

The Soviets have raised the specter that other space weapons which they call "space strike weapons" are being developed as part of the US Strategic Defense Initiative. The fact that the Soviets emphasize such a threat at a time when the US has no concepts, let alone a technology which could produce them, raises the concern that the Soviets are developing them, because the Soviets often accuse the US of developing and deploying weapons which they themselves are developing.

Several years after the initial Soviet assertions that SDI raised the spectre of such weapons, the Soviets defined them for Ambassador Henry Cooper, head of the US negotiating team on defense and space talks, as : (1) Ground to space weapons, (2) Space to space weapons; and (3) Space to ground weapons. The U.S.S.R. has demonstrated all three: Galosh interceptors against satellites; co-orbital ASATs; and FOBs, which are bombs in orbit.

If space and ground based ICBM defenses could give us a decisive advantage, they would confer no less advantage on the Soviets if we allow our enemies to develop them without any counter on our part.

This is the unique feature of the Technological War. Military superiority or even supremacy is not permanent, and never ends the conflict unless it is used. The United States considers the Technological War as an infinite game: one which is not played out to a decisive victory. We are committed to a grand strategy of defense, and will never employ a decisive advantage to end the conflict by destroying our enemies. Consequently, we must maintain not only military superiority but technological supremacy.

In summary, proper conduct of the Technological War requires that strategy drive technology most forcefully; that there be an overall strategy of the Technological War, allocating resources according to well-defined objectives and an operational plan, not merely strategic elements which make operational use of the products of technology. Instead of the supply officer and the munitions designer controlling the conduct of this decisive war, command must be placed in the hands of those who understand the Technological War; and this requires that they first understand the nature of war.

Lest the reader be confused, we do not advocate that the Technological War be given over to the control of the scientists, or that scientists should somehow create a strategy of technological development. We mean that an understanding of the art of war is more important than familiarity with one or another of the specialties of technology. It is a rare scientist who makes a good strategist; and the generals of the Technological War need not be scientists any more than the generals of the past needed to be good riflemen or railroad engineers.

Like all wars, the Technological War must be conducted by a *commander* who operates with a strategy. It is precisely the lack of such a strategy that brought the United States to the 1970's low point in prestige and power, with her ships seized across the world, her Strategic Offensive Forces (SOF) threatened by the growing Soviet SOF — and with the United States perplexed by as simple a question as whether to attempt to defend her people from enemy thermonuclear bombs, and unable to win a lesser war in South East Asia.

We had neither generals nor strategy, and muddled through the most decisive conflict in our national history.

Much of this changed in 1981. President Reagan's 1983 call for SDI was in response to strategic analyses presented by General Daniel O. Graham and others.

There always were exceptions to this unsatisfactory record of American performance. General Bernard Schriever created a military organization for strategic analysis which was responsible for our early commanding lead over the Soviets in ballistic missiles, despite the fact that the U.S. had allowed the U.S.S.R. many years' head start in missile development after World War II. The Air Force's Project Forecast and later Project 75, was an attempt to let strategy react to, then drive, technology; these, too, were creations of General Schriever's.

In the Navy there have also been notable attempts to allow strategy to influence technology and produce truly modern weapons systems.

4

Environmental Effects of Warfare

THE IMPACT OF WAR ON THE ENVIRONMENT AND HUMAN HEALTH

The application of weapons, the destruction of structures and oil fields, fires, military transport movements and chemical spraying are all examples of the destroying impact war may have on the environment. Air, water and soil are polluted, man and animal are killed, and numerous health affects occur among those still living. This page is about the environmental effects of wars and incidents leading to war that have occurred in the 20th and 21st century.

TIMELINE OF WARS

In Africa many civil wars and wars between countries occurred in the past century, some of which are still continuing. Most wars are a result of the liberation of countries after decades of colonialization. Countries fight over artificial borders drawn by former colonial rulers. Wars mainly occur in densely populated regions, over the division of scarce resources such as fertile farmland. It is very hard to estimate the exact environmental impact of each of these wars. Here, a summary of some of the most striking environmental effects, including biodiversity loss, famine, sanitation problems at refugee camps and over fishing is given for different countries.

Congo war (II) – Since August 1998 a civil war is fought in former Zaire, now known as the Democratic Republic of the Congo (DRC). The war eventually ended in 2003 when a Transitional Government took power. A number of reasons are given for the conflict, including access and control of water resources and rich minerals and political agendas. Currently over 3 million people have died in the war, mostly from disease and starvation. More than 2 million people have become refugees. Only 45% of the people had access to safe drinking water. Many women were raped as a tool of intimidation, resulting in a rapid spread of sexually transmitted diseases such as HIV-AIDS. The war has a devastating effect on the environment. National parks housing endangered species are often affected for exploitation of minerals and other resources. Refugees hunt wildlife for bush meat, either to consume or sell it. Elephant populations in Africa have seriously declined as a result of ivory poaching. Farmers burn parts of the forest to apply as farmland, and corporate logging contributes to the access of poachers to bush meat. A survey by the WWF showed that the hippopotamus population in one national park decreased from 29,000 thirty years previously, to only 900 in 2005. The United Nations Educational, Scientific and Cultural Organization (UNESCO) listed all five parks as 'world heritage in danger'.

Ethiopia & Eritrea – Before 1952, Eritrea was a colony of Italy. When it was liberated, Ethiopia annexed the country. Thirty years of war over the liberation of Eritrea followed, starting in 1961 and eventually ending with the independence of Eritrea in 1993. However, war commenced a year after the country introduced its own currency in 1997. Over a minor border dispute, differences in ethnicity and economic progress, Ethiopia again attacked Eritrea. The war lasted until June 2000 and resulted in the death of over 150,000 Eritrean, and of hundreds of thousands of Ethiopians. During the war severe drought resulted in famine, particularly because most government funds were spend on weapons and other war instrumentation. The government estimated that after the war only 60% of the country received adequate food supplies. The war resulted in over 750,000 refugees. It basically destroyed the entire infrastructure. Efforts to disrupt agricultural production in Eritrea resulted in changes in habitat. The placing of landmines has caused farming or herding to be very dangerous in most parts of the country. If floods occur landmines may be washed into cities. This has occurred earlier in Mozambique.

Rwanda civil war - Between April and July 1994 extremist military Hutu groups murdered about 80,000-1,000,000 Tutsis and moderate Hutus in Rwanda. Over 2,000,000 people lost their homes and became refugees.

Rwanda has a very rich environment, however, it has a particularly limited resource base. About 95% of the population lives on the countryside and relies on agriculture. Some scientists believe that competition for scarce land and resources led to violence prior to and particularly after the 1994 genocide. It is however stated that resource scarcity only contributed limitedly to the conflict under discussion. The main cause of the genocide was the death of the president from a plane-crash caused by missiles fires from a camp.

The many refugees from the 1994 combat caused a biodiversity problem.

When they returned to the already overpopulated country after the war, they inhabited forest reserves in the mountains where endangered gorillas lived. Conservation of gorilla populations was no longer effective, and refuges destroyed part of the habitat. Despite the difficulties still present in Rwanda particularly concerning security and resource provision, an international gorilla protection group is now working on better conditions for the gorillas in Rwanda.

Somalia civil war – A civil war was fought in Somalia 1991. One of the most striking effects of the war was over fishing. The International Red Cross was encouraging the consumption of seawater fish to improve diets of civilians. For self-sufficiency they provided training and fishing equipment. However, as a consequence of war Somali people ignored international fishing protocols, thereby seriously harming ecology in the region. Fishing soon became an unsustainable practise, and fishermen are hard to stop because they started carrying arms. They perceive over fishing as a property right and can therefore hardly be stopped.

Sudan (Darfur & Chad) – In Sudan civil war and extreme droughts caused a widespread famine, beginning in 1983. Productive farmland in the southern region was abandoned during the war. Thousands of people became refugees that left behind their land, possibly never to return. Attempts of remaining farmers to cultivate new land to grow crops despite the drought led to desertification and soil erosion. The government failed to act for fear of losing its administrative image abroad, causing the famine to kill an estimated 95,000 of the total 3,1 million residents of the province Darfur.

As farmers started claiming more and more land, routes applied by herders were closed off. This resulted in conflicts between farmers and rebels groups. In 2003, a conflict was fought in Darfur between Arab Sudanese farmers and non-Arab Muslims.

The Muslim group is called Janjaweed, a tribe mainly consisting of nomadic sheep and cattle herders. Originally the Janjaweed were part of the Sudanese and Darfurian militia, and were armed by the Sudanese government to counter rebellion. However, they started utilizing the weapons against non-Muslim civilians. The tribe became notorious for massacre in 2003-2004.

In December 2005 the conflict continued across the border, now involving governmental army troops from Chad, and the rebel groups Janjaweed and United Front for Democratic Change from Sudan. In February 2006 the governments of Chad and Sudan signed a peace treaty called the Tripoli Agreement. Unfortunately a new rebel assault of the capital of Chad in April made Chad break all ties with Sudan. The Darfur Conflict so far caused the death of between 50,000 and 450,000 civilians. It caused over 45,000 people to flea the countries of Sudan and Central Africa, into north and east Chad. Most refugees claim they fled civilian attacks from rebel forces, looting food and recruiting young men to join their troops.

AMERICA

Pearl Harbor (WWII) – When World War II began, Japan signed the Tripartite Pact with Nazi Germany and Fascist Italy. Consequentially, the United States closed the Panama Canal to Japanese shipping, and initiated a complete oil embargo. Japan, being dependent on US oil, responded to the embargo violently. On December 1941, Japanese troops carried out a surprise attack on Pearl Harbor, Hawaii, aimed at the US Navy stationed there. Despite the awareness that Japan might attack, the US was surprisingly unprepared for the Japanese aggression. There were no aircraft patrols, and anti-aircraft weapons were not manned.

For the attack five Japanese submarines were present in the harbor to launch torpedos. One was discovered immediately, and attacked by the USS Ward. All five submarines sank, and at least three of them have not been located since. As Japanese bombers arrived they began firing at US marine airbases across Hawaii, and subsequently battle ships in Pearl Harbor. Eighteen ships sank, including five battleships, and a total of more than 2,000 Americans were killed in action. The explosion of the USS Arizona caused half of the casualties. The ship was hit by a bomb, burned for two days in a row, and subsequently sank to the bottom. The cloud of black smoke over the boat was mainly caused by burning black powder from the magazine for aircraft catapults aboard the ship.

Leaking fuel from the Arizona and other ships caught fire, and caused more ships to catch fire. Of the 350 Japanese planes taking part in the attack, 29 were lost. Over sixty Japanese were killed in actions, most of them airmen.

Today, three battle ships are still at the bottom of the harbor. Four others were raised and reused. The USS Arizona, being the most heavily damaged ship during the attack, continues to leak oil from the hulk into the harbor. However, the wreck is maintained, because it now serves as part of a war memorial.

World Trade Centre explosion - The so-called 'War on Terrorism' the United States are fighting in Asia currently all started with the event we recall so well from the shocking images projected on news bulletins. On September 11, 2001, terrorists flew airplanes into the buildings of the World Trade Centre. It is now claimed that the attack and simultaneous collapse of the Twin Towers.

As the planes hit the Twin Towers more than 90.000 litres of jet fuel burned at temperatures above 1000oC. An atmospheric plume formed, consisting of toxic materials such as metals, furans, asbestos, dioxins, PAH, PCB and hydrochloric acid. Most of the materials were fibres from the structure of the building. Asbestos levels ranged from 0.8-3.0% of the total mass. PAH comprised more than 0.1% of the total mass, and PCBs less than 0.001% of total mass. At the site now called Ground Zero, a large pile of smoking rubble burned intermittently for more than 3 months. Gaseous and particulate particles kept forming long after the towers had collapsed.

The day of the attacks dust particles of various sizes spread over lower Manhattan and Brooklyn, for many miles. Fire fighters and medics working at the WTC were exposed, but also men and women on the streets and in nearby buildings, and children in nearby schools. In vivo inhalation studies and epidemiological studies pointed out the impact of the dust cloud. Health effects from inhaling dust included bronchial hyper reactivity, because of the high alkalinity of dust particles. Other possible health effects include coughs, an increased risk of asthma and a two-fold increase in the number of small-for-gestational-age baby's among pregnant women present in or nearby the Twin Towers at the time of the attack. After September, airborne pollutant concentrations in nearby communities declined.

Many people present at the WTC at the time of the attacks are still checked regularly, because long-term effects may eventually show. It is thought there may be an increased risk of development of mesothelioma, consequential to exposure to asbestos. This is a disease where malignant cells develop in the protective cover of the body's organs. Airborne dioxins in the days and weeks after the attack may increase the risk of cancer and diabetes. Infants of women that were pregnant on

September 11 and had been in the vicinity of the WTC at the time of the attack are also checked for growth or developmental problems.

ASIA

Afghanistan War

In October 2001, the United States attacked Afghanistan as a starting chapter of the 'War on terrorism', which still continues today. The ultimate goal was to replace the Taliban government, and to find apparent 9/11 mastermind and Al-Qaeda member Osama Bin Laden. Many European countries assisted the US in what was called 'Operation Enduring Freedom'.

During the war, extensive damage was done to the environment, and many people suffered health effects from weapons applied to destroy enemy targets. It is estimated that ten thousand villages, and their surrounding environments were destroyed. Safe drinking water declined, because of a destruction of water infrastructure and resulting leaks, bacterial contamination and water theft. Rivers and groundwater were contaminated by poorly constructed landfills located near the sources.

Afghanistan once consisted of major forests watered by monsoons. During the war, Taliban members illegally trading timber in Pakistan destroyed much of the forest cover. US bombings and refugees in need of firewood destroyed much of what remained. Less than 2% of the country still contains a forest cover today.

Bombs threaten much of the country's wildlife. One the world's important migratory thoroughfare leads through Afghanistan. The number of birds now flying this route has dropped by 85%. In the mountains many large animals such as leopards found refuge, but much of the habitat is applied as refuge for military forces now. Additionally, refugees capture leopards and other large animals are and trade them for safe passage across the border.

Pollution from application of explosives entered air, soil and water. One example is cyclonite, a toxic substance that may cause cancer. Rocket propellants deposited perchlorates, which damage the thyroid gland. Numerous landmines left behind in Afghan soils still cause the deaths of men, women and children today.

Cambodia Civil War

In 1966 the Prince of Cambodia began to lose the faith of many for failure to come to grips with the deteriorating economic situation. In 1967 rebellion started in a wealthy province where many large landowners lives. Villagers began attacking the tax collection brigade, because taxes were invested in building large factories, causing land to be taken. This led to a bloody civil war. Before the conflict could be repressed 10,000 people had died.

The rebellion caused the up rise of the Khmer Rouge, a Maoist-extremist organization that wanted to introduce communism in the country. In 1975 the organization, led by Pol Pot, officially seized power in Cambodia. The Khmer considered farmers (proletarians) to be the working class, as did Mao in China earlier. Schools, hospitals and banks were closed, the country was isolated from all foreign influence, and people were moved to the countryside for forced labor. People were obligated to work up to 12 hours a day, growing three times as many crops, as was usually the case. Many people died there from exhaustion, illness and starvation, or where shot by the Khmer on what was known as 'The Killing Fields'.

The Khmer Rouge regime resulted in deforestation, caused by extensive timber logging to finance war efforts, agricultural clearance, construction, logging concessions and collection of wood fuels. A total 35% of the Cambodian forest cover was lost under the Maoist regime. Deforestation resulted in severe floods, damaging rice crops and causing food shortages. In 1993, a ban on logging exports was introduced to prevent further flooding damage.

In 1979 the Khmer Rouge regime ended with an invasion by Vietnam, and the installation of a pro-Vietnamese puppet government. Subsequently, Thai and Chinese forces attempted to liberate the country from Vietnamese dominance. Many landmines were placed in the 1980's, and are still present in the countryside. They deny agricultural use of the land where they are placed. In 1992 free elections were introduced, but the Khmer Rouge resumed fighting. Eventually, half of the Khmer soldiers left in 1996, and many officials were captured. Under the Khmer regime, a total of 1.7 million people died, and the Khmer was directly responsible for about 750,000 of those casualties.

Hiroshima & Nagasaki Nuclear Explosions

Atomic bombs are based on the principle of nuclear fission, which was discovered in Nazi Germany in 1938 by two radio chemists. During the process, atoms are split and energy is released in the form of heat. Controlled reactions are applied in nuclear power plants for production of electricity, whereas unchecked reactions occur during nuclear bombings.

The invention in Germany alarmed people in the United States, because the Nazi's in possession of atomics bombs would be much more dangerous than they already where. When America became involved in WWII, the development of atomic bombs started there in what was called the 'Manhattan Project'. In July 1945 an atomic bomb was tested in the New Mexico desert. The tests were considered a success, and America was now in possession of one of the world's deadliest weapons.

In 1945, at the end of World War II and the beginning of the Cold War, nuclear weapons were applied to kill for the first time in Japan. On August 6, a uranium bomb by the name of Little Boy was dropped on Hiroshima, followed by a plutonium bomb by the name of Fat Man on Nagasaki on August 9. The reason Hiroshima was picked was that it was a major military centre. The bomb detonated at 8.15 p.m. over a Japanese Army parade field, where soldiers were already present. Nagasaki was picked because it was an industrial centre. The bomb, which was much larger than that used on Hiroshima, exploded at 11.02 a.m. at an industrial site. However, the hills on and the geographical location of the bombing site caused the eventual impact to be smaller than days earlier in Hiroshima.

The first impact of the atomic bombings was a blinding light, accompanied by a giant wave of heat. Dry flammable materials caught fire, and all men and animals within half a mile from the explosion sites died instantly. Many structures collapsed, in Nagasaki even the structures designed to survive earthquakes were blasted away. Many water lines broke. Fires could not be extinguished because of the water shortage, and six weeks after the blast the city still suffered from a lack of water. In Hiroshima a number of small fires combined with wind formed a firestorm, killing those who did not die before but were left immobile for some reason. Within days after the blasts, radiation sickness started rearing its ugly head, and many more people would die from it within the next 5 years.

The total estimated death toll:

In Hiroshima 100,000 were killed instantly, and between 100,000 and 200,000 died eventually.

In Nagasaki about 40,000 were killed instantly, and between 70,000 and 150,000 died eventually.

The events of August 6 and August 9 can be translated into environmental effects more literally. The blasts caused air pollution from dust particles and radioactive debris flying around, and from the fires burning everywhere. Many plants and animals were killed in the blast, or died moments to months later from radioactive precipitation. Radioactive sand clogged wells used for drinking water winning, thereby causing a drinking water problem that could not easily be solved. Surface water sources were polluted, particularly by radioactive waste. Agricultural production was damaged; dead stalks of rice could be found up to seven miles from ground zero. In Hiroshima the impact of the bombing was noticeable within a 10 km radius around the city, and in Nagasaki within a 1 km radius.

Iraq & Kuwait

The Gulf War was fought between Iraq, Kuwait and a number of western countries in 1991. Kuwait had been part of Iraq in the past, but was liberated by British imperialism, as the Iraqi government described it. In August 1990, Iraqi forces claimed that the country was illegally extracting oil from Iraqi territory, and attacked. The United Nations attempted to liberate Kuwait. Starting January 1991, Operation Desert Storm began, with the purpose of destroying Iraqi air force and anti-aircraft facilities, and command and control facilities. The battle was fought in Iraq, Kuwait and the Saudi-Arabian border region. Both aerial and ground artillery was applied. Late January, Iraqi aircraft were flown to Iran, and Iraqi forces began to flee.

The Gulf War was one of the most environmentally devastating wars ever fought. Iraq dumped approximately one million tons of crude oil into the Persian Gulf, thereby causing the largest oil spill in history. Approximately 25,000 migratory birds were killed. The impact on marine life was not as severe as expected, because warm water sped up the natural breakdown of oil. Local prawn fisheries did experience problems after the war. Crude oil was also spilled into the desert, forming oil lakes covering 50 square kilometres. In due time the oil percolated into groundwater aquifers.

Fleeing Iraqi troops ignited Kuwaiti oil sources, releasing half a ton of air pollutants into the atmosphere. Environmental problems caused by the oil fires include smog formation and acid rain. Toxic fumes originating from the burning oil wells compromised human health, and threatened wildlife. A soot layer was deposited on the desert, covering plants, and thereby preventing them from breathing. Seawater was applied to extinguish the oil fires, resulting in increased salinity in areas close to oil wells. It took about nine months to extinguish the fires.

During the war, many dams and sewage water treatment plants were targeted and destroyed. A lack of possibilities for water treatment resulting from the attacks caused sewage to flow directly into the Tigris and Euphrates rivers. Additionally, pollutants seeped from bombed chemical plants into the rivers. Drinking water extracted from the river was polluted, resulting in widespread disease. For example, cases of typhoid fever have increased tenfold since 1991.

Movement of heavy machinery such as tanks through the desert damaged the brittle surface, causing soil erosion. Sand was uncovered that formed gradually moving sand dunes. These dunes may one day cause problems for Kuwait City. Tanks fired Depleted Uranium (DU) missiles, which can puncture heavy artillery structures. DU is a heavy metal that causes kidney damage and is suspected to be teratogenic and carcinogenic. Post-Gulf War reports state an increase in birth defects for children born to veterans. The impact of Depleted Uranium could not be thoroughly investigated after the Gulf War, because Saddam Hussein refused to cooperate. Its true properties were revealed after the Kosovo War in 2001. DU has now been identified as a neurotoxin, and birth defects and cancers are attributed to other chemical and nerve agents. However, it is stated that DU oxides deposited in the lungs of veterans have not been thoroughly researched yet. It was later found that this may cause kidney and lung infections for highly exposed persons.

After the Gulf War many veterans suffered from a condition now known as the Gulf War Syndrome. The causes of the illness are subject to widespread speculation. Examples of possible causes are exposure to DU, chemical weapons (nerve gas and mustard gas), an anthrax vaccine given to 41% of US soldiers and 60-75% of UK soldiers, smoke from burning oil wells and parasites. Symptoms of the GWS included chronic fatigue, muscle problems, diarrhoea, migraine, memory loss, skin problems and shortness of breath. Many Gulf War veterans have died of illnesses such as brain cancer, now acknowledged as potentially connected to service during the war.

Iraq & the United States

The war in Iraq started by the United States in 2003 as part of the War on Terrorism causes poverty, resulting in environmental problems. Long-term environmental effects of the war remain unclear, but short-term problems have been identified for every environmental compartment. For example, some weapons are applied that may be extremely damaging to the environment, such as white phosphorus ammunition. People around the world protest the application of such armoury.

Water

Damage to sanitation structures by frequent bombing, and damage to sewage treatment systems by power blackouts cause pollution of the River Tigris. Two hundred blue plastic containers containing uranium were stolen from a nuclear power plant located south of Baghdad. The radioactive content of the barrels was dumped in rivers and the barrels were rinsed out. Poor people applied the containers as storage facility for water, oil and tomatoes, or sold them to others. Milk was transported to other regions in the barrels, making it almost impossible to relocate them.

Air

Oil trenches are burning, as was the case in the Gulf War of 1991, resulting in air pollution. In Northern Iraq, a sulphur plant burned for one month, contributing to air pollution. As fires continue burning, groundwater applied as a drinking water source may be polluted.

Soil

Military movements and weapon application result in land degradation. The destruction of military and industrial machinery releases heavy metals and other harmful substances.

Israel & Lebanon

In July 2006, Hezbollah initiated a rocket attack on Israeli borders. A ground patrol killed and captured Israeli soldiers. This resulted in open war between Israel and Lebanon.

The war caused environmental problems as Israelis bombed a power station south of Beirut. Damaged storage tanks leaked an estimated 20,000 tons of oil into the Mediterranean Sea. The oil spill spread rapidly, covering over 90 km of the coastline, killing fish and affecting the habitat of the endangered green sea turtle. A sludge layer covers Beaches across Lebanon, and the same problem may occur in Syria as the spill continues to spread. Part of the oil spill burned, causing widespread air pollution. Smog affects the health of people living in the city of Beirut. So far problems limiting the clean-up operation of oil spills have occurred, because of ongoing violence in the region.

Another major problem were forest fires in Northern Israel caused by Hezbollah bombings. A total of 9,000 acres of forest burned to the ground, and fires threaten tree reserves and bird sanctuaries.

Russia & Chechnya

In 1994 the First Chechen War of independence started, between Russian troops, Chechen guerrilla fighters and civilians. Chechnya has been a province of Russia for a very long time and now desires independence. The First War ended in 1996, but in 1999 Russia again attacked Chechnya for purposes of oil distribution.

The war between the country and its province continues today. It has devastating effects on the region of Chechnya. An estimated 30% of Chechen territory is contaminated, and 40% of the territory does not meet environmental standards for life. Major environmental problems include radioactive waste and radiation, oil leaks into the ground from bombarded plants and refineries, and pollution of soil and surface water. Russia has buried radioactive waste in Chechnya. Radiation at some sites is ten times its normal level. Radiation risks increase as Russia bombs the locations, particularly because after 1999 the severeness of weaponry increased. A major part of agricultural land is polluted to the extent that it can no longer meet food supplies. This was mainly caused by unprofessional mini-refineries of oil poachers in their backyards, not meeting official standards and causing over 50% of the product to be lost as waste. Groundwater pollution flows into the rivers Sunzha and Terek on a daily basis. On some locations the rivers are totally devoid of fish. Flora and fauna are destroyed by oil leaks and bombings.

Vietnam War

The Vietnam War started in 1945 and ended in 1975. It is now entitled a proxy war, fought during the Cold War between the United States and the Soviet Union to prevent the necessity for the nations to fight each other directly. North Vietnam fought side by side with the Soviet Union and China, and South Vietnam with the United States, New Zealand and South Korea. It must be noted that the United States only started to be actively involved in the battle after 1963. Between 1965 and 1968 North Vietnam was bombed under Operation Rolling Thunder, in order to force the enemy to negotiate. Bombs destroyed over two million acres of land. North Vietnam forces began to strike back, and the Soviet Union delivered anti-aircraft missiles to North Vietnam. The ground war of US troops against the Viet Cong began. The United States would not retreat from Vietnam until 1973, and during those years extremely environmentally damaging weapons and war tactics were applied.

A massive herbicidal programme was carried out, in order to break the forest cover sheltering Viet Cong guerrillas, and deprive Vietnamese peasants of food. The spraying destroyed 14% of Vietnam's forests, diminished agricultural yield, and made seeds unfit for replanting. If agricultural yield was not damaged by herbicides, it was often lost because military on the ground set fire to haystacks, and soaked land with aviation fuel en burned it. A total of 15,000 square kilometres of land were eventually destroyed. Livestock was often shot, to deprive peasant of their entire food supply. A total of 13,000 livestock were killed during the war.

The application of 72 million litres of chemical spray resulted in the death of many animals, and caused health effects with humans. One chemical that was applied between 1962 and 1971, called Agent Orange, was particularly harmful. Its main constituent is dioxin, which was present in soil, water and vegetation during and after the war. Dioxin is carcinogenic and teratogenic, and has resulted in spontaneous abortions, chloracne, skin and lung cancers, lower intelligence and emotional problems among children. Children fathered by men exposed to Agent Orange during the Vietnam War often have congenital abnormalities. An estimated half a million children were born with dioxin-related abnormalities. Agent Orange continues to threaten the health of the Vietnamese today.

Today, agriculture in Vietnam continues to suffer problems from six million unexploded bombs still present. Several organisations are attempting to remove these bombs. Landmines left in Vietnam are not removed, because the Vietnamese government refuses to accept responsibility.

EUROPE

Kosovo War

The Kosovo war can be divided up in two separate parts: a conflict between Serbia and Kosovo, and a conflict between Kosovo and the North Atlantic Treaty Organisation (NATO). The first conflict originated in 1996 from the statement of Slobodan Milocevic that Kosovo was to remain a part of Serbia, and from the resulting violent response of Albanian residents. When Serbian troops slaughtered 45 Albanians in the village of Racak in Kosovo in 1999, the NATO intervened. NATO launched a 4-month bombing campaign upon Serbia as a reply to the massacre at Racak.

The United Nations Environment Programme (UNEP) investigated the environmental impact of the Kosovo war. It was concluded that the war did not result in an environmental disaster affecting the entire Balkan region. Nevertheless, some environmental hot spots were identified, namely Belgrade, Pancevo, Kragujevac, Novi Sad and Bor.

Bombings carried out by the United States resulted in leakages in oil refineries and oil storage depots. Industrial sites containing other industries were also targeted. EDC (1,2-dichloroethane), PCBs en mercury escaped to the environment. Burning of Vinyl Chloride Monomer (VCM) resulted in the formation of dioxin, hydrochloric acid, carbon monoxide and PAHs, and oil burning released sulphur dioxide, nitrogen dioxide, carbon monoxide, lead and PAHs into the air. Heavy clouds of black smoke forming over burning industrial targets caused black rain to fall on the area around Pancevo. Some damage was done to National Parks in Serbia by bombings, and therefore to biodiversity. EDC, mercury and petroleum products (e.g. PCBs) polluted the Danube River. These are present in the sediments and may resurface in due time. EDC is toxic to both terrestrial and aquatic life. Mercury may be converted into methyl mercury, which is very toxic and bio accumulates. As a measure to prevent the consequences of bombing, a fertilizer plant in Pancevo released liquid ammonia into the Danube River. This caused fish kills up to 30 kilometres downstream.

In 1999 when NATO bombed Belgrade, the capital of Serbia, the resulting environmental damage was enormous. Petrochemical plants in suburbs started leaking all kinds of hazardous chemicals into air, water and soil. Factories producing ammonia and plastics released chlorine, hydrochloric acid, vinyl chloride and other chlorine substances, resulting in local air pollution and health problems. Water sources were polluted by oil leaking from refineries. The Danube River was polluted by oil more severely, but this time hydrochloric acid and mercury compounds also ended up there. These remained in the water for a considering period of time and consequently ended up in neighbouring countries Rumania and Bulgaria.

Clean drinking water supplies and waste treatment plants were damaged by NATO bombings. Many people fled their houses and were moved to refugee camps, where the number of people grew rapidly. A lack of clean drinking water and sanitation problems occurred.

Like in the Gulf War, Depleted Uranium (DU) was applied in the Kosovo War to puncture tanks and other artillery. After the war, the United Kingdom assisted in the removal of DU residues from the environment. Veterans complained of health effects. It was acknowledged by the UK and the US that dusts from DU can be dangerous if inhaled. Inhalation of dust most likely results in chemical poisoning.

World War I: Trench Warfare – In 1914, the assassination of archduke Franz Ferdinand of Austria-Hungary resulted in the First World War, otherwise known as The Great War, or WWI. It started with Austria-Hungary invading Serbia, where the assassin came from, and Germany invading Belgium. The war was mostly in Europe, between the Allies and the Central Powers.

Allies: France, United Kingdom, Italy, Belgium, Luxembourg, Russia, Poland, Serbia, Montenegro, Rumania, Albania, Greece, Portugal, Finland, United States, Canada, Brazil, Armenia, Australia, India, New Zealand, South Africa, Liberia, China, Japan, Thailand, Guatemala, Haiti, Honduras, Nicaragua, and Panama

CENTRAL POWERS: AUSTRIA-HUNGARY, GERMANY, TURKISH EMPIRE, AND BULGARIA

The war was fought from trenches, dug from the North Sea to the border of Switzerland. In 1918 when the war was over, empires disintegrated into smaller countries, marking the division of Europe today. Over 9 million people had died, most of which perished from influenza after the outbreak of the Spanish Flu. The war did not directly cause the influenza outbreak, but it was amplified. Mass movement of troops and close quarters caused the Spanish Flu to spread quickly. Furthermore, stresses of war may have increased the susceptibility of soldiers to the disease.

In terms of environmental impact, World War I was most damaging, because of landscape changes caused by trench warfare. Digging trenches caused trampling of grassland, crushing of plants and animals, and churning of soil. Erosion resulted from forest logging to expand the network of trenches. Soil structures were altered severely, and if the war was never fought, in all likelihood the landscape would have looked very differently today.

Another damaging impact was the application of poison gas. Gases were spread throughout the trenches to kill soldiers of the opposite front. Examples of gases applied during WWI are tear gas (aerosols causing eye irritation), mustard gas (cell toxic gas causing blistering and bleeding), and carbonyl chloride (carcinogenic gas). The gases caused a total of 100,000 deaths, most caused by carbonyl chloride (phosgene). Battlefields were polluted, and most of the gas evaporates into the atmosphere. After the war, unexploded ammunition caused major problems in former battle areas.

Environmental legislation prohibits detonation or dumping chemical weapons at sea, therefore the cleanup was and still remains a costly operation. In 1925, most WWI participants signed a treaty banning the application of gaseous chemical weapons. Chemical disarmament plants are planned in France and Belgium.

World War II: Gas Chambers

World War II was a worldwide conflict, fought between the Allies (Britain, France and the United States as its core countries) and the Axis Powers (Germany, Italy and Japan as its core countries). It started with the German invasion of Poland and Czechoslovakia in 1939, and ended with the liberation of Western Europe by the allies in 1945.

Between 1941 and 1945, over 1 million people were killed in the gas chambers of the extermination camp Auschwitz-Birkenau in Nazi Germany. Over 90% of the victims were Jews, and the other 10% consisted of Poles, Soviet prisoners of war and gypsies. The substance applied was Zyklon-B, a cyanide-based insecticide that is lethal to humans in large doses. It was stored as crystals in closed containers, but when exposed to air it released the lethal hydrogen cyanide gas (HCN). As Zyklon-B was poured into the gas chambers through small openings, it took only 10-15 minutes to kill all people inside.

The insecticide was supplied to Nazi Germany by two firms, Tesch-Stabenow and Degesh. After the war the firms claimed they were unaware of the application of the product to kill people in large numbers. However, it was later stated that the company had to have known, because they supplied enough substance to kill 2 million people, and additionally gave some advise on how to use the ventilating and heating equipment.

World War II: Hunger Winter

In late 1944, the allied troops attempted to liberate Western Europe. As they reached The Netherlands, German resistance caused the liberation to be halted in Arnhem, as allied troops failed to occupy a bridge over the River Rhine. As the Dutch government in exile in Britain called for railway strikes, the Germans responded by putting embargo on food transport to the west. This resulted in what is now known as the Hunger Winter, causing an estimated 20,000-25,000 Dutch to starve to death. A number of factors caused the starvation: a harsh winter, fuel shortages, the ruin of agricultural land by bombings, floods, and the food transport embargo. Most people in the west lived off tulip bulbs and sugar beet. Official food rations were below 1000 cal per person per day. In May 1945 the Hunger Winter ended with the official liberation of the west of The Netherlands.

5

Effects of Nuclear Explosions

BASIC EFFECTS OF NUCLEAR WEAPONS

Nuclear explosions produce both immediate and delayed destructive effects. Blast, thermal radiation, and prompt ionizing radiation cause significant destruction within seconds or minutes of a nuclear detonation.

The delayed effects, such as radioactive fallout and other possible environmental effects, inflict damage over an extended period ranging from hours to years. Each of these effects are calculated from the point of detonation.

Ground Zero

The term "ground zero" refers to the point on the earth's surface immediately below (or above) the point of detonation. For a burst over (or under) water, the corresponding point is generally called "surface zero". The term "surface zero" or "surface ground zero" is also commonly used for ground surface and underground explosions. In some publications, ground (or surface) zero is called the "hypocenter" of the explosion.

Blast Effects

Most damage comes from the explosive blast. The shock wave of air radiates outward, producing sudden changes in air pressure that can crush objects, and high winds that can knock objects down. In general, large buildings are destroyed by the change in air pressure, while people and objects such as trees and utility poles are destroyed by the wind. The magnitude of the blast effect is related to the height of the burst above ground level. For any given distance from the center of the explosion, there is an optimum burst height that will produce the greatest change in air pressure, called overpressure, and the greater the distance the greater the optimum burst height. As a result, a burst on the surface produces the greatest overpressure at very close ranges, but less overpressure than an air burst at somewhat longer ranges.

When a nuclear weapon is detonated on or near Earth's surface, the blast digs out a large crater. Some of the material that used in be in the crater is deposited on the rim of the crater; the rest is carried up into the air and returns to Earth as radioactive fallout. An explosion that is farther above the Earth's surface than the radius of the fireball does not dig a crater and produces negligible immediate fallout. For the most part, a nuclear blast kills people by indirect means rather than by direct pressure.

Thermal Radiation Effects

Approximately 35 percent of the energy from a nuclear explosion is an intense burst of thermal radiation, i.e., heat. The effects are similar to the effect of a two-second flash from an enormous sunlamp. Since the thermal radiation travels at roughly the speed of light, the flash of light and heat precedes the blast wave by several seconds, just as lightning is seen before thunder is heard.

The visible light will produce "flashblindness" in people who are looking in the direction of the explosion. Flashblindness can last for several minutes, after which recovery is total. If the flash is focused through the lens of the eye, a permanent retinal burn will result. At Hiroshima and Nagasaki, there were many cases of flashblindness, but only one case of retinal burn, among the survivors. On the other hand, anyone flashblinded while driving a car could easily cause permanent injury to himself and to others.

Skin burns result from higher intensities of light, and therefore take place closer to the point of explosion. First-degree, second-degree and third-degree burns can occur at distances of five miles away from the blast or more.

Third-degree burns over 24 percent of the body, or second-degree burns over 30 percent of the body, will result in serious shock, and will probably prove fatal unless prompt, specialized medical care is available. The entire United States has facilities to treat 1,000 or 2,000 severe burn cases. A single nuclear weapon could produce more than 10,000.

The thermal radiation from a nuclear explosion can directly ignite kindling materials. In general, ignitable materials outside the house, such as leaves or newspapers, are not surrounded by enough combustible material to generate a self-sustaining fire. Fires more likely to spread are those caused by thermal radiation passing through windows to ignite beds and overstuffed furniture inside houses. Another possible source of fires, which might be more damaging in urban areas, is indirect. Blast damage to Stores, water heaters, furnaces, electrical circuits or gas lines would ignite fires where fuel is plentiful.

DIRECT NUCLEAR RADIATION EFFECTS

Direct radiation occurs at the time of the explosion. It can be very intense, but its range is limited. For large nuclear weapons, the range of intense direct radiation is less than the range of lethal blast and thermal radiation effects. However, in the case of smaller weapons, direct radiation may be the lethal effect with the greatest range. Direct radiation did substantial damage to the residents of Hiroshima and Nagasaki. Human response to ionizing radiation is subject to great scientific uncertainty and intense controversy. It seems likely that even small doses of radiation do some harm.

Fallout

Fallout radiation is received from particles that are made radioactive by the effects of the explosion, and subsequently distributed at varying distances from the site of the blast. While any nuclear explosion in the atmosphere produces some fallout, the fallout is far greater if the burst is on the surface, or at least low enough for the fireball to touch the ground. The significant hazards come from particles scooped up from the ground and irradiated by the nuclear explosion. The radioactive particles that rise only a short distance (those in the "stem" of the familiar mushroom cloud) will fall back to earth within a matter of minutes, landing close to the center of the explosion. Such particles are unlikely to cause many deaths, because they will fall in areas where most people have already been killed. However, the radioactivity will complicate efforts at rescue or eventual reconstruction. The radioactive particles that rise higher will be carried some distance by the wind before returning to Earth, and hence the area and intensity of the fallout is strongly influenced by local weather conditions. Much of the material is simply blown downwind in a long plume. Rainfall also can have a significant influence on the ways in which radiation from smaller weapons is deposited, since rain will carry contaminated particles to the ground. The areas receiving such contaminated rainfall would become "hot spots," with greater radiation intensity than their surroundings.

TYPES OF NUCLEAR EXPLOSIONS

The effects of a nuclear explosion depend in part to the height of the detonation. There five general classifications of bursts: air, high-altitude, underwater, underground, and surface bursts.

An air burst is defined as one in which the explosion occurs in the air at an altitude below 100,000 feet (30,480 meters), but at such a height that the fireball does not touch the surface of the earth. A detontation above that altitude is generally refered to as a high-altitude burst.

A nuclear explosion that occurs at or slightly above the actual surface of the land or water is known as a surface burst. If the explosion happens beneath the surface of the land or water, then it is known as underground or underwater respectively. The design of Robust Nuclear Earth Penetrator (RNEP) uses the charaterastics of an underground burst in an attempt to destroy buried targets.

One of the greatest results of the type of burst is the amount of radioactive debris and fallout, and the force of the blast wave.

The Blast Wave

A fraction of a second after a nuclear explosion, the heat from the fireball causes a high-pressure wave to develop and move outward producing the blast effect. The front of the blast wave, i.e., the shock front, travels rapidly away from the fireball, a moving wall of highly compressed air.

The air immediately behind the shock front is accelerated to high velocities and creates a powerful wind. These winds in turn create dynamic pressure against the objects facing the blast. Shock waves cause a virtually instantaneous jump in pressure at the shock front.

The combination of the pressure jump (called the overpressure) and the dynamic pressure causes blast damage. Both the overpressure and the dynamic pressure reach to their maximum values upon the arrival of the shock wave. They then decay over a period ranging from a few tenths of a second to several seconds, depending on the blast's strength and the yield.

Overpressure

Blast effects are usually measured by the amount of overpressure, the pressure in excess of the normal atmospheric value, in pounds per square inch (psi).

Peak overpressure	*Maximum Wind Speed*
50 psi	934 mph
20 psi	502 mph
10 psi	294 mph
5 psi	163 mph
2 psi	70 mph

After 10 seconds, when the fireball of a 1-megaton nuclear weapon has attained its maximum size (5,700 feet across), the shock front is some 3 miles farther ahead. At 50 seconds after the explosion, when the fireball is no longer visible, the blast wave has traveled about 12 miles. It is then traveling at about 784 miles per hour, which is slightly faster than the speed of sound at sea level.

As a general guide, city areas are completely destroyed by overpressures of 5 psi, with heavy damage extending out at least to the 3 psi contour.

These many different effects make it difficult to provide a simple rule of thumb for assessing the magnitude of injury produced by different blast intensities. A general guide is given below:

Overpressure	*Physical Effects*
20 psi	Heavily built concrete buildings are severely damaged or demolished.
10 psi	Reinforced concrete buildings are severely damaged or demolished. Most people are killed.
5 psi	Most buildings collapse. Injuries are universal, fatalities are widespread.
3 psi	Residential structures collapse. Serious injuries are common, fatalities may occur.
1 psi	Window glass shatters Light injuries from fragments occur.

Blast Effects on Humans

Blast damage is caused by the arrival of the shock wave created by the nuclear explosion. Humans are actually quite resistant to the direct effect of overpressure. Pressures of over 40 psi are required before lethal effects are noted.

The danger from overpressure comes from the collapse of buildings that are generally not as resistant. Urban areas contain many objects that can become airborne, and the destruction of buildings generates many more. The collapse of the structure above can crush or suffocate those caught inside.

Serious injury or death can also occur from impact after being thrown through the air.

The blast also magnifies thermal radiation burn injuries by tearing away severely burned skin. This creates raw open wounds that readily become infected.

The Mach Stem

If the explosion occurs above the ground, when the expanding blast wave strikes the surface of the earth, it is reflected off the ground to form a second shock wave traveling behind the first. This reflected wave travels faster than the first, or incident, shock wave since it is traveling through air already moving at high speed due to the passage of the incident wave. The reflected blast wave merges with the incident shock wave to form a single wave, known as the Mach Stem. The overpressure at the front of the Mach wave is generally about twice as great as that at the direct blast wave front.

At first the height of the Mach Stem wave is small, but as the wave front continues to move outward, the height increases steadily. At the same time, however, the overpressure, like that in the incident wave, decreases because of the continuous loss of energy and the ever-increasing area of the advancing front. After about 40 seconds, when the Mach front from a 1-megaton nuclear weapon is 10 miles from ground zero, the overpressure will have decreased to roughly 1 psi.

Thermal Radiation

A primary form of energy from a nuclear explosion is thermal radiation. Initially, most of this energy goes into heating the bomb materials and the air in the vicinity of the blast. Temperatures of a nuclear explosion reach those in the interior of the sun, about 100,000,000° Celsius, and produce a brilliant fireball.

Two pulses of thermal radiation emerge from the fireball. The first pulse, which lasts about a tenth of a second, consists of radiation in the ultraviolet region. The second pulse which may last for several seconds, carries about 99 percent of the total thermal radiation energy. It is this radiation that is the main cause of skin burns and eye injuries suffered by exposed individuals and causes combustible materials to break into flames.

Thermal radiation damage depends very strongly on weather conditions. Clouds or smoke in the air can considerably reduce effective damage ranges versus clear air conditions.

The Fireball

The fireball, an extremely hot and highly luminous spherical mass of air and gaseous weapon residues, occurs within less than one millionth of one second of the weapon's detonation. Immediately after its formation, the fireball begins to grow in size, engulfing the surrounding air. This growth is accompanied by a decrease in temperature because of the accompanying increase in mass. At the same time the fireball rises, like a hot-air balloon. Within seven-tenths of one millisecond from the detonation, the fireball from a 1-megaton weapon is about 440 feet across, and this increases to a maximum value of about 5,700 feet in 10 seconds. It is then rising at a rate of 250 to 350 feet per second. After a minute, the fireball has cooled to such an extent that it no longer emits visible radiation. It has then risen roughly 4.5 miles from the point of burst.

The Mushroom Cloud

As the fireball increases in size and cools, the vapors condense to form a cloud containing solid particles of the weapon debris, as well as many small drops of water derived from the air sucked into the rising fireball.

Depending on the height of burst, a strong updraft with inflowing winds, called "afterwinds," are produced. These afterwinds can cause varying amounts of dirt and debris to be sucked up from the earth's surface into the cloud. In an air burst with a moderate (or small) amount of dirt and debris drawn up into the cloud, only a relatively small proportion become contaminated with radioactivity. For a burst near the ground, however, large amounts of dirt and debris are drawn into the cloud during formation.

The color of the cloud is initially red or reddish brown, due to the presence of nitrous acid and oxides of nitrogen. As the fireball cools and condensation occurs, the color changes to white, mainly due to the water droplets (as in an ordinary cloud).

The cloud consists chiefly of very small particles of radioactive fission products and weapon residues, water droplets, and larger particles of dirt and debris carried up by the afterwinds.

The eventual height reached by the radioactive cloud depends upon the heat energy of the weapon and upon the atmospheric conditions. If the cloud reaches the tropopause, about 6-8 miles above the Earth's surface, there is a tendency for it to spread out. But if sufficient energy remains in the radioactive cloud at this height, a portion of it will ascend into the more stable air of the stratosphere.

The cloud attains its maximum height after about 10 minutes and is then said to be "stabilized." It continues to grow laterally, however, to produce the characteristic mushroom shape. The cloud may continue to be visible for about an hour or more before being dispersed by the winds into the surrounding atmosphere where it merges with natural clouds in the sky.

Thermal Pulse Effects

One of the important differences between a nuclear and conventional weapon is the large proportion of a nuclear explosion's energy that is released in the form of thermal energy. This energy is emitted from the fireball in two pulses. The first is quite short, and carries only about 1 percent of the energy; the second pulse is more significant and is of longer duration (up to 20 seconds).

The energy from the thermal pulse can initiate fires in dry, flammable materials, such as dry leaves, grass, old newspaper, thin dark flammable fabrics, etc. The incendiary effect of the thermal pulse is also substantially affected by the later arrival of the blast wave, which usually blows out any flames that have already been kindled. However, smoldering material can reignite later.

The major incendiary effect of nuclear explosions is caused by the blast wave. Collapsed structures are much more vulnerable to fire than intact ones. The blast reduces many structures to piles of kindling, the many gaps opened in roofs and walls act as chimneys, gas lines are broken open, storage tanks for flammable materials are ruptured. The primary ignition sources appear to be flames and pilot lights in heating appliances (furnaces, water heaters, stoves, etc.). Smoldering material from the thermal pulse can be very effective at igniting leaking gas.

Thermal radiation damage depends very strongly on weather conditions. Cloud cover, smoke, or other obscuring material in the air can considerably reduce effective damage ranges versus clear air conditions.

Thermal radiation also affects humans both directly - by flash burns on exposed skin - and indirectly - by fires started by the explosion.

Firestorms

Under some conditions, the many individual fires created by a nuclear explosion can coalesce into one massive fire known as a "firestorm." The combination of many smaller fires heats the air and causes winds of hurricane strength directed inward toward the fire, which in turn fan the flames. For a firestorm to develop:

- There must be at least 8 pounds of combustibles per square foot.
- At least one-half of the structures in the area are on fire simultaneously.
- There is initially a wind of less than 8 miles per hour.
- The burning area is at least 0.5 square miles.

In Hiroshima, a firestorm did develop and about 4.4 square miles were destroyed. Although there was some damage from uncontrolled fires at Nagasaki, a firestorm did not develop. One reason for this was the difference in the terrain. Hiroshima is relatively flat, while Nagasaki has uneven terrain. Firestorms can also be caused by conventional bombing. During World

War II, the cities of Dresden, Hamburg, and Tokyo all suffered the effects of firestorms.

Flash Burns

Flash burns are one of the serious consequences of a nuclear explosion. Flash burns result from the absorption of radiant energy by the skin of exposed individuals. A distinctive feature of flash burns is the fact they are limited to exposed areas of the skin facing the explosion.

A 1-megaton explosion can cause first-degree burns (a bad sunburn) at a distance of about 7 miles, second-degree burns (producing blisters and permanent scars) at distances of about 6 miles, and third-degree burns (which destroy skin tissue) at distances up to 5 miles. Third-degree burns over 24 percent of the body, or second-degree burns over 30 percent, will result in serious shock, and will probably prove fatal unless prompt, specialized medical care is available.

It has been estimated that burns caused some 50 percent of the deaths at Hiroshima and Nagasaki.

Flash blindness

Flash blindness is caused by the initial brilliant flash of light produced by the nuclear detonation. The light is received on the retina than can be tolerated, but less than is required for irreversible injury. The retina is particularly susceptible to visible and short wavelength infrared light. The result is a bleaching of visual pigment and temporary blindness. Vision is completely recovered as the pigment is regenerated.

During the daylight hours, flash blindness does not persist for more than 2 minutes, but generally lasts a few seconds. At night, when the pupil is dilated, flashblindness will last for a longer period of time.

A 1-megaton explosion can cause flash blindness at distances as great as 13 miles on a clear day, or 53 miles on a clear night. If the intensity is great enough, a permanent retinal burn will result. Retinal injury is the most far-reaching injury effect of nuclear explosions, but it is relatively rare since the eye must be looking directly at the detonation. Retinal injury results from burns in the area of the retina where the fireball image is focused.

Nuclear Radiation

The release of radiation is a phenomenon unique to nuclear explosions. There are several kinds of radiation emitted; these types include gamma, neutron, and ionizing radiation, and are emitted not only at the time of detonation (initial radiation) but also for long periods of time afterward (residual radiation).

THERMAL RADIATION

Formation of Thermal Radiation

Large amounts of electromagnetic radiation in the visible, infrared, and ultraviolet regions of the electromagnetic spectrum are emitted from the surface of the fireball within the first minute or less after detonation.

This thermal radiation travels outward from the fireball at the speed of light, 300,000 km/sec. The chief hazard of thermal radiation is the production of burns and eye injuries in exposed personnel. Such thermal injuries may occur even at distances where blast and initial nuclear radiation effects are minimal.

Absorption of thermal radiation will also cause the ignition of combustible materials and may lead to fires which then spread rapidly among the debris left by the blast. The range of thermal effects increases markedly with weapon yield.

Propagation of Thermal Energy

a. Most of the energy released in the fission or fusion processes is initially in the form of the kinetic energy of the products of the reactions (e.g., fission fragments, etc.). Within millionths of a second after detonation, numerous inelastic collisions of these vaporized atoms give rise to a plasma of intensely hot weapon residues. Since the temperature of this system is of several tens of million degrees centigrade, it emits enormous quantities of energy in the form of electromagnetic radiation. This radiation is subsequently absorbed by the surrounding atmosphere, which is heated to extremely high temperatures, causing it to emit additional radiation of slightly lower energy. This complex process of radiative transfer of energy is the basic mechanism by which the fireball is formed and expands.

b. Because this thermal radiation travels at the speed of light, and its mean free path (distance between point of emission and point of absorption) is relatively long, the initial expansion of the fireball is extremely rapid, much more so than the outward motion of gaseous material from the center of the burst responsible for production of the blast wave. Consequently, the blast wave front at first lags behind the radiative front (surface of the fireball).

c. However, as the fireball expands and its energy is deposited in an ever-increasing volume its temperature decreases and the transfer of energy by thermal radiation becomes less rapid. At this point, the blast wave front begins to catch up with the surface of the fireball and t h e n moves ahead of it, a process called hydrodynamic separation. Due to the tremendous compression of the atmosphere by the blast wave, the air in front of the fireball is heated to incandescence. Thus, after hydrodynamic separation, the fireball actually consists of two concentric regions: the hot inner core known as the isothermal sphere; and an outer layer of luminous shock-heated air.

d. The outer layer initially absorbs much of the radiation from theisothermal sphere and hence the apparent surface temperature of the fireball and the amount of radiation emitted from it decreases after separation. But, as the shock front advances still farther, the temperature of the shocked air diminishes and it becomes increasingly transparent. This results in an unmasking of the still incandescent isothermal region and an increase in the apparent surface temperature of the fireball. This phenomena is referred to as breakaway.

Rate of Thermal Emission

a. The rate of thermal emission from the fireball is governed by its apparent surface temperature. From the foregoing discussion, it should be apparent that the thermal output of a nuclear air burst will then occur in two pulses, an initial pulse, consisting primarily of ultraviolet radiation, which contains only about 1% of the total radiant energy of the explosion and is terminated as the shock front moves ahead of the fireball, and a second pulse which occurs after breakaway.

b. The thermal radiation emitted from the fireball surface during the second thermal pulse is responsible for most of the thermal effects. It consists chiefly of radiation in the infrared, visible, and ultraviolet regions of the electromagnetic spectrum. Thermal exposure (measured in joules per unit area of exposed surface) will be less farther from the center of the explosion because the radiation is spread over a greater area and is attenuated in passing through the intervening air. Since the fireball is very close to a point source of thermal radiation, the quantity of thermal radiation at any given point varies approximately with the square of the distance from the explosion. The inverse square law does not apply exactly because thermal radiation, particularly ultraviolet, will also be absorbed and scattered by the atmosphere. The degree of atmospheric visibility affects the attenuation of thermal energy with distance to a limited degree, but less than would be expected from the purely absorptive properties of the atmosphere, because the decrease in transmission is largely compensated by an increase in scattered radiation.

Shielding

Since thermal radiation travels in straight lines from the fireball (unless scattered) any opaque object interposed between the fireball and the target will act as a shield and provide significant protection from thermal radiation. If a significant amount of scattering is present, as is the case when visibility is poor, thermal radiation will be received from all directions and shielding will be less effective.

Yield and Altitude

a. *Yield.* The total amount of thermal radiation, the period of time during which it is emitted, and the range for thermal effects increase with the yield of the nuclear explosion.

b. *Altitude Effects.* The thermal radiation intensity at a given point will depend on the altitude and the type of burst. In general, the thermal hazard is greatest in the case of a low altitude air burst. General thermal effects will be less for surface bursts and frequently nonexistent for subsurface bursts. In surface bursts a large part of the thermal energy is absorbed by the ground or water around ground zero. In addition, shielding due to terrain irregularities of dust, moisture, and various gases in the air near the surface of the earth will tend to reduce the amount of thermal energy reaching a target. In subsurface bursts without appreciable penetration, most of the thermal energy is absorbed and dissipated in heating and vaporizing soil and water below the surface.

c. *High Altitude Effects.* In high altitude air bursts (above 30 km), the low density of the atmosphere alters the nature of the thermal radiation process because the primary thermal radiation is absorbed in a much larger volume of air, and the temperature of the system is correspondingly less. While a greater percentage of the yield of the explosion appears in the form of thermal radiation, much of the radiation is emitted so slowly that it is ineffective. About 25-35% of the total yield is emitted in a single pulse of very short duration. Moreover, because of the relatively great distance between the center of the burst and the earth's surface, the intensity of thermal radiation at ground level is generally low.

Thermal Effects

a. When thermal radiation strikes an object, part will be reflected, part will be transmitted, and the rest will be absorbed. The fraction of the incident radiation that is absorbed depends on the nature and color of the material. A thin material may transmit a large part of the radiant energy striking it. A light colored object may reflect much of the incident radiation and thus escape damage. Thermal damage and injury is due to the absorption of large amounts of thermal energy within relatively short periods of time. The absorbed thermal radiation raises the temperature of the absorbing surface and results in scorching, charring, and possible ignition of combustible organic materials, such as wood, paper, fabrics, etc. If the target material is a poor thermal conductor, the absorbed energy is largely confined to a superficial layer of the material.

b. The radiation exposure (# Joules/sq/cm) required for the ignition of materials and other thermal effects increases with the yield of the weapon. This is so because increased thermal energy is required to compensate for energy lost via conduction and convection during the longer thermal pulse of higher yield weapons. For lower yield weapons, the thermal pulse is so short that there is not much time for these processes to cool the exposed surface. Hence, a much higher percentage of the deposited thermal energy is effective in producing thermal damage. This increased thermal requirement does not mean that the thermal hazard is less significant for higher yields. On the contrary, the total thermal energy released during a nuclear explosion increases markedly with yield, and the effects extend over much greater distances. Therefore, although more thermal energy is required to produce a given thermal response for a large yield explosion, the effective range to which this level extends is very much greater.

c. Actual ignition of materials exposed to thermal radiation is highly dependent on the width of the thermal pulse (which is dependent on weapon yield) and the nature of the material, particularly its thickness and moisture content. At locations close to ground zero where the radiant thermal exposure exceeds 125 Joules/sq cm, almost all ignitable materials will flame, although burning may not be sustained. On the other hand, at greater distances only the most easily ignited materials will flame, although charring of exposed surfaces may occur. The probability of significant fires following a nuclear explosion depends on the density of ignition points, the availability and condition of combustible material (whether hot, dry, wet), wind, humidity, and the character of the surrounding area. Incendiary effects are compounded by secondary fires started by the blast wave effects such as from upset stoves and furnaces, broken gas lines, etc. In Hiroshima, a tremendous fire storm developed within 20 minutes after detonation. A fire storm burns in upon itself with great ferocity and is characterized by gale force winds blowing in towards the center of the fire from all points of the compass. It is not, however, a phenomenon peculiar to nuclear explosions, having been observed frequently in large forest fires and following incendiary raids during World War II.

NUCLEAR RADIATION

Sources of Nuclear Radiation

Blast and thermal effects occur to some extent in all types of explosions, whether conventional or nuclear. The release of ionizing radiation, however, is a phenomenon unique to nuclear explosions and is an additional casualty producing mechanism superimposed on blast and thermal effects. This radiation is basically of two kinds, electromagnetic and particulate, and is emitted not only at the time of detonation (initial radiation) but also for long periods of time afterward (residual radiation). Initial or prompt nuclear radiation is that ionizing radiation emitted within the first minute after detonation and results almost entirely from the nuclear processes occurring at detonation. Residual radiation is defined as that radiation which is emitted later than 1 minute after detonation and arises principally from the decay of radioisotopes produced during the explosion.

Initial Radiation

About 5% of the energy released in a nuclear air burst is transmitted in the form of initial neutron and gamma radiation. The neutrons result almost exclusively from the energy producing fission and fusion reactions, while the initial gamma radiation includes that arising from these reactions as well as that resulting from the decay of short-lived fission products. The intensity of initial nuclear radiation decreases rapidly with distance from the point of burst due to the spread of radiation over a larger area as it travels away from the explosion, and to absorption, scattering, and capture by the atmosphere.

The character of the radiation received at a given location also varies with distance from the explosion. Near the point of the explosion, the neutron intensity is greater than the gamma intensity, but with increasing distance the neutron-gamma ratio decreases. Ultimately, the neutron component of initial radiation becomes negligible in comparison with the gamma component. The range for significant levels of initial radiation does not increase markedly with weapon yield and, as a result, the initial radiation becomes less of a hazard with increasing yield. With larger weapons, above 50 Kt, blast and thermal effects are so much greater in importance that prompt radiation effects can be ignored.

Residual Radiation

The residual radiation hazard from a nuclear explosion is in the form of radioactive fallout and neutron-induced activity. Residual ionizing radiation arises from:

a. *Fission Products.* These are intermediate weight isotopes which are formed when a heavy uranium or plutonium nucleus is split in a fission reaction. There are over 300 different fission products that may result from a fission reaction. Many of these are radioactive with widely differing half-lives. Some are very short, i.e., fractions of a second, while a few are long enough that the materials can be a hazard for months or years. Their principal mode of decay is by the emission of beta and gamma radiation. Approximately 60 grams of fission products are formed per kiloton of yield. The estimated activity of this quantity of fission products 1 minute after detonation is equal to that of 1.1×10^{21} Bq (30 million kilograms of radium) in equilibrium with its decay products.

b. *Unfissioned Nuclear Material.* Nuclear weapons are relatively inefficient in their use of fissionable material, and much of the uranium and plutonium is dispersed by the explosion without undergoing fission. Such unfissioned nuclear material decays by the emission of alpha particles and is of relatively minor importance.

c. *Neutron-Induced Activity.* If atomic nuclei capture neutrons when exposed to a flux of neutron radiation, they will, as a rule, become radioactive (neutron-induced activity) and then decay by emission of beta and gamma radiation over an extended period of time. Neutrons emitted as part of the initial nuclear radiation will cause activation of the weapon residues. In addition, atoms of environmental material, such as soil, air, and water, may be activated, depending on their composition and distance from the burst. For example, a small area around ground zero may become hazardous as a result of exposure of the minerals in the soil to initial neutron radiation. This is due principally to neutron capture by sodium (Na), manganese, aluminum, and silicon in the soil. This is a negligible hazard because of the limited area involved.

Fallout

a. *Worldwide Fallout.* After an air burst the fission products, unfissioned nuclear material, and weapon residues which have been vaporized by the heat of the fireball will condense into a fine suspension of very small particles 0.01 to 20 micrometers in diameter. These particles may be quickly drawn up into the stratosphere, particularly so if the explosive yield exceeds 10 Kt. They will then be dispersed by atmospheric winds and will gradually settle to the earth's surface after weeks, months, and even years as worldwide fallout. The radiobiological hazard of worldwide fallout is essentially a long-term one due to the potential accumulation of long-lived radioisotopes, such as strontium-90 and cesium-137, in the body as a result of ingestion of foods which had incorporated these radioactive materials. This hazard is much less serious than those which are associated with local fallout and, therefore, is not discussed at length in this publication. Local fallout is of much greater immediate operational concern.

b. *Local Fallout.* In a land or water surface burst, large amounts of earth or water will be vaporized by the heat of the fireball and drawn up into the radioactive cloud. This material will become radioactive when it condenses with fission products and other radiocontaminants or has become neutron-activated. There will be large amounts of particles of less than 0.1 micrometer to several millimeters in diameter generated in a surface burst in addition to the very fine particles which contribute to worldwide fallout. The larger particles will not rise into the stratosphere and consequently will settle to earth within about 24 hours as local fallout. Severe local fallout contamination can extend far beyond the blast and thermal effects, particularly in the case of high yield surface detonations. Whenever individuals remain in a radiologically contaminated area, such contamination will lead to an immediate external radiation exposure as well as a possible later internal hazard due to inhalation and ingestion of radiocontaminants. In severe cases of fallout contamination, lethal doses of external radiation may be incurred if protective or evasive measures are not undertaken. In cases of water surface (and shallow underwater) bursts, the particles tend to be rather lighter and smaller and so produce less local fallout but will extend over a greater area. The particles contain mostly sea salts with some water; these can have a cloud seeding affect causing local rainout and areas of high local fallout. For subsurface bursts, there is an additional phenomenon present called "base surge." The base surge is a cloud that rolls outward from the bottom of the column produced by a subsurface explosion. For underwater bursts the visible surge is, in effect, a cloud of liquid (water) droplets with the property of flowing almost as if it were a homogeneous fluid. After the water evaporates, an invisible base surge of small radioactive particles may persist. For subsurface land bursts, the surge is made up of small solid particles, but it still behaves like a fluid. A soil earth medium favors base surge formation in an underground burst.

c. *Meteorological Effects.* Meteorological conditions will greatly influence fallout, particularly local fallout. Atmospheric winds are able to distribute fallout over large areas. For example, as a result of a surface burst of a 15 Mt thermonuclear device at Bikini Atoll on March 1, 1954, a roughly cigar-shaped area of the Pacific extending over 500 km downwind and varying in width to a maximum of 100 km was severely contaminated. Snow and rain, especially if they come from considerable heights, will accelerate local fallout. Under special meteorological conditions, such as a local rain shower that originates above the radioactive cloud, limited areas of heavy contamination may be formed.

INITIAL NUCLEAR RADIATION

Initial nuclear radiation is defined as the radiation that arrives during the first minute after an explosion, and is mostly gamma radiation and neutron radiation.

The level of initial nuclear radiation decreases rapidly with distance from the fireball to where less than one roentgen may be received five miles from ground zero. In addition, initial radiation lasts only as long as nuclear fission occurs in the fireball. Initial nuclear radiation represents about 3 percent of the total energy in a nuclear explosion.

Though people close to ground zero may receive lethal doses of radiation, they are concurrently being killed by the blast wave and thermal pulse. In typical nuclear weapons, only a relatively small proportion of deaths and injuries result from initial radiation.

Residual Nuclear Radiation

The residual radiation from a nuclear explosion is mostly from the radioactive fallout. This radiation comes from the weapon debris, fission products, and, in the case of a ground burst, radiated soil. There are over 300 different fission products that may result from a fission reaction. Many of these are radioactive with widely differing half-lives. Some are very short, i.e., fractions of a second, while a few are long enough that the materials can be a hazard for months or years. Their principal mode of decay is by the emission of beta particles and gamma radiation.

Radiation Effects on Humans

Certain body parts are more specifically affected by exposure to different types of radiation sources. Several factors are involved in determining the potential health effects of exposure to radiation. These include:

- The size of the dose (amount of energy deposited in the body)
- The ability of the radiation to harm human tissue
- Which organs are affected

The most important factor is the amount of the dose - the amount of energy actually deposited in your body. The more energy absorbed by cells, the greater the biological damage. Health physicists refer to the amount of energy absorbed by the body as the radiation dose.

The absorbed dose, the amount of energy absorbed per gram of body tissue, is usually measured in units called rads. Another unit of radation is the rem, or roentgen equivalent in man. To convert rads to rems, the number of rads is multiplied by a number that reflects the potential for damage caused by a type of radiation. For beta, gamma and X-ray radiation, this number is generally one. For some neutrons, protons, or alpha particles, the number is twenty.

Hair

The losing of hair quickly and in clumps occurs with radiation exposure at 200 rems or higher.

Brain

Since brain cells do not reproduce, they won't be damaged directly unless the exposure is 5,000 rems or greater. Like the heart, radiation kills nerve cells and small blood vessels, and can cause seizures and immediate death.

Thyroid

The certain body parts are more specifically affected by exposure to different types of radiation sources. The thyroid gland is susceptible to radioactive iodine. In sufficient amounts, radioactive iodine can destroy all or part of the thyroid. By taking potassium iodide can reduce the effects of exposure.

Blood System

When a person is exposed to around 100 rems, the blood's lymphocyte cell count will be reduced, leaving the victim more susceptible to infection. This is often refered to as mild radiation sickness. Early symptoms of radiation sickness mimic those of flu and may go unnoticed unless a blood count is done.According to data from Hiroshima and Nagaski, show that symptoms may persist for up to 10 years and may also have an increased long-term risk for leukemia and lymphoma. For more information, visit Radiation Effects Research Foundation.

Heart

Intense exposure to radioactive material at 1,000 to 5,000 rems would do immediate damage to small blood vessels and probably cause heart failure and death directly.

Gastrointestinal Tract

Radiation damage to the intestinal tract lining will cause nausea, bloody vomiting and diarrhea. This is occurs when the victim's exposure is 200 rems or more. The radiation will begin to destroy the cells in the body that divide rapidly. These including blood, GI tract, reproductive and hair cells, and harms their DNA and RNA of surviving cells.

Long Term Effects on Humans

Long after the acute effects of radiation have subsided, radiation damage continues to produce a wide range of physical problems. These effects- including leukemia, cancer, and many others- appear two, three, even ten years later.

Blood Disorders

According to Japanese data, there was an increase in anemia among persons exposed to the bomb. In some cases, the decrease in white and red blood cells lasted for up to ten years after the bombing.

Cataracts

There was an increase in cataract rate of the survivors at Hiroshima and Nagasaki, who were partly shielded and suffered partial hair loss.

Reproductive Tract

Because reproductive tract cells divide rapidly, these areas of the body can be damaged at rem levels as low as 200. Long-term, some radiation sickness victims will become sterile.

Dose-rem	*Effects*
5-20	Possible late effects; possible chromosomal damage.
20-100	Temporary reduction in white blood cells.
100-200	Mild radiation sickness within a few hours: vomiting, diarrhea, fatigue; reduction in resistance to infection.
200-300	Serious radiation sickness effects as in 100-200 rem and hemorrhage; exposure is a Lethal Dose to 10-35% of the population after 30 days (LD 10-35/30).
300-400	Serious radiation sickness; also marrow and intestine destruction; LD 50-70/30.
400-1000	Acute illness, early death; LD 60-95/30.
1000-5000	Acute illness, early death in days; LD 100/10.

Malignant Tumors

All ionizing radiation is carcinogenic, but some tumor types are more readily generated than others. A prevalent type is leukemia.

The cancer incidence among survivors of Hiroshima and Nagasaki is significantly larger than that of the general population, and a significant correlation between exposure level and degree of incidence has been reported for thyroid cancer, breast cancer, lung cancer, and cancer of the salivary gland.

Often a decade or more passes before radiation-caused malignancies appear.

Keloids

Beginning in early 1946, scar tissue covering apparently healed burns began to swell and grow abnormally. Mounds of raised and twisted flesh, called keloids, were found in 50 to 60 percent of those burned by direct exposure to the heat rays within 1.2 miles of the hypocenter. Keloids are believed to be related to the effects of radiation.

Radioactive Fallout

Fallout is the radioactive particles that fall to earth as a result of a nuclear explosion. It consists of weapon debris, fission products, and, in the case of a ground burst, radiated soil. Fallout particles vary in size from thousandths of a millimeter to several millimeters.

Much of this material falls directly back down close to ground zero within several minutes after the explosion, but some travels high into the atmosphere. This material will be dispersed over the earth during the following hours, days (and) months. Fallout is defined as one of two types: early fallout, within the first 24 hours after an explosion, or delayed fallout, which occurs days or years later.

Most of the radiation hazard from nuclear bursts comes from short-lived radionuclides external to the body; these are generally confined to the locality downwind of the weapon burst point. This radiation hazard comes from radioactive fission fragments with half-lives of seconds to a few months, and from soil and other materials in the vicinity of the burst made radioactive by the intense neutron flux.

Most of the particles decay rapidly. Even so, beyond the blast radius of the exploding weapons there would be areas (*hot spots*) the survivors could not enter because of radioactive contamination from long-lived radioactive isotopes like strontium 90 or cesium 137. For the survivors of a nuclear war, this lingering radiation hazard could represent a grave threat for as long as 1 to 5 years after the attack.

Predictions of the amount and levels of the radioactive fallout are difficult because of several factors. These include; the yield and design of the weapon, the height of the explosion, the nature of the surface beneath the point of burst, and the meteorological conditions, such as wind direction and speed.

An air burst can produce minimal fallout if the fireball does not touch the ground. On the other hand, a nuclear explosion occurring at or near the earth's surface can result in severe contamination by the radioactive fallout.

Fallout Particles

Many fallout particles are especially hazardous biologically. Some of the principal radioactive elements are as follows:

Strontium 90 is very long-lived with a half-life of 28 years. It is chemically similar to calcium, causing it to accumulate in growing bones. This radiation can cause tumors, leukemia, and other blood abnormalities.

Iodine 131 has a half-life of 8.1 days. Ingestion of it concentrates in the thyroid gland. The radiation can destroy all or part of the thyroid. Taking potassium iodide can reduce the effects.

The amount of tritium released varies by bomb design. It has a half-life of 12.3 years and can be easily ingested, since it can replace a hydrogen in water. The beta radiation can cause lung cancer.

Cesium 137 has a half-life of 30 years. It does not present as large a biological threat as Strontium 90. It behaves similar to potassium, and will distribute fairly uniformly thoughout the body. This can contribute to gonadal irradiation and genetic damage.

When a plutonium weapon is exploded, not all of the plutonium is fissioned. Plutonium 239 has a half-life of 24,400 years. Ingestion of as little as 1 microgram of plutonium, a barely visible speck, is a serious health hazard causing the formation of bone and lung tumors.

The Fallout Pattern

The actual fallout pattern depend on wind speed and direction and on the terrain. The fallout will contain about 60 percent of the total radioactivity. The largest particles will fall within a short distance of ground zero. Smaller particles will require many hours to return to earth and may be carried hundreds of miles. This means that a surface burst can produce serious contamination far from the point of detonation.

From the 15-megaton thermonuclear device tested at Bikini Atoll on March 1, 1954 - the BRAVO shot of Operation CASTLE - the fallout caused substantial contamination over an area of more than 7,000 square miles. The contaminated region was roughly cigar-shaped and extended more than 20 miles upwind and over 350 miles downwind.

Fallout can also enter into the stratosphere. In this stable region, radioactive particles can remain from 1 to 3 years before returning to the surface.

The OTA Study

The Office of Technology Assessment (1979) estimated the effects of a large-scale nuclear attack on U.S. military and economic targets. This scenario assumes a direct attack on 250 U.S. cities, with a total yield of 7,800 megatons. The most immediate effects would be the loss of millions of human lives, accompanied by similar incomprehensible levels of injuries, and the physical destruction of a high percentage of U.S. economic and industrial capacity. The full range of effects resulting from several thousand warheads - most having yields of a megaton or greater - impacting on or near U.S. cities can only be discussed in terms of uncertainty and speculation. It is estimated that 100 million to 165 million people would be killed.

Although this type of attack is less likely than during the Cold War, the risk of a limited nuclear strike by one of the smaller nuclear powers still remains a possibility.

Electromagnetic Pulse

Electromagnetic pulse (EMP) is an electromagnetic wave similar to radio waves, which results from secondary reactions occurring when the nuclear gamma radiation is absorbed in the air or ground. It differs from the usual radio waves in two important ways. First, it creates much higher electric field strengths. Whereas a radio signal might produce a thousandth of a volt or less in a receiving antenna, an EMP pulse might produce thousands of volts. Secondly, it is a single pulse of energy that disappears completely in a small fraction of a second. In this sense, it is rather similar to the electrical signal from lightning, but the rise in voltage is typically a hundred times faster. This means that most equipment designed to protect electrical facilities from lightning works too slowly to be effective against EMP.

There is no evidence that EMP is a physical threat to humans. However, electrical or electronic systems, particularly those connected to long wires such as power lines or antennas, can undergo damage. There could be actual physical damage to an electrical component or a temporary disruption of operation.

An attacker might detonate a few weapons at high altitudes in an effort to destroy or damage the communications and electric power systems. It can be expected that EMP would cause massive disruption for an indeterminable period, and would cause huge economic damages.

On July 8, 1962, the EMP from the high altitude (250 miles above Johnston Island) "Starfish Prime" test (1.4 Mt) turned off 300 streetlights in Oahu, Hawaii (740 miles away).

6

A Post-War Disaster for Environment and Health

CYLINDER STORAGE OF DEPLETED URANIUM HEXAFLUORIDE

Most of the depleted uranium produced to date is being stored as UF_6 in steel cylinders in the open air in so-called cylinder yards located adjacent to the enrichment plants. The cylinders contain up to 12.7 tonnes of UF_6. In the US alone, 560,000 metric tonnes of depleted UF_6 have accumulated until 1993; they are currently stored in 46,422 cylinders. Meanwhile, their number has grown by another 8,000 new cylinders.

At ambient temperature, UF_6 is a crystalline solid, but at a temperature of 56.4°C, it sublimates (becomes a gas). Chemically, UF_6 is very reactive: with water (atmospheric humidity!) it forms the extremely corrosive hydrofluoric acid and the highly toxic uranyl fluoride (UO_2F_2). The hydrofluoric acid causes skin burns, and, after inhalation, damages the lungs. Further health hazards result from the chemical toxicity of the uranium to the kidneys, and from the radiation of the uranium (an alpha emitter).

In the storage yards, the cylinders are subject to corrosion. The integrity of the cylinders must therefore be monitored and the painting must be refreshed from time to time. This maintenance work requires moving of the cylinders, causing further hazards from breaching of corroded cylinders, and from handling errors. As a worst-case scenario, the crash of an airplane into a cylinder yard must be assumed. If cylinders are involved in long-lasting fires, large amounts of UF_6 can be released within a short time. If the whole contents of a cylinder is released during a fire, lethal air concentrations of toxic substances can occur within distances of 500 to 1,000 meters.

Civilian uses of depleted uranium

Historically, uranium has been used as a colouring matter in pottery. More recent civilian uses include the use of uranium as a steel-alloying constituent, and the use of several uranium compounds in chemical processes, for example as a catalyst. For its high density of 18.9 g/cm^3 (67% higher than that of lead and slightly lower than that of tungsten), uranium can be used in dense metal applications such as counterweights or flywheels. For example, the first 550 Boeing 747 aircrafts built utilized depleted uranium weights for mass balance of outboard elevator and upper rudder assemblies. But this use of depleted uranium in the form of uranium metal also included drawbacks: over 20% of these weights were corroded at each major aircraft overhaul and had to be reprocessed, although nickel and cadmium plated. In more recent aircraft designs, however, the use of counterweights has been minimized due to advanced design technology.

During the production process of uranium metal applications, the pyrophoric behaviour of small uranium metal particles constitutes a problem. These particles, such as finely divided metallic saw turnings and chips, sawdust, and abrasive saw sludge are capable of spontaneous ignition, and have caused many incidents. Inhalation of dust from fires involving uranium metal can cause high radiation doses.

Another possible use of depleted uranium based on its high density is the use in radiation shields: though an alpha-radioactive material itself, it is suitable for shielding penetrating gamma-radiation better than lead.

For all of the uses mentioned, it doesn't matter other than for use as nuclear fuel, that the uranium is depleted in uranium-235.

To date, none of the civilian uses of depleted uranium has brought an appreciable decrease of the existing stockpiles of this material. In the US, however, the Department of Energy (DOE), urged by the increasing maintenance problems of its cylinder yards, is now performing the first steps towards a large-scale civilian use of depleted uranium. The DOE's preferred alternative for the management of its 560,000-metric-tonne stockpile is to use the entire inventory of material in the form of metal or oxide, mainly for radiation shielding in casks for spent fuel and high-level waste, but also for other industrial uses to be developed. The depleted uranium, now contained at a few sites, would then be dispersed over a wide range of products. The DOE now plans to build two plants to convert the $UF_6$to more stable forms that could be manufactured to marketable products or used for disposal, at costs of nearly $200 million each.

LONG-TERM STORAGE OR DISPOSAL

The portion of the depleted uranium for which no use can be identified must be disposed of, or must be safely stored in the long term for possible future uses. According to the nuclear industry, changes in the market or new enrichment technologies might allow for an economical recovery of the residual uranium-235 still contained in the depleted uranium in the future.

For long-term storage or disposal, the depleted UF_6 must be converted to a less reactive chemical form: candidates are UF_4, U_3O_8, and UO_2. UF_4 has the advantage of being easily reconvertible to UF_6, while U_3O_8 is the most stable form, also existing as a natural mineral.

The depleted uranium long-term storage project at Bessines (France)

France's nuclear fuel company Cogéma is going to store 199,900 metric tonnes of depleted uranium at the site of the former uranium mill of Bessines-sur-Gartempe (Haute Vienne) near Limoges. The project was licensed on December 20, 1995. This license was revoked by the Administrative Tribunal of

Limoges on July 9, 1998, mainly for the reason that the depleted uranium had to be regarded as a waste under current conditions, though an extraction of the residual uranium-235 might be viable in the future.

On Nov. 5, 1998 however, a Bordeaux appeals court ruled that the material is no waste, but a "directly usable raw material that is effectively used for multiple uses". Following the court decision, Cogéma sent the first depleted uranium shipment to Bessines on Nov. 12, 1998.

Originally, Cogéma had applied for the storage of 265,000 tonnes, but during the hearings held on the project, it became obvious that Cogéma had "forgotten" to consider some radionuclides (artificial uranium-236, among others) in its calculation of the total activity inventory: the specific activity of the depleted uranium is 21,100 Bq/g instead of 15,902 Bq/g. The project would therefore have exceeded the 100,000 Curie ($3.7 \cdot 10^{15}$ Bq) limit, requiring a different type of license (Installation Nucléaire de Base) involving wider public participation. Cogéma was not able to provide a reasonable explanation for the presence of the uranium-236.

The depleted uranium is a residue of the Eurodif Tricastin gaseous diffusion enrichment plant in the Rhône valley. Its residual contents of uranium-235 is 0.2 to 0.3% and it has the chemical form of uranium hexafluoride (UF_6). Cogéma doesn't declare it a waste, but wants to store it for possible future use. Cogéma hopes that the stored depleted uranium can be useful, if future enrichment techniques would allow for economic extraction of the residual uranium-235, or if uranium prices would rise significantly.

For storage, the UF_6 is converted to the chemically more stable form of U_3O_8 at Cogéma's Pierrelatte facility. Then it is transported by rail to the Bessines site and stored as a powder in iron containers. The containers (8.5 or 11 tonnes each) are to be stored in 11 special storage buildings. Each building can store 2,500 containers. The maximum dose that an individual would be exposed to at the fence of the facility is calculated at 0.7 mSv (70 mrem) per year, far below the (extremely high)

French limit of 5 mSv (500 mrem) for the public. The total investment is planned at 60 million French Francs (approximately US$ 10 million) over a period of 15 years.

Re-enrichment

Surprisingly, the recovery of the residual uranium-235 contained in the depleted uranium no longer is a matter of the future: it has been practised for several years now.

Depleted uranium from European uranium enricher Urenco (with plants operating in the United Kingdom, The Netherlands, and Germany) and others is now being enriched in Russia. The centrifuge enrichment plant of Minatom's Ural Electrochemical Integrated Plant (UEChK, formerly Sverdlovsk-44) at Novouralsk near Ekaterinburg is enriching tails for Urenco. Minatom, while further depleting ("stripping") Urenco's depleted uranium, produces uranium of natural contents (0.71%) in uranium-235. It thus *re-enriches* or *upgrades* the tails to natural uranium-235 grade. This product is then delivered back to Urenco for further enrichment to reactor grade. In 1996 alone, more than 6,000 metric tonnes of tails were upgraded.

The economics of tails re-enrichment

Assuming 1997 world market prices for uranium and enrichment services, the break-even point for tails upgrading according to the assumptions made above would be reached at a recovery rate of "natural" uranium of 2.63 kg U/SWU at Minatom. The obtained recovery rate of 1.57 kg U/SWU only reaches 60% of this value. So additional factors must be taken into consideration to understand the economics of re-enrichment.

Minatom possibly does not charge the full enrichment cost

Minatom has an estimated 9 million SWU/year of enrichment capacity in excess of Russia's needs [*Nuclear Fuel* Oct. 19, 1998]. It is therefore possible that Minatom does not charge the full enrichment cost, but its operating cost only. The US DOE's *Engineering Analysis Report for the Long-Term Management of Depleted Uranium Hexafluoride* of May 1997 estimates operating costs of $20-$30/SWU for centrifuge enrichment plants (there are no such plants in the US though). With US$30/SWU, for example, the break-even point would be reached at 0.88 kg U/SWU. The obtained recovery rate is 78% higher for the case shown above. The highest absolute cost savings would be obtained at a tails assay of 0.21% at Minatom, in this case.

Minatom possibly strips the tails further than contracted

In case of Minatom not quoting the full enrichment cost, also another consideration can be made: According to George White, a consultant with Uranium Exchange Co., it is likely the Russians have contracted with Urenco to strip tails from 0.3% to 0.25% U-235. But the Russians are then probably stripping the tails further to 0.12% U-235 to produce uranium for their own account, White has suggested [*Nuclear Fuel*, Oct. 19, 1998].

If Russia used all of its excess 9 million SWU/year to strip Urenco's tails in the described way from 0.3% to 0.12% U-235, then 7,290 tonnes/year of uranium of natural isotope composition would be recovered, 4,680 tonnes of which would be on Russia's own account.

Urenco's avoided disposal cost

The new tails produced during the upgrading process remain in Russia, according to the answer of the German government to a parliamentary question in 1997. This, together with the fact that the upgrading process results only in a minor reduction of the amount of tails, gives reason to have a look at Urenco's avoided disposal cost.

Assuming market conditions, the tails upgrading does not make an economic sense, if the recovery of the uranium were its only purpose: the recovered uranium would be 68% more expensive than fresh uranium.

The re-enrichment does, however, make sense, if the avoided disposal cost for the tails are taken into consideration. For the German branch of Urenco, for example, disposal in the proposed Gorleben HLW deposit must be assumed, since the German LLW deposits don't allow for storage of such amounts of uranium. The excess upgrading cost over the market value of the uranium recovered would be about 10% only of the storage cost at Gorleben.

Urenco's main purpose of the deal, therefore, seems to be to "solve" its waste management problem by transferring the depleted uranium to Russia.

The German Federal Government, however, stresses the results of an investigation it has conducted together with the governments of the United Kingdom and The Netherlands. The study has approved that the re-enrichment in Russia is not connected to a management of residues violating international rules, standards, or obligations.

Re-enrichment would also be an option for the management of the depleted uranium stockpile of the US DOE - in particular, since roughly 30% of the DOE inventory has a rather high tails assay in the 0.3 - 0.4% range. But, since there exist no low-cost enrichment plants such as centrifuge plants in the US, this option is not seen viable at present.

DEPLETED URANIUM WEAPONS

The 1991 Persian Gulf War included an array of the twentieth century's most frightening and devastating weapons. Nuclear, chemical, and biological weapons were all poised for use, each with the ability to cause massive casualties among friend and foe alike. When hostilities subsided in March, 1991, the world breathed a collective sigh of relief that weapons of mass destruction had not been used. Or had they?

During the Gulf War, American and British forces introduced armor-piercing ammunition made of depleted uranium, a radioactive and toxic waste. By war's end, more than 290,000 kilograms (640,000 pounds) of depleted uranium contaminated equipment and the soil on the battlefields of Saudi Arabia, Kuwait, and southern Iraq. Though investigations are ongoing and additional research is needed, it now appears that some veterans and civilians exposed to depleted uranium contamination are suffering health problems including kidney damage and cancers.

The use of a radioactive and toxic waste in ammunition heralds a dangerous new era in land warfare, one in which the line between conventional and unconventional warfare is irreversibly blurred. The increasing proliferation and use of depleted uranium weapons ensure their part in armed conflict for the foreseeable future. Accordingly, we must learn from the lessons of the use of depleted uranium weapons in the Gulf War and take steps to minimize and prevent the adverse effects on soldiers, civilians, and food and water supplies.

Depleted uranium (DU) is the waste product of the process to enrich uranium ore for use in nuclear weapons and reactors. Depleted uranium is chemically toxic like other heavy metals such as lead, but it is also primarily an alpha particle emitter with a radioactive half-life of 4.5 billion years. The U.S. Army Environmental Policy Institute states "DU is a low-level radioactive waste, and, therefore must be disposed in a licensed repository."

In the 1950's, the United States Department of Defense became interested in using depleted uranium metal in weapons because it is extremely dense, pyrophoric, cheap, and available in huge quantities in the United States. During the 1960's and 1970's, research and open-air testing at various locations in the United States demonstrated the effectiveness of using depleted uranium in kinetic energy penetrators, which are rods of solid metal shot from guns. Kinetic energy penetrators do not explode; they fragment and burn through armor "due to the pyrophoric nature of uranium metal and the extreme flash temperatures generated on impact." In the 1980's, depleted uranium was also developed for use in tank armor.

During Operation Desert Storm, American M1A1, M1, and M60 tanks and British Challenger tanks fired thousands of large caliber depleted uranium penetrators. American A-10 and AV-8B aircraft shot hundreds of thousands of small caliber depleted uranium rounds. American snipers shot 7.62mm and possibly.50 caliber depleted uranium bullets. In addition, one-third (654) of the American tanks used in the war (2,054) were equipped with depleted uranium armor. Depleted uranium penetrators enhanced the tactical advantage of American and

British forces over the Iraqi Army's inventory of tanks, but the effectiveness of depleted uranium tank armor was never tested on the field of battle. Iraq did not have DU armor or munitions in its inventory.

Amidst post-war hype over the success of expensive, high tech weaponry, depleted uranium weapons received surprisingly little public praise from Pentagon and U.S. defense industry officials. A possible motivation for this cautious silence is expressed in pre-war U.S. Army reports which warned the use of DU weapons could have severe health and environmental consequences and create "adverse international reaction." However, post-war reports have promoted a policy of "proponency" to guarantee the unrestricted use and proliferation of depleted uranium weapons. The Pentagon's focus on proponency has forestalled investigation and research of illnesses among veterans of the American-led expeditionary force and populations in southern Iraq possibly related to exposure to depleted uranium.

The lessons of the use of depleted uranium weapons in the Gulf War are unsettling, but understanding them will enable us to prevent or minimize the effects of depleted uranium weapons in the future.

LESSON 1: Depleted uranium weapons contaminate impact areas with extremely fine radioactive and toxic dust. U.S. Army testing found that 18 to 70% of a depleted uranium penetrator rod burns and oxidizes into extremely small particles during impact. The impact of one 120mm depleted uranium penetrator fired from an American Abrams tank therefore creates between 900 and 3,400 grams (roughly 2 to 7 pounds) of uranium oxide dust. U.S. Army testing further found "he DU oxide aerosol formed during the impact of DU into armor has a high percentage of respirable size particles (50 to 96%)," and 52 to 83% of those respirable size particles are insoluble in lung fluids. Respirable size particles (less than 5 microns in diameter) are easily inhaled or ingested. Insoluble particles are not readily excreted from the body, and may remain in the lungs or other organs for years.

U.S. Army research recently found that some respirable size uranium dust remains suspended in the air for hours after an impact. As demonstrated in the 1970's by the release of depleted uranium during the manufacture of DU ammunition near Albany, New York, depleted uranium dust can be carried downwind for 40 kilometers (25 miles) or more. Most of the dust created by an impact comes to rest inside, on, or within 50 meters of the target. However, U.S. Army testing also discovered depleted uranium dust can be resuspended by the wind, or the movement of people and vehicles.

The long-term dangers of depleted uranium contamination are discussed in a U.S. Army Chemical School training manual:

DU's mobility in water is due to how easily it dissolves. Soluble compounds of DU will readily dissolve and migrate with surface or ground water. Drinking or washing or other contact with contaminated water will spread the contamination... The end result of air and water contamination is that DU is deposited in the soil. Once in the soil, it stays there unless moved. This means that the area remains contaminated, and will not decontaminate itself.

No cleanup of depleted uranium in the soil has taken place in Iraq or Kuwait. Surprisingly, the U.S. Department of Defense claims it tested soil in Kuwait and found no presence of depleted uranium contamination. However, in 1995 and 1997, documentary film teams detected depleted uranium contamination on destroyed vehicles and in the soil in southern Iraq.

In addition to the fine uranium dust created by impacts, depleted uranium fragments and intact DU penetrators also pose a hazard. In March, 1991, an internal U.S. Defense Nuclear Agency memorandum noted: "Alpha particles (uranium oxide dust) from expended rounds is a health concern but Beta particles from fragments and intact rounds is a serious health threat, with a possible exposure rate of 200 millirads per hour on contact." One depleted uranium penetrator found in April, 1991 at the Port of Dammam, Saudi Arabia had a radiation reading of 260-270 mrad/hour. The corrosion rate for a DU penetrator in soil depends upon the chemical makeup of the soil and other environmental conditions. Weathered DU penetrators principally corrode into uranium dust that is soluble in water.

Established limits on intake of depleted uranium dust attest that just a small amount poses a serious health threat. The limit for intake by an occupational worker has been set at 0.01 gram/one week (U.S. Nuclear Regulatory Commission) and 0.008 gram/one year (UK Ministry of Defense). The limit on intake for a member of the public is set at 0.002 gram/one year (UK Atomic Energy Authority).

The route of depleted uranium in the body depends upon the method of exposure (inhalation, ingestion, implantation, or wound contamination), and the size and solubility of the particles. Recent research found depleted uranium particles may remain in the lungs if inhaled, or travel in the bloodstream and deposit in the brain, kidney, bone, reproductive organs, muscle and spleen. Insoluble depleted uranium particles (up to 83% by volume of the total dust created by an impact), if inhaled, "pose primarily a radiological, as opposed to a chemical, toxicological hazard." In 1997, depleted uranium was found in the semen of five out of twenty two American veterans who had been wounded by depleted uranium fragments in 1991.

Though additional studies on depleted uranium's health effects are needed, internalized DU is acknowledged to cause kidney damage, cancers of the lung and bone, non-malignant respiratory disease, skin disorders, neurocognitive disorders, chromosomal damage, and birth defects. A July, 1990 report from the U.S. Army Armament, Munitions, and Chemical Command notes depleted uranium is a "low level alpha radiation emitter which is linked to cancer when exposures are internal, [and] chemical toxicity causing kidney damage." In August, 1993, the U.S. Army Surgeon General's Office confirmed the "[e]xpected physiological effects from exposure to DU dust include possible increased risk of cancer (lung or bone) and kidney damage." A June, 1995 U.S. Army Environmental Policy Institute report adds: "The radiation dose to critical organs depends upon the amount of time that DU resides in the organs. When this value is known or estimated, cancer and hereditary risk estimates can be determined."

The end result of the use of depleted uranium weapons is contamination of damaged equipment and the environment with dangerous levels of depleted uranium dust and debris. Respirable size particles formed during impacts and soluble uranium oxide dust formed by corroding penetrators may be transported by the wind or water, and may contaminate food and water supplies. Friend and foe alike may inhale or ingest depleted uranium dust and suffer severe short and long term health problems.

LESSON 2: Armed forces are unlikely to be protected from exposure to depleted uranium contamination. As far back as 1974 - seventeen years before depleted uranium weapons were used in the Gulf War - a U.S. Department of Defense study group predicted: "In combat situations involving the widespread use of DU munitions, the potential for inhalation, ingestion, or implantation of DU compounds may be locally significant." In July, 1990, a U.S. Army contractor further warned: "Aerosol DU exposures to soldiers on the battlefield could be significant with potential radiological and toxicological effects... Under combat conditions, the MEI's [most exposed individuals] are probably the ground troops that re-enter a battlefield following the exchange of armor-piercing munitions, either on foot or motorized transports."

Despite the blunt admonitions of pre-war U.S. Army reports, no warnings about the dangers of depleted uranium were provided to the U.S. and coalition forces expected to encounter DU contamination on Gulf War battlefields. Combatants and support person-nel were not informed of the need to check soldiers' wounds for depleted uranium contamination, or told of the requirement to don full protective suits during contact with contaminated equipment and soil. In violation of operative U.S. Army and U.S. Nuclear Regulatory Commission regulations, no medical testing or follow-up was provided to soldiers who were wounded by depleted uranium fragments, or who may have inhaled or ingested DU dust.

Though American military commanders have never offered an explanation for their failure to warn troops about the hazards of depleted uranium weapons, it appears their inaction was inspired by a desire to avoid creating concern within the ranks and among the public. After a 1992 inquiry, U.S. General Accounting Office investigators reported that "[U.S.] Army officials believe that DU protective methods can be ignored during battle and other life-threatening situations because DU-related health risks are greatly outweighed by the risks of combat." When it became clear U.S. military commanders disregarded all DU protective methods during and after the Gulf War, the U.S. Army Environmental Policy Institute expressed concern about the costs of providing medical care to exposed veterans: "When DU is indicted as a causative agent for Desert Storm illness, the Army must have sufficient data to separate fiction from reality. Without forethought and data, the financial implications of long-term disability payments and health care costs would be excessive."

In January, 1998, the U.S. Department of Defense expressed its first and only admission of responsibility for Gulf War depleted uranium exposures:

Our investigations into potential health hazards of depleted uranium point to serious deficiencies in what our troops understood about the health effects DU posed on the battlefield... Combat troops or those carrying out support functions generally did not know that DU contaminated equipment, such as enemy vehicles struck by DU rounds, required special handling... The failure to properly disseminate such information to troops at all levels may have resulted in thousands of unnecessary exposures.

A map released by the U.S. Department of Defense in November, 1998 shows both the primary areas where depleted uranium was released during the Gulf War, and the movements of hundreds of thousands of American and coalition fighting forces through these contaminated areas. Though the U.S. Department of Defense admits "thousands" of American forces may have been unnecessarily exposed to depleted uranium contamination, it also asserts that not even one American veteran could possibly be sick from a depleted uranium exposure.

The case of the July, 1991 munitions fire at the U.S. Army base in Doha, Kuwait illustrates the hazards of accidental releases of depleted uranium. Among the large quantity of equipment and munitions destroyed in the twenty-four hour fire were 660 tank rounds containing 3,200 kg (7,000 lbs) of depleted uranium. While the fire raged, the U.S. Central Command acknowledged that "burning depleted uranium puts off alpha radiation. Uranium particles when breathed can be hazardous. 11ACR [The U.S. Army command at Doha] has been informed to treat the area as though it were a chemical area, i.e. stay upwind and wear protective mask in the vicinity." Despite this and other warnings, U.S. soldiers were not informed of DU's hazards or instructed to wear protective gear, even during post-fire cleanup operations. Further, the smoke from the fire drifted toward nearby Kuwait City, potentially exposing downwind populations to airborne depleted uranium.

Adequately protecting armed forces from exposure to depleted uranium contamination requires training, use of protective suits in a contaminated environment, and distribution of radiation detection devices to medical personnel. Unfortunately, since cancers and other health problems related to a depleted uranium exposure may not develop until after a battle or war is over, military commanders have little incentive to adhere to safety procedures which could impinge on a soldier or Marine's battlefield performance. The Gulf War proved that military commanders will not be held accountable for the uncontrolled release of a radioactive and toxic waste, or for violating safety regulations requiring medical testing and care of exposed troops.

The 1991 Gulf War demonstrated that members of armed forces are unlikely to receive adequate protection from exposure to depleted uranium during or after future conflicts or accidental releases. In addition, governments are unlikely to provide long-term medical care for depleted uranium-related health problems among war veterans.

LESSON 3: Local civilian populations are unlikely to be warned when depleted uranium weapons are used - even if depleted uranium contaminates their food or water supplies. Prior to the Gulf War, the U.S. Army was aware of the potential for depleted uranium contamination to cause health problems among civilian populations. However, during and after the Gulf War, the U.S. Department of Defense took no steps to warn the inhabitants of Kuwait, Saudi Arabia and Iraq about depleted uranium contamination on their lands. In contrast, U.S. Army reports express more concern about public outcry and future restrictions on the use of depleted uranium weapons than with contaminating foreign lands and poisoning civilians.

A July, 1990 U.S. Army report predicted: "Following combat, the condition of the battlefield, and the long-term health risks to natives and combat veterans may become issues in the acceptability of the continued use of DU kinetic energy penetrators for military applications." This concern was reiterated in March, 1991 just as the war was ending: "There has been and continues to be a concern regarding the impact of DU on the environment. Therefore, if no one makes a case for the effectiveness of DU on the battlefield, DU rounds may become politically unacceptable and thus, be deleted from the arsenal... I believe we should keep this sensitive issue at mind when after action reports are written."

Once hostilities subsided and the scale of the depleted uranium contamination in southern Iraq and Kuwait became known, further concern was expressed by the U.S. Defense Nuclear Agency: "As Explosive Ordnance Disposal (EOD), ground combat units, and the civil populations of Saudi Arabia, Kuwait, and Iraq come increasingly into contact with DU ordnance, we must prepare to deal with the potential problems. Toxic war souvenirs, political furor, and post conflict clean-up (host nation agreement) are only some of the issues that must be addressed."

In April, 1991, the United Kingdom Atomic Energy Authority also expressed concern about depleted uranium contamination in Kuwait:

It would be unwise for people to stay close to large quantities of DU for long periods and this would obviously be of concern to the local population if they collect this heavy metal and keep it. There will be specific areas in which many rounds will have been fired where localized contamination of vehicles and the soil may exceed permissible limits and these could be hazardous to both clean up teams and the local population...Furthermore, if DU gets into the food chain or water then this will create potential health problems.

Potential political problems were also noted:

"The whole issue of contamination in Kuwait is emotive and thus must be dealt with in a sensitive manner. It is necessary to inform the Kuwait Government of the problem in a tactful way and this... is probably best done in conjunction with the UK Ambassador to Kuwait."

The United States established a precedent during the Gulf War which permits an armed force to use depleted uranium weapons without warning civilian populations about contamination of the land. The United States is continuing this practice in the Kosovo war. Nations involved in conflicts in which depleted uranium weapons are used may find themselves faced with the "excessive" costs of long-term health care for exposed soldiers and civilians. The health and environmental consequences of depleted uranium weapons will likely receive less attention in nations where the populations are unaware of its use, or unable to voice their concerns and assert their rights.

LESSON 4: Depleted uranium weapons are proliferating and are likely to become commonly used in land warfare. A 1995 U.S. Army Chemical School training manual notes: "The United States' success with using DU in combat leads us to conclude that other nations, not all of them friendly, will be using DU in the future." Further, "it is likely that DU may also become the primary tank-killing munition for our potential enemies... in the next battle, potentially all stricken tanks or fighting vehicles will possibly contain DU contamination." Another 1995 U.S. Army report notes: "Since DU weapons are openly available on the world arms market, DU weapons will be used in future conflicts... The number of DU patients on future battlefields probably will be significantly higher because other countries will use systems containing DU." American soldiers and Marines are likely to be among the DU patients on future battlefields, as noted in a 1998 U.S. Department of Defense report: "DU's battlefield effectiveness has encouraged its steady proliferation into the arsenals of allies and adversaries alike. There is little doubt, therefore, that DU will be used against our troops in some future conflict."

Since 1991, the United States has led the world in using and proliferating depleted uranium weapons. After Operation Desert Storm, the U.S. started using depleted uranium rounds in the M2 and M3 Bradley Fighting Vehicles (25mm), the Light Amphibious Vehicle (25mm), the Apache attack helicopter (30mm), and the AH-1W "Whiskey Cobra" helicopter gunship (20mm). In 1994 and 1995, American fighter planes fired depleted uranium rounds against Serb targets in Bosnia, and during training near Okinawa, Japan.

In April, 1999, the US Department of Defense would neither confirm nor deny the use of depleted uranium ammunition by the A-10 aircraft in Kosovo. Interestingly, however, the US Army stated the Apache helicopter would not fire depleted uranium rounds because their analysts determined high explosive rounds were sufficient to destroy Serb tanks. Increased public and media interest in the use of DU weapons in the Kosovo war has evidently forced military commanders to reconsider their use of depleted uranium ammunition.

The growing list of nations possessing or manufacturing depleted uranium weapons includes the United States, the United Kingdom, France, Russia, Greece, Turkey, Israel, Saudi Arabia, Kuwait, Bahrain, Egypt, Kuwait, Thailand, Taiwan and Pakistan. The 'interoperability' of NATO military forces could also enable armed forces throughout Europe to obtain and use depleted uranium weapons.

With little discussion or fanfare, depleted uranium weapons have found their way into the arsenals of nations powerful and poor in some of the world's most volatile regions. The U.S. Department of Defense anticipates the use of depleted uranium weapons in future conflicts, and increasing numbers of depleted uranium exposures among friend and foe alike. Long after the guns fall silent and the survivors march home, the casualties and costs of using depleted uranium weapons will continue to mount.

LESSON 5: Depleted uranium contamination is unlikely to be cleaned up by victor or vanquished because of the extreme cost and the prospect of further environmental damage. As noted by the U.S. Army, " contaminated soil... should be scraped up and containerized for removal as radioactive waste." This is the procedure used in the United States during cleanup of depleted uranium contamination at the Starmet plant in Concord, Massachusetts (where DU penetrators are manufactured), and at Sandia National Laboratory and Kirkland Air Force Base in New Mexico (where DU penetrators were test fired).

The U.S. Army states cleanup involves removing the "the top layer of soil," which could be potentially devastating to an environment, especially if depleted uranium contaminates arable land or wetlands. Further, the cost involved in removing the topsoil from contaminated areas could be astronomical. As an example, the cost of cleaning up and disposing of the estimated 69,000 kg (152,000 lbs) of depleted uranium dust and debris on 200 hectares (500 acres) of the U.S. Army's Jefferson Proving Ground in Indiana has been placed at $4 to 5 billion (U.S.$). The cost of cleaning up 290,000 kg (640,000 lbs) of depleted uranium on thousands of hectares in Saudi Arabia, Kuwait, and Iraq could therefore easily be tens of billions of dollars (U.S.$).

A July, 1990 U.S. Army report warned: "Assuming U.S. regulatory standards and health physics practices are followed, it is likely that some form of remedial action will be required in a DU post-combat environment." However, once the scale and cost of cleaning up depleted uranium in the Persian Gulf region became clear, the U.S. Army Environmental Policy

Institute informed American policymakers that "no international law, treaty, regulation, or custom requires the United States to remediate the Persian Gulf War battlefields." As the most powerful nation in the world today, the United States established a standard of behavior in the Gulf War which allows nations and armed forces to use depleted uranium weapons without taking any responsibility for cleanup, environmental restoration, or provision of health care to exposed combatants or civilians.

In the last hundred years since the first The Hague conference, the devastating results of war have been multiplied in proportion to the increased mobility of armed forces, and the unparalleled destructiveness of the weapons used. In the conflicts of the next century and beyond, huge expanses of land and countless numbers of soldiers and civilians may be poisoned by radioactive and toxic waste shot from armored vehicles, aircraft, small arms, and ships. Depleted uranium weapons are the offspring of nuclear weapons, and the newest weapon capable of causing mass destruction. If the international community accepts the use of depleted uranium weapons in warfare, it must also accept the moral obligation to fully address the health and environmental consequences, regardless of the cost.

GULF WAR VETERANS AND DEPLETED URANIUM

Uranium metal is autopyrophoric and can burn spontaneously at room temperature in the presence of air, oxygen and water. At temperatures of 200-400 degrees Centigrade, uranium powder may self-ignite in atmospheres of carbon dioxide and nitrogen. Oxidation of uranium under certain conditions may generate sufficient energy to cause an explosion (Gindler 1973). Friction caused by bullet or missile entry into a tank or armored car, for example, can cause the uranium to ignite, forming a concentrated ceramic aerosol capable of killing most personnel in the vehicle. Depleted uranium was used extensively in place of thungsten for ordnance by the US and UK in the Gulf War.

There is no dispute of the fact that at least 320 tons of depleted uranium (DU) was "lost" in the Gulf war, and that much of that was converted at high temperature into an aerosol, that is, minute insoluble particles of uranium oxide, UO_2 or UO_3, in a mist or fog. It would have been impossible for ground troops to identify this exposure if or when it occurred in war, as this would require specialized detection equipment. However, veterans can identify situations in which they were likely to have been exposed to DU. Civilians working at military bases where live ammunition exercises are conducted may also have been exposed.

Uranium oxide and its aerosol form are insoluble in water. The aerosol resists gravity, and is able to travel tens of kilometres in air. Once on the ground, it can be resuspended when the sand is disturbed by motion or wind. Once breathed in, the very small particles of uranium oxide, those which are 2.5 microns or less in diameter, could reside in the lungs for years, slowly passing through the lung tissue into the blood. Uranium oxide dust has a biological half life in the lungs of about a year. According to British NRPB experiments with rats, the ceramic or aerosol form of uranium oxide takes "twice as long" or about a two year biological half life in the lungs, before passing into the blood stream. [Stradling et al 1988]

Because of coughing and other involuntary mechanisms by which the body keeps large particles out of the lungs, the larger particles are excreted through the gastro-intestinal tract in feces. The uranium compounds which enter the body either through the wall of the gastro-intestinal tract or the lungs, can be broken down in the body fluids, and tetravalent uranium is likely to oxidize to the hexavalent form, followed by the formation of uranyl ions. Uranium generally forms complexes with citrate, bicarbonates or protein in plasma, and it can be stored in bone, lymph, liver, kidney or other tissues. Eventually this uranium which is taken internally is excreted through urine. Presence of depleted uranium in urine seven or eight years after exposure is sufficient evidence to substantiate long term internal contamination and tissue storage of this radioactive substance.

Uranium is both a chemical toxic and radioactive hazard: Soluble uranium is regulated because of its chemical toxicity, measured by damage to the kidney and tubules. Uranium is a heavy metal, known to cause uranium nephritis. Insoluble uranium, such as was released in the Gulf War, is regulated by its radiological properties, and not its chemical properties. Because of its slow absorption through the lungs and long retention in body tissues, its primary damage will be due to its radiological damage to internal organs rather than chemical damage to the renal system. Obviously, both types of damage occur simultaneously, therefore it is a matter of judgement which severe damage, radiological or chemical, occurs at the lowest dose level. However, with the lengthening of the time during which the contaminant resides in the body and the low overall dose, the risk of cancer death becomes greater than the risk of significant damage to the renal system.

Uranium decays into other radioactive chemicals with statistical regularity. There-fore, in its natural and undisturbed state, it always occurs together with a variety of other radioactive chemical, some of the best known being thorium, radium, polonium and lead.

Natural uranium in soil is about 1 to 3 parts per million, whereas in uranium ore it is about 1,000 times more concentrated, reaching about 0.05 to 0.2% of the total weight. Depleted uranium concentrate is almost 100% uranium. More than 99% of both natural and depleted uranium consists of the isotope U-238. One gram of pure U-238 has a specific activity of 12.4 kBq, which means there are 12,400 atomic transformations every second, each of which releases an energetic alpha particle. Uranium 238 has a half life of 4.51 E+9 (or 4.51 times 10^9, equivalent to 4,510,000,000 years). Each atomic transformation produces another radioactive chemical: first, uranium 238 produces thorium 234, (which has a half life of 24.1 days), then the thorium 234 decays to protactinium 234 (which has a half life of 6.75 hours), and then protactinium decays to uranium 234 (which has a half life of 2.47E+5 or 247,000 years). The first two decay radioisotopes together with the U 238 count for almost all of the radioactivity in the depleted uranium. Even after an industrial process which separates out the uranium 238 has taken place, it will continue to produce these other radionuclides. Within 3 to 6 months they will all be present in equilibrium balance. Therefore one must consider the array of radionuclides, not just uranium 238, when trying to understand what happened when veterans inhaled depleted uranium in the Gulf War.

It should be noted that uranium 235, the more fissionable fraction which was partially removed in enrichment, makes up only 0.2 to 0.3% of the depleted uranium, whereas it was 0.7% of natural uranium. It is this deficit which enables one to use analytical methods to identify the uranium found in veteran's urine as depleted and not natural uranium. The U 235 was extracted for use in nuclear weapons and nuclear reactor fuel. Depleted uranium is considered nuclear waste, a by-product of uranium enrichment.

The difference in radioactivity between natural and depleted uranium is that given equal quantities, depleted uranium has about half the radioactivity of the natural mixture of uranium isotopes. However, because of the concentration of the uranium in the depleted uranium waste, depleted uranium is much more radioactive than uranium in its natural state.

Uranium and all of its decay products, with the exception of radon which is a gas, are heavy metals. Unlike some other heavy metals which are needed in trace quantities by the human body, there is no known benefit to having uranium in the body. It is always a contaminant. Ingesting and inhaling some uranium, usually from food, is inescapable however, in the normal Earth environment, and we humans basically take in, on average, 5 Bq per year of uranium 238 in equilibrium with its decay products. This gives an effective radiation dose equivalent to the whole body of 0.005 mSv. Using a quantitative measure, we normally ingest about 0.000436 g a year.[UNSCEAR 1988, 58-59] This is a mixture of soluble and insoluble compounds, absorbed mostly through the gut.

Regulatory limits recommended by the International Commission on Radiological Protection [ICRP] assume that the maximum permissible dose for members of the public will be the one which gives the individual 1 mSv dose per year. This is in addition to the natural exposure dose from uranium in the food web. Assuming that this dose come entirely from an insoluble inhaled uranium oxide, and using the ICRP dose conversion factor for uranium 238 in equilibrium with its decay products, one can obtain a factor of 0.84 mSv per mg, or a limit of intake of 1.2 mg (0.0012 g) per year for the general public. This would give an added radiation dose of 1.0 mSv from uranium, and an increase of almost 2.75 times the natural uranium intake level. Nuclear workers would be allowed by the ICRP maximum permissible level, to reach an annual dose of 20 mSv, comparable to an intake of 24 mg of uranium, 55 times the normal yearly intake.

The US has not yet conformed to the 1990 international recommendations which were used for this calculation, and it is still permitting the general public to receive five times the above general public amount, and the worker to receive 2.5 times the above occupational amount. The US may have used its domestic "nuclear worker" limits during the Gulf War, if it used any protective regulations at all. The military manual discusses the hazards of depleted uranium as less than other hazardous conditions on an active battle field!

The maximum dose per year from anthropogenic sources can be converted to the maximum concentration permissible in air using the fact that the adult male breathes in about 23 cu m air in a day [ICRP 1977]. The maximum permissible concentration in air for the general public would be: 0.14 microgram per cu metre, and for workers: 2.9 micrograms per cu m assuming the Gulf War situation of continuous occupancy rather than a 40 hour work week, and 8 hour day.

It is common in the US and Canada to refer to 2000 pounds as a "ton", whereas the British "ton" is 2240 pounds. Both are roughly 1000 kg. Just in order to understand the scale of the ceramic uranium released in Desert Storm, at least 300 million grams were "lost", and breathing in only 0.023 g would be equivalent to the maximum permissible inhalation dose for a nuclear worker to receive in a year under the 1990 recommendations of ICRP.

Medical Testing for Depleted Uranium Contamination

Potential testing includes: chemical analysis of uranium in urine, feces, blood and hair; tests of damage to kidneys, including analysis for protein, glucose and non-protein nitrogen in urine; radioactivity counting; or more invasive tests such as surgical biopsy of lung or bone marrow.

Experience with Gulf War veterans indicates that a 24 hour urine collection analysis shows the most promise of detecting depleted uranium contamination seven or eight years after exposure. However, since this test only measures the amount of depleted uranium which has been circulating in the blood or kidneys within one or two weeks prior to the testing time, rather than testing the true body burden, it cannot be directly used to reconstruct the veteran's dose received during the Gulf War. However, this seems to be the best diagnostic tool at this time, eight years after the exposure.

Feces tests for uranium are used for rapid detection of intake in an emergency situation, and in order to be useful for dose reconstruction, must be undertaken within hours or days of the exposure. Blood and fecal analysis are not advised except immediately after a known large intake of uranium.

Whole body counting for uranium, using the sodium iodide or hyper pure germanium detectors, is designed to detect the isotope uranium 235, the isotope of uranium partially removed from depleted uranium. For lung counting, again it is the uranium 235 which is detected, and the minimum detection limit is about 7.4 Bq or 200 pCi. Since normally humans take in only 5 Bq per year, this is not a very sensitive measure. Seven or eight years after the Gulf War exposure, this method of detection is most likely useless for veterans.

Routine blood counts shortly after exposure, or during a chelating process for decontamination of the body are useful. This is not a search for uranium in blood, but rather a complete blood count with differential. This is done to discover potentially abnormal blood counts, since the stem cells which produce the circulating lymphocytes and erythrocytes are in the bone marrow, near to where uranium is normally stored in the body.

The monocyte stem cells in bone marrow are known to be among the most radiosensitive cells. Their depletion can lead to both iron deficient anemia, since they recycle heme from discarded red blood cells, and to depressed cellular immune system, since monocytes activate the lymphocyte immune system after they detect foreign bodies.

Hair tests need to be done very carefully since they tend to reflect the hair products used: shampoos, conditioners, hair coloring or permanent waves. Pubic hair would likely be the best material for analysis. I am not aware of good standards against which to test the Uranium content of hair, or how the analysis would differentiate between the various uranium isotopes.

Testing of lymph nodes or bone on autopsy would be helpful. However, invasive biopsies on live patients carry no benefit for the patient and are usually not recommended because of ethical considerations about experimentation on humans. If a veteran is recommended for bronchoscopy for medical reasons, it would be advisable to also take tissue samples for analysis for depleted uranium.

When chelation processes have been initiated the rate of excretion of uranium in urine will be increased and there is a risk of damage to kidney tubules. Therefore careful urine analysis for protein, glucose and non-protein nitrogen is important. Some researchers have also reported specifically finding B-2-microglobulinuria and aminoaciduria in urine due to uranium damage.

Relating Depleted Uranium Contamination with Observed Health Effects in Veterans

There are two ways of documenting the radiological health effects of a veteran's exposure to depleted uranium. The first, and the one usually attempted in a compensation argument, would be to reconstruct the original dose and then appeal to regulatory limits or dose-response estimates available in the scientific literature. This methodology is not recommended for the Gulf War veterans, because the uranium excretion rate seven or eight years after exposure cannot be used to estimate the original lung and body burden of depleted uranium. Moreover, no dose-response estimates for the chronic health effects of such exposure are available from the literature, as will be seen later in this paper. Recognized dose-response estimates for radioactive materials are unique to fatal cancers (and even these are disputed). It is not clear whether regulatory limits for exposure to ionizing radiation apply in a war situation, or, if they do, whether the veteran should be considered to have been "general public" or a "nuclear worker". Beyond this, the question of whether international or US standards should be used for a multinational situation needs to be addressed.

The second methodology would require ranking veterans on an ordinal scale for their original exposure, based on their current excretion rate of depleted uranium. This involves the reasonable assumption that the original contamination, although not precisely measurable, was proportional to the current excretion rate. The analysis of a 24 hour urine sample, for example, could be rated on a specific research scale as having "high", "medium" or "low" quantities of the contaminate. By collecting detailed health and exposure data on each veteran, one can use biostatistical methods to determine firstly, whether any medical problems show an increase with the ordinal scale increase in exposure, determined through urine analysis; and secondly, whether there is a correlation between the descriptive accounts of potential depleted uranium exposure and the assigned ordinal scale determined on the basis of the urine analysis.

Using Non-Parametric Statistics one could determine the statistical significance of various medical problems being depleted uranium exposure related. This would undoubtedly eliminate some medical problems from consideration and highlight others. It could point to future research questions. It could also provide a fair method of dealing with the current suffering of the veterans using the best scientific methodology available at this time. Risk estimates based on radiation related cancer death are obviously unable to provide a reasonable response to current veteran medical problems.

Known Occupational Health Problems Related to Uranium Exposure:

"Uranium poisoning is characterized by generalized health impairment. The element and its compounds produce changes in the kidneys, liver, lungs and cardiovascular, nervous and haemopoietic systems, and cause disorders of protein and carbohydrate metabolism....... Chronic poisoning results from prolonged exposure to low concentrations of insoluble compounds and presents a clinical picture different from that of acute poisoning. The outstanding signs and symptoms are pulmonary fibrosis, pneumoconiosis, and blood changes with a fall in red blood count; haemoglobin, erythrocyte and reticulocyte levels in the peripheral blood are reduced. Leucopenia may be observed with leucocyte disorders (cytolysis, pyknosis, and hypersegmentosis). There may be damage to the nervous system. Morphological changes in the lungs, liver, spleen, intestines and other organs and tissues may be found, and it is reported that uranium exposure inhibits reproductive activity and affects uterine and extra-uterine development in experimental animals. Insoluble compounds tend to be retained in tissues and organs for long periods."

Human and Animal Studies on Uranium Exposure

In a study of uranium toxicity by the US Agency for Toxic Substances and Disease Registry [ATSDR 1998], released for public review and comments by 17 February 1998, exposure times were divided into three categories: acute, less than 15 days; intermediate, 15 to 365 days; and chronic more than a year. Most of the Gulf War Veterans would have had chronic duration exposure from the point of view of the length of time the material remained in the body. However, this ATSDR division was based on the duration of the presence of the external source of contamination, not its residence time in the body, therefore it would, in most cases be considered intermediate duration exposure. There is very little human research available to clarify the effects of intermediate duration exposure to humans.

It should not be assumed that lack of research implies lack of effect on that particular system. It should also be noted that although one or more paper may exist for acute and chronic duration exposures, these do not necessarily cover the questions which one might like to raise. No comments on the quality or extent of the research is implied by this table.

Health Effects which have been associated with inhalation of uranium

The more soluble compounds of uranium, namely, uranium hexafluoride, uranyl fluoride, uranium tetrachloride, uranyl nitrate hexahydrate, are likely to be absorbed into the blood from the alveolar pockets in the lungs within days of exposure. Although inhalation products also are transported through coughing and mucocilliary action to the gastro-intestinal tract only about 2% of this fraction is actually absorbed into the body fluids through the intestinal wall. Therefore all of the research papers on acute effects of uranium refer to these soluble uranium compounds via inhalation. The main acute effect of inhalation of soluble uranium compounds is damage to the renal system, and the main long term storage place of these compounds in the body is bone. These research findings do not apply easily to the insoluble uranium compounds to which the Gulf Veterans were exposed when the depleted uranium ordnance was used in battle.

The uranium compound used for ordnance is DU-metal. When it burns it forms uranium dioxide or less likely, uranium trioxide. Particles of these compounds smaller than 2.5 microns are usually deposited deep in the lungs and pulmonary lymph nodes where they can remain for years. According to research done in the UK by the NRPB, the ceramic uranium formed when uranium ignites through friction, as happened in the Gulf War. In this form, it is twice as slow to move from the lungs to the blood than would be the non-ceramic uranium dioxide. Of the portion of inhaled uranium oxide which passes through the gastro-intestinal tract, only 0.2% is normally absorbed through the intestinal wall. This may be an even smaller portion for ceramic uranium. This fraction of the inhaled compound can, of course, do damage to the GI tract as it passes through because it emits damaging alpha particles with statistical regularity. The residence time of the insoluble uranium compounds in the GI tract (the biological half life) is estimated in years.[ibid.]

The chemical action of all isotopic mixtures of uranium (depleted, natural and enriched) is identical. Current evidence from animal studies suggests that the chemical toxicity is largely due to its chemical damage to kidney tubular cells, leading to nephritis.

The differences in toxicity based on the solubility of the uranium compound (regardless of which uranium isotope is incorporated in the compound) are more striking: water soluble salts are primarily renal and systemic chemical toxicants; insoluble chemical compounds are primarily lung chemical toxicants and systemic radiological hazards. Once uranium dioxide enters the blood, hexavalent uranium is formed, which is also a systemic chemical toxicant.

It is important to note that there is no scientific evidence which supports the US Veteran Administration claim that the insoluble uranium oxide to which the Gulf War Veterans were exposed will be primarily a renal chemical toxicant. Yet this is the criteria which the VA proposes for attributing any health problems of the Veteran to depleted uranium. Intermediate and chronic exposure duration to insoluble uranium is regulated in the US by its radiological property. The slow excretion rate of the uranium oxide allows for some kidney and tubule repair and regeneration. Moreover, because of the long biological half life, much of the uranium is still being stored in the body and has not yet passed through the kidneys. The direct damage to lungs and kidneys by uranium compounds is thought to be the result of the combined radiation and chemical properties, and it is difficult to attribute a portion of the damage to these separate factors which cannot be separated in life.

There is human research indicating that inhalation of insoluble uranium dioxide is associated with general damage to pulmonary structure, usually non-cancerous damage to alveolar epithelium. With acute duration exposure this can lead to emphysema or pulmonary fibrosis. Animal studies demonstrate uranium compounds can cause adverse hematological disturbances.

With respect to ORAL exposure, there is no human data but a great deal of animal data. This was not as likely a pathway in the Gulf War as was inhalation, but possible contamination of food, and water can not be totally ignored. DERMAL exposure was researched in humans only in the acute duration of exposure case. Animal studies on dermal exposure include acute, intermediate and chronic duration of exposure, and immunologic/-lymphoreticular and neurologic effects.

Mortality Within 30 Days of Exposure

The lowest acute duration lethal dose observed, with exposure to the soluble uranium hexafluoride, was 637 mg per cu metre of air. No acute dose deaths were found using insoluble compounds. Since there were acute deaths in the Iraqi tanks in persons not directly hit, one can assume concentrations of uranium aerosol were greater than this amount. It should also be noted that it was the radiation protection units of the military which designated these contaminated tanks off bounds. They were acting because of radiological (not chemical) properties of the aerosol.

The intermediate duration exposure, 15 to 365 days, dose level for mortality with insoluble uranium oxide, was 15.8 mg per cu metre of air. With soluble uranium hexachloride it was much lower, 2 mg per cu metre air. The dose resulting in lung cancer in the dog study, with chronic duration inhalation of the insoluble uranium oxide, was 5.1 mg per cu metre air, for 1 to 5 years, 5 day a week and 5.4 hours a day.

Systemic Damage

Damage to body organs occurred with intermediate or chronic exposure at doses as low as 0.05 mg per cu metre air. A generally sensitive indicator of exposure seems to be loss of body weight. However this finding is sometimes attributed to the unpleasant taste of the uranium laced food given to animals. There is also damage to the entrance portals: respiratory and gastro-intestinal systems; and the exit portals: intestinal and renal systems. Uranium oxide was associated with fibrosis and other degenerative changes in the lung. It was also associated with proteinuria, and increased NPN (non-protein nitrogen) and slight degenerative changes in the tubules. The more severe renal damage was associated with the soluble compounds uranium tetrafluoride and uranium hexafluoride (not thought to have been used in the Gulf War ordnance).

Focal necrosis of the liver was only associated with uranium oxide. This may be a clue to one of its storage places in body tissue. Uranium oxide is also associated with hematological changes, lymph node fibrosis, severe muscle weakness and lassitude at intermediate or chronic dose rates in 0.2 to 16 mg per cu metre air.

None of the uranium research dealt with the synergistic, additive or antagonistic effects potentially present in the Gulf War mixture of iatrogenic, pathological, toxic chemical and electromagnetic exposures.

Potential US Government administration of radio-protective substances to combat military

It is obvious that the US had some expectation of the health effects related to using depleted uranium ordnance in the Gulf War. This is evident based on military research and manuals. They would also have had access to information on chemical and biological agents which could protect against some of the harmful side effects. These agents might also "confuse" the toxicology of this exposure. Some potential radio-protective agents are thiols (also called mercaptans, these are organosulfur compounds that are derivatives of hydrogen sulfide), nitroxides (used as a food aerosol and an anesthetic), cytokines (non-antibody proteins released by one cell population, e.g T-lymphocytes, generating an immune response), eicosanoids (biologically active substances derived from arachidonic acid, including the prostaglandins and leukotrienes), antioxidants and modifiers of apoptosis (fragmentation of a cell into small membrane bound particle which are then eliminated by phagocytes).

Just in case this is the reality and not merely a suspicion, it would be good to examine the after effects of exposure to ceramic depleted uranium in Iraqi veterans and in the survivors of the El Al crash near Schiphol Airport, Amsterdam. It is unlikely that these two populations were given any protective agents.

Proposal for assisting the Gulf War veterans

In keeping with the above findings, it is proposed to undertake an analysis of both questionnaire and clinical data for a sample of each of the following populations: US, Canadian and British Gulf War veterans or civilian base workers exposed to DU; US, Canadian and British military personnel not exposed to DU; Iraqi Veterans exposed to DU; Iraqi Veterans not exposed to DU; and firemen and civilians exposed to the El Al crash.

Sampling strategy and sample size to be determined. Each participant should complete a questionnaire covering general background variables, exposure profile and medical problems and symptoms. Each participant will agree to collect a 24 hour urine sample for analysis, and to take 500 mg blue-green algae (Spirulina) 48 hours before beginning the collection. This is a mild chelating agent. Each participant will agree to the analysis of this data for the benefit of all exposed persons, and to the release of the results of the analysis without identifying characteristics for individuals.

All questionnaire data will be entered into computer using Epi Info Software (WHO) and transferred on disc to the Biostatistical Support Unit of the University of Toronto for analysis.

Research Hypotheses to be tested: (to be written as a null hypothesis)

There will be a high correlation between the questionnaire exposure estimates and the level of depleted uranium found in urine.

Medical problems related to damage of the blood and/or hepatic systems will show an association with exposure data and urine sample analysis for depleted uranium.

Preliminary work to be accomplished:

- Identification of principal investigators for each identified study group.
- Development of a Grant Proposal, including the null hypotheses and protocols.
- Development of a budget for each population study group.
- Agreement of the Research team to undertake the study.
- Raising of funds or assignment of costs for the study.
- Identification and training of data entry processors for each group.

THE NEXT TESTING SITE FOR DEPLETED URANIUM WEAPONRY

During the Gulf War, munitions and armour made from depleted uranium (DU) were used for the first time in military action. Since they proved unmatchable in their armour piercing capacity and are very cheap, uranium waste, they became the weapon of choice. They were further used in Bosnia and presently in Yugoslavia.

The US military, like the British military, do not hide the fact that they use DU weapon systems. The US Army has the A-10 Thunderbolt II, nicknamed "the Warthog", responsible for most of the fired DU munitions during the Gulf War. They have the M1A1 Abrams tank and the new M1A2 Abrams tank, the Marines the M-60, the Navy the Phalanx missile. Many cruise missiles contains DU balance weights. The British have the Challenger tank. And now for their latest testing scenario for DU weapons systems in the Balkans, British Harriers can fire DU. The US F-16 has been modified to fire DU. The increasing number of US Apache helicopters deployed to the region can now fire DU rounds. Most of these weapons systems are now deployed in the neighbouring countries around Yugoslavia.

No, the use of DU weaponry is not being covered up. What is being covered up are the effects of DU on the health of people and their environments. The Clinical Chief of the Department of Nuclear Medicine of the US Veterans Administration, Dr. Asaf Durakovic, was terminated from his position after diagnosing DU contamination of some of the 24 sick US Gulf War Vets sent to him by the military soon after the war ended in 1991; two of the soldiers who were referred to him for observation later died from unknown causes. In December 1998, the homes of two British Gulf War Vets were raided by the Ministry of Defence Police and their computer equipment confiscated. The apparent object for the raid was a search for documents obtained by the Vets that showed that the Ministry of Defence was carrying out its own research into the effects of DU contamination of Gulf Vets which it did not want the general public know about.

Throughout 1998 and into 1999, Dr. Hari Sharma of the University of Waterloo, Ontario, Canada, conducted tests using new techniques for the presence of DU in Gulf Vets and found DU contamination in the urine of his subjects 8 years after the end of the war, contrary to the MoD and DoD'd assertion that DU passes through the body very quickly. And recently, representatives from the Defense Departments of five countries (England, US, Australia, New Zealand and Canada) coordinated their enquiries and jointly interviewed Sharma, intent on knowing what techniques he had used in testing for DU, his methodology of analysis, and findings.

In the Gulf more than a million rounds were fired, between 300-800 tons being consumed in 1991 alone. When a DU penetrator hits its target, it explodes and vaporises. From 10-70% burns up and forms micrometer-size uranium oxide particles that can be inhaled or ingested. The fall-out of uranium aerosol is virtually unlimited. In the fine sand of the Gulf, uranium micro-particles, because they are electrically charged attach themselves to the sand, and remain suspended in the air for very long periods. Wind storms will resuspend the settled particles and transport them to new locations far and wide. There is a noted massive rise in cancers in Saudi-Arabia, in most of the Emirates all the way to Bahrain. Incalculable collateral damage to veterans, civilians, and neighbouring countries, now and for all future generations is the result of using radioactive weapons. Nuclear explosions cause massive damage at the time, while radioactive weapons cause more prolonged devastation to humans and the environment for tens of years, or maybe till the end of time, since the half life of DU is the life of the solar system.

All over Iraq but especially in the South, there has been a sixfold rise in cancers of all kinds, but especially leukaemias and lymphomas. Birth defects from being a rarity have become so common that there can be three children in one family with birth defects. Plants and animals are also showing signs of genetic mutations. British and American veterans show very similar disorders.

In a veterans community in Mississippi, 67% of the children were born without eyes, ears, brain, thyroid and other organ malformations. In Bosnia after the NATO war, there was a massive rise of instant deaths for huge numbers of people in the war zone (acute radiation poisoning). Alterations in plant, animal and a horrendous rise of birth defects has been reported. Veterans with Gulf War Syndrome report symptons similar to the Iraqi and Bosnian groups, namely multiple organ failure, AIDS like syndrome with very low immunity. There are multiple causes from chemical and bacteriological pollutants in the war zone, but definitely DU with its radiological and chemical toxicity is one of the main culprits.

Knowing that DU on exposion forms insoluble particles of uranium oxixe that can be inhaled, the particles would lodge in the lung for long periods of time (depending on the biological half life). Uranium and its daughter products radiate the lung killing and mutating neighbouring cells. Some particles get washed into the blood, causing devastating effects all over the body but mainly to the reproductive system and the bone marrow (rapidly dividing cells). This results in the birth defects and the anaemias, leukaemias and immune deficience disorders.

We tested urine samples from 30 veterans from the USA, UK, Canada and Iraq. Their locations covers the whole of the ground war region. The samples were analysed for isotopic composition of uranium isotopes by the delayed neutron activation method and confirmed by surface ionization mass spectometry.

All those tested showed DU in their urine with values ranging between 3-18 micrograms for a 24 hour period. The values collorated positively with where they were located, whether their job entailed travelling between sites (more exposure) and how long they stayed in the Gulf. It also matches perfectly the morbidity and mortality picture.

Samples from the population of Baghdad and Basra were also tested. They also show the presence of DU in the urine over the whole geographical regions. The risk factor from exposure to the oxide inside the lungs depends on the biological half life (time tissues remain irradiated). The half life seems much longer that suggested by the DoD.

It is more likely 10 years or longer instead of the mentioned 500 days. Six to ten percent, ie. 36,000 of the 600,000 veterans exposed would succumb to fatal cancers. In Basra the percentage could be much higher since people are continuing to breath, drink and eat radio-active material. The risk factor could be 20% or even higher. The tests were carried out in three labs.

DEPLETED URANIUM

On learning that I had tested positive for depleted uranium not only was I devastated but my wife and family too, it was like having a real smack on the chin. Quite naturally I imagined all sorts of cancers etc. developing; I have seen some horrendous carcinomas in the 20 years that I have worked in Operating Theatres as a Technician.

After the initial shock, it sank in, and I was horrified at what has actually happened. To some it up; the Coalition Forces stood shoulder to shoulder against a tyrannical regime, a regime that we were aware had an arsenal of weapons of mass destruction together with the knowledge that not only had those weapons previously been used, but used against their own people. A committee of the United Nations has already declared that depleted uranium is a weapon of mass destruction.

The British and American Forces were the only forces during the Persian Gulf War to use depleted uranium to increase the effectiveness of their armour piercing shells. This has not only left a terrible legacy of cancers with the Iraqi casualties who survived conventional wounds. The contamination of thousands of our own troops with depleted uranium must make this the Greatest Friendly Fire incident in the history of warfare. It has also left a terrible legacy much worse than any land mine for the civilian population.

It is an outrageous scandal that depleted uranium was ever used, it was not necessary, it was over-kill, and was not worth the cost to the Soldiers Health. I cannot in any way accept that the Ministry of Defence (MoD) would not have been aware of the consequences following the use of depleted uranium. In my eyes this puts the British and American Governments in the same league as the regime we were sent to fight, one that is willing to use a weapon of Mass Destruction that has serious heath consequences against their own people and for what? To stabilise the price of oil, that's what! Just what kind of society is Britain? I don't know anymore.

Veterans now require the Medical Practitioners of the National Health Service to take their illnesses seriously and not to discount everything unknown as psychological. Veterans are being denied the health care to which they are entitled because Medical Practitioners are being deliberately misled and having vital information withheld by the MoD.

It is about time that those responsible for this continuing outrage in the MoD are held accountable and the Gulf Veterans Illness Unit is run by civilians and overseen by Professor Malcolm Hooper, one of the few people Gulf Veterans trust. I would also like to see that both the MoD and the War Pensions Agency stop the deliberate bullying of ill veterans and ensure that they receive their full pension entitlements. Also an apology from the MoD, DoD, British and American governments wouldn't come a miss either. Raymond Bristow, Former Warrant Officer, 1st Field Surgical Team, 32 Field Hospital, Royal Army Medical Corps, Saudi Arabia, January to March 1991.

THE HEALTH OF THE IRAQI PEOPLE

United Nations sanctions imposed on Iraq since August 1990 are described even by UN officials as unique in ferocity. Prior to 1990, according to World Health Organization figures, the population had 92% access to high quality free health care in some of the finest hospitals in the Middle East, 93% access to clean water, high nutritional status and a free education system described as unique by UNESCO, since of standard such that a child born into abjects poverty could leave graduate school as a doctor, engineer or architect.

Nine years on, the human toll taken by the sanctions is on a unparallelled scale. "We have a new phenomenon", remarked one doctor. "People are just dying, they are not ill, they just give up - especially young men between the ages of about 30 to 35, their youth has been sacrificed to the sanctions, and they see middle age approaching with no hope, dreams, aspirations or ability to provide for those they love."

I had telephoned Mustafa from Jordan, old friend, gentle academic, whose childlike joy of life illuminated every experience. During the December 1998 bombing his voice broke as he described the destruction of some of the most ancient buildings - world heritage sites - in his beloved Baghdad.

Mustafa always celebrated my arrival with an aubergine dish to dream of. Surprisingly the call connected immediately and Doha, his daughter, answered: "I'm on my way, get the aubergine ready...".

There was a silence, then: "We have had a catastrophe, Mustafa is dead." He had died five minutes earlier. A month before he had undergone a full medical and been told he had 'the heart of lion'. "He was haunted by the thought we would be bombed again after the Ramadan and he had no way to protect us" said Nasra, his wife. He died on 17th January, the anniversary of the start of the Gulf War.

He was buried within twelve hours in accordance with Islam. Since the bus from Amman took 20 hours (flights are vetoed by the UN Sanctions Committee), I could only attend the mourning - a four day grieving of an intensity defying description. Friends, relatives colleagues called, shared the pain. When Nasra, feisty, gutsy, witty, beautiful and beloved friend entered, she was unrecognisable: 'the weight of grief' encapsulated. "It is killing us all, one by one', she gasped, "we lost five friends this year." All were under forty, all had 'just died'.

Bashir. Where ever one looked was the manifestation of his statement. Six month old Yacoub Yusif, with his small hand twisted at the right angle, with no thumb on his small foreshortened right arm, was comparitively lucky. Six year old Mustafa Ahmed with his bright, intelligent face and great dark eyes had gross deformities of all his stick like limbs, of his facial bones, his hands pathetically turned. Sitting on the examination table like a frail broken doll he said: "I van write." Hunched over, a tiny piece of pencil (pencils are vetoed by the Sanctions Committee, since they contain graphite) and minute square of paper (also vetoed) he wrote, the stub clutched between his knucles, in beautiful Arabic, laughing with triumph at his achievement.

Ali Samir, seven, shuffled in like a tiny, bird like old man, the expression in his eyes was of one who has seen all the trials of the world. He was covered with head to toe ulcerations which as they healed tightened his skin - or ruptured. His fingers were turned inwards, seared in to his palms, he had no toes. When his gay 'Route 97' top was liften up, the terrible, searing ulcerations on his back brought tears to the eyes. "Surgery is counter indicated, since he won't heal - this is a genetic malformation caused by environmental changes in pregnancy' said Consultant, Dr. Harith. The Zafaranya district of Baghdad where he lives was bombed relentlessly in the Gulf War and a nuclear reactor reportedly hit. It was bombed again in 1993 and Ali was still recovering from this terror in the December bombings when the district was hit again. He too could write and did so with pride - but he was unable to tell us - he had no tongue.

In the southern, beautiful, relentlessly bombarded city of Basrah where the biblical Tigris and Euphrates rivers meet the Shat Al Arab, the state of health takes another dimension again. One doctor has completed a thesis comparing the congenital abnormalities, cancers and malignancies since the Gulf War with Hiroshima. Dr. Jenan Ali has been keeping a record of 'mysterious' congenital anomalies. Her photographs for 1998 were chilling. Full term babies undeveloped, the so-called 'bunch of grapes' babies reminiscent of the nuclear testing areas of the South Pacific. A baby with no face, another with no eyes, twisted limbs, or no limbs. A tiny mite with a huge head - and no brain. Page after page of tragedy. "All young parents, with no history of abnormalities in the family as far as we can tell - since we have few laboratory facilities now" further, many she felt "not recorded in the text books - but we cannot be sure since we have had no text books since 1990." (Text books and medical journals are vetoed by the UN Sanctions Committee.)

There were haunting human tales of the December bombing. Jameel, father of Zena a teenager who has severe psychological problems linked to her terror in the Gulf War, when she was six, recountered another tragedy. Zena was inseperable from her cat Sudar (Sugar). It slept by her, ate with her, followed her every move. Sudar shared her most intimate secrets, quietly purring with pleasure at every contact. When the bombing started, Sudar lost her mind, tearing around the garden, attacking, defying all attempts to catch and comfort, tearing and scratching at Zena in her terror. Sudar is still mindless and Zena inconsolable.

"There is something else, which I hope won't affend you", said Jameel. "We had seven children in out house during the bombing, the youngest 6 months, the oldest 7 years. Their terror was such that when the bombs stopped, we were left in the dark (the electricity sub-station was reportedly hit again) with great pools of urine and faeces."

At the Saddam Paediatric Hospital Sahara, aged 3, was dying. She had acute myeloid leukaemia and was bleeding internally from the nose and gums. She needed 10-15 units of platelets a day - the doctors could obtain just one. "In the UK and US leukaemia is a treatable disease, yet due to a lack of chemotherapy we have not achieved one cure - only some remissions - in the last eight years" said Dr. Rad Aljanabi, Chief Resident. "In '94, '95 and '96, we had no treatment at all, so every single patient died." Iraq's cancer, leukaemia and malignancy rate has risen up to sevenfold since the Gulf War, a rise associated with the depleted uranium weapons used primarily by the US and UK, which left a residue of radioactive dust throughout the country, which according to studies, including by John Hopkins University in the US has entered the food chain via the water table and soil.

Leukaemias were a rarity prior to 1991: "This is my first residency" said one doctor. "I saw 39 new cases in three months. I admitted eight in the last month, I remember all their names. We are suffering, the patients are suffering - I cry so often." He wrote down their names: Hussein, Tuness, Mahmood, Tabarik - 11 months old - Lara, Hussan and Sahira. The oldest was 4 years. There were other horrors. Heider Latif, 5 years old, weighing just 13 kgs. Starvation, multiple congenital abnormalities, cancers, heart defects, leprosy, water borne diseases: death stalks Iraq's children from the moment of birth.

Cases at the Centre for Reconstructive Surgery would break a heart of stone. "We are seeing an astonishing rise in even the rarest of abnormalities' said British trained plastic surgeon Professor Ala. "I can show you a baby born one hour ago if you are strong and not prone to fainting" said Dr. Janeen.

A nurse brought in a small bundle wrapped in cloth - sterile wrappings, baby clothing is just a memory in another formerly internationally renowned hospital. Unwrapped the tiny being, making a little bleating noises, had no eyes, no nose, a sweet little mouth, but no tongue or osophegus, no hands or genitalia. Hopelessly twisted small legs were joined together from the knees upwards by a thick 'web' of flesh. "We see many similar" commented Dr. Janeen. In the maternity unit, midwife Bushra Nasser said: "My colleague delivered the baby you saw, I am frightened of what I might deliver." With no ultra sound or scanning facilities (vetoed) there is no knowledge until birth. "Sometimes the mothers attack us in their agony." In the event, the baby we watched born was a healthy eight pounds - but the conditions so insanitary, without hot water, with cockroaches crawling over the metal of the delivery bed - disinfectant is vetoed, electricity and thus water heating off eighteen hours a day - odds were stacked against him from the moment of birth. When mothers ask: "Is it alright?" there is terror in the question. Some soil samples in areas of Basrah show 84 times (sic) background radiation from uranium elements.

Twentyfive percent (sic) of babies are now born prematurely or of premature weight due to malnutrition and/or environmental factors. There is no oxygen, no incubators working at optimum capacity, no rehydration, no gastronasal nutrition. As we stood in the premature unit, containing 17 babies the doctor remarked: "We have not had one premature weight birth survive since 1994." I looked round the ward at each small life, at twins sharing an incubator, noted each face and tiny form. Each is by now almost certainly now another statistic in embargo-related deaths.

There are three unforgettable incidents. A doctor running up and saying: "Do any of you" (photographer Karen Robinson, myself and our interpreter) "have O-negative blood?" A newly born baby, bright yellow, with acute jaundice would die without an exchange transfusion. There was no blood. I thought I might have the blood type, but then was unsure if it was positive or negative. "Test me" I said. There were no laboratory facilities to do so. If I was wrong, the baby would die anyway.

The 23 day old baby which died two minutes before we reached the ward. His mother had run, inconsolable, screaming, from the hospital. The grandmother, upright, proud, Shia, in her black abaya, tears streaming down her face, stood by his cot, as I vainly stroked his small, perfect head and face, so warm, feeling somehow he could be brought back. All he had needed was oxygen. There was none. The two doctors and the soldier who screamed at us as we left: "You want a story, you want pictures: there is a two year old baby dead on the sixth floor - the doctors did everything they could, all he needed was oxygen - two years old. What more do you want of us?"

As we left, Dr. Ali - Glasgow trained, world renowned surgeon: "I still have a bank account in the Bank of Scotland, but it is frozen under sanctions", shook hands. "You have seen the state of our hospitals, what will we do if they bombed again?" The hospital, founded by British General Maude, had been hit in the Iran/Iraq War and two doctors killed. In the Gulf War, it was pounded so relentlessly people often were unable to col-lect the dead said Dr. Ali: "Dogs were eating bodies in the street." I said it was impossible to believe it could happen again. For what? We left Basra and returned to Baghdad. The following morning Basra was bombed.

There is a monument in Basra to Iraqi Airways. It reads: "Iraqi Airways, 1947 - 1990." It could be a metaphor for Iraq.

URANIUM POLLUTION FROM THE AMSTERDAM 1992 PLANE CRASH

On October 4, 1992, an El Al Boeing 747 crashed in Amsterdam's Bijlmermeer, killing 43 people. In recent years questions have remained about the cause of the crash, health problems among citizens and rescue workers, the exact cargo, depleted uranium counterweights, and other issues. Last year a Parliamentarian Inquiry (called Commission Meijer, after its chairman) was started to resolve these questions. On 22 April 1999 the Commission Meijer published its results.

One of the Bijlmer crash issues was the presence of depleted uranium (DU) in the plane's counterweights. A total of 282 kilograms was constructed in the plane's tail wings. Laka made this public in October 1993 after which a discussion started on the potential burning of DU and the risks for citizens and rescue workers.

From the beginning, Laka pointed out emphatically that bystanders and Bijlmer residents ran potential health risks as a result of airborne uranium from the burning wreck. The presence of DU is among others based on a publication by Paul Loewenstein, then technical director and vice-president of the American company Nuclear Metals Inc. (currently named Starmet), the supplier of the DU to Boeing. Loewenstein says in this document that each Boeing 747 contained DU in the form of counterweights. Loewenstein says in his article that "large pieces of uranium will oxidize rapidly and will sustain slow combustion when heated in air to temperatures of about 500 degrees celcius".

The great danger from this chemical reaction is that the escaping cloud of dust with thousands of microparticles of uranium oxide can be inhaled or swallowed by bystanders. The American physicist Robert L. Parker wrote in *Nature*, in a worst-case scenario involving the crash of a Boeing 747, that about 250,000 people would run health risks (or near-poisoning) as a result of inhalation or swallowing of uranium oxide particles. Parker's conclusion assumed the presence of 450 kilos of DU in a Boeing 747. He says: "Extended tests by the American Navy and NASA showed that the temperature of the fireball in a plane crash can reach 1,200C. Such temperatures are high enough to cause very rapid oxidation of depleted uranium."

Paul Loewenstein said that DU would disperse particles in a fire, depending on the following factors: temperature, the surface condition of the fragments (a measure of the accessibility of the metal to surrounding oxygen), and wind speed. This means that the weather at the time of the Bijlmer crash was conducive to the dispersion of burning uranium and that there was every reason for concern. The temperature of the jet fuel fire apparently went higher than 500C, sufficient for the likely combustion of the outer surfaces of the DU fragments. Moreover, there was a strong northeast wind blowing at the time (windspeed 7). People should have been concerned because a big part of the uranium in the form of dust clouds could have spread across the area, especially towards the southwest. It is known that dust particles can be blown by the wind for kilometers.

To calm troubled minds in the Amsterdam suburb Bijlmermeer, the radiation expert A.S. Keverling Buisman of the Energy Research Center (ECN) issued a press release the same day that the news of the uranium contamination swept the world. He confirmed the presence of DU in the wrecked plane, but denied any hazard to public health or the environment. He declared that the uranium remained intact. A day later, the same expert spoke in the town hall in the Zuidoost (Southeast) district, where the Amsterdam Research Service on Environmental Protection and Soil Mechanics (Omegam) presented a definitive version of its investigation on the polluted soil in the immediate surroundings of the flats named Kruitberg and Groeneveen where the plane crashed. Throughout the hearing, Keverling Buisman was pressed to answer all kinds of questions about uranium, and to calm the uneasiness of the Zuidoost population.

Neither the Zuidoost-council nor the Amsterdam Environmental Service nor Omegam was aware at that time of the extent of the presence of DU in the accident. The clearly nervous radiation expert did not convince the neighborhood people that uranium carried no risks. The Bijlmer working group on Air Traffic and associated neighborhood groups like Service Platform and Sounding Board were already in possession of a variety of documents in which it was clear that depleted uranium in a jet fuel fire is definitely harmful to public health and the environment. The district council had obviously not grasped the message from the information, because in cooperation with the ECN the next day (October 14), a letter was carried door-to-door with the advice that all was well and that there was not a single reason for concern: "It is possible that recent publications on the presence of uranium-bearing materials in the unfortunate plane crash have led to unease among neighborhood residents. The concern is misplaced. From the information of the Dutch Aviation Administration it was already known that depleted uranium metal is used as a ballast in airframes. About 400 kg of uranium metal was incorporated into the unfortunate Boeing plane for this purpose. The uranium metal was simultaneously removed with other fragments from the plane crash in the week after the accident. Uranium metal is not dangerous to the public health. The surrounding effects were therefore not influenced by the accident."

Spokesmen for Boeing, El Al, the Dutch Ministry of Traffic and Water Supply, and the Dutch Aviation Administration admitted immediately that there were DU counterweights in the tail rudder of the ill-starred aircraft. They claimed that the plane contained 390 kg of DU. El Al declared that during the maintainance work on the plane, 45 kg of a total of 435 kg of DU was replaced by tungsten. Last year it appeared that the total amount of DU at the crash time must be 282 kg rather than 390 kg, because of measurement faults. The 90 kg of DU retrieved from the wreckage by KLM was transported in the eginning of 1993 to COVRA, the Dutch national agency for radioactive waste management. After the October 1993 media attention, a new search started into the missing DU. In the remaining wreckage a counterweight of 37 kilograms was found and on a polluted-soil repository, another broken weight of 3 kilograms was found. No search was conducted at the waste repository, where a lot of debris from the flats and cargo was dumped after the crash.

On September 13, 1994, the Amsterdam Health Service (GG and GD) declared that effects on the health of neighbors by the DU are unlikely. In a letter to the city council of Zuidoost, the Health Service wrote: "The complaints which were put forward by a group of residents were not such as these that a relationship was acceptable with the plane crash." The physicians of the municipal service based this conclusion on information of family doctors in this part of the city and on declarations of industrial doctors. Additionally they mentioned that the service personnel who were thrown into gear for the rescue work had also experienced no disadvantageous consequences. Even when small particles of DU oxides have been spread by burning, the Health Service said, nobody would run any risk to inhale or to ingest the radioactive particles, because "the airstream is always directed to the seat of fire".

The research results of the Health Service made part of the final report on the DU by the city council of Zuidoost, published on October 4, 1994. On a public hearing about this report, Laka made many critical comments on the function of the Dutch Aviation Administration (RLD), the city council, the Environment Service of Zuidoost and the Amsterdam Health Service. Especially the last service had to pay to it. Together with Bijlmer residents and the Dutch Greens, Laka called for a long-term in-depth epidemiological search for the presence of uranium in the bodies of the service personnel and residents.

Since the publication of the final report from the city council, which strongly played down the health and environmental effects of DU, Laka has obtained more and more documents which strongly emphasized the chemical and radiological toxicity of DU. One interesting aspect about this particular case is probably the report, "Health risks during exposure of uranium", made by radiation expert Leonard A. Hennen from the Dutch Ministry of Defense. By accident, this report was published just a week after the final report on DU from the city council of Zuidoost. The author is very thorough about the radiotoxic nature of DU in the human body.

The findings of Hennen strongly contradicts the findings in the final DU report of Zuidoost. He said that people in a DU crash site are running risks. In his report, he proposed the taking of urine samples and in vivo measurements when there is suspicion of internal contamination of the DU. This is exactly what Laka has been insisting upon. In the last six years, Laka has continuously referred to the possibility that DU had been burned, causing a potential risk for people. Besides, Laka repeated the need to conduct medical tests to get clearance on the relation with observed health problems.

The ongoing publications and rumors on the plane crash, also called "the disaster after the disaster", was reason to appoint a Parliamentarian Inquiry Commission in September 1998. This Commission had to give clarity on questions about the cargo, the exact cause of the crash, the depleted uranium issue, observed men in white protective suits, etc. The

Parliamentarian Inquiry Commission investigated the DU issue intensively. On request of the commission, research was conducted and people were heard (among them from Laka).

From the Parliamentarian Inquiry Commission Bijlmer Disaster, chaired by the Christian-Democrat Meijer, it appeared that some authorities were aware of the DU issue but never informed responsible ministers and others. For instance, the Dutch Aviation Administration found DU weights at the third day after the crash but failed to inform rescue workers at the crash site.

For as long as a year, the Ministry of Environment's Inspection Environmental Health failed to inform its own minister on the presence of the DU weights in the plane. From October 7, 1993, three days after the disaster, the Inspection knew about the presence of DU, but didn't forwarded it to the fire brigade, the police and the people on the place of the disaster.

As well as the Minister for Environment, the chiefs of the fire brigade and the police and others only learned about it after media publications one year after the crash. The Commission called this "inconceivable" and "negligent". In their final conclusions, the Commission stated: "The risks of DU were not recognized sufficiently."

Apart from the finding and recognition of DU weights three days after the crash, it also became clear that one day after the crash, the possible presence was already recognized by the Dutch Royal Airways (KLM). From maintainance manuals, the KLM knew about DU weights in 747s and informed the Dutch Aviation Administration and the Ministry of Environment (likely the Environmental Health Inspection) immediately. So, one day after the crash, safety measures could have been taken when people at the crash site were informed. This information was given directly by the KLM to Laka, which informed the Inquiry Commission about it. However, in its final report the Commission did not mention this.

Another remarkable absence in the report of the Commission is the discussion about the behavior of DU in a fire. In fact, the heart of the whole matter. Until last year, all concerned ministers repeated again and again the statement of the radiation expert Keverling Buisman that the DU could not have been burned, and thus therefore no health risks were present. After repeated claims by Laka and others that temperatures of a few hundred degrees would be sufficient to cause rapid oxidation and dispersion, the Minister of Traffic announced a new research on this matter.

The research was conducted by ECN and Laka acted as an advisor on request of the Minister.

The outcome, mainly based on US Army research, confirmed low-temperature burning. Between 350 and 600 degrees Celsius DU will oxidize and loosen it as fine powder. From 650 to 800 degrees, however, the formed oxides mainly stuck to the surface of a weight.

At higher temperatures, the counterweights would oxidize completely. The day the report was published, a lot of media attention was given to a conflict that had risen between Laka and ECN on the final text of the conclusions that could be made from the study. This conflict is said to be the reason to undertake a full Parliamentarian Inquiry, instead of a much smaller "Parliamentarian Research".

As DU was found in dust in the hangar, where the plane's remains were stored, the Commission concluded that: "In the crash, particles of depeleted uranium were formed and released. The Commission expects that a release of DU particles has taken place at the crash site and in hangar 8. In all probability, the particles had been inhaled by rescue workers and citizens."

But the Commission refers to scientific research reports that state that inhaled particles does not necessarily mean that people are at great risk, as the exact radiation dose is related to the amount of DU inhaled.

Apart from the cancer risk, the Commission refers to the possible relation between uranium and the observed increase in auto-immune diseases. Pathologist Weening of the Academical Medical Center mentioned uranium one of the possible causes for this disease.

The final conclusion on the health aspects of DU

Although the Commission thinks that the partly or total oxidation and dispersion of the DU could be real, it concludes: "Based on exsisting scientific literature, research on the Bijlmer crash, its hearings and own research, that it is unlikely that big groups of citizens and rescue workers have contracted a uranium poisoning." But: "The Commission explicitly states that it can not be excluded that in specific circumstances, some individuals have inhaled that much respirable uranium oxide particles that a contamination has taken place.".

7

The Global Health Effects of Nuclear War

ALTERATIONS OF THE GLOBAL ENVIRONMENT

A nuclear war would involve such prodigious and concentrated short term release of high temperature energy that it is necessary to consider a variety of potential environmental effects. It is true that the energy of nuclear weapons is dwarfed by many natural phenomena. A large hurricane may have the power of a million hydrogen bombs. But the energy release of even the most severe weather is diffuse; it occurs over wide areas, and the difference in temperature between the storm system and the surrounding atmosphere is relatively small. Nuclear detonations are just the opposite—highly concentrated with reaction temperatures up to tens of millions of degrees Fahrenheit. Because they are so different from natural processes, it is necessary to examine their potential for altering the environment in several contexts.

High Altitude Dust

It has been estimated that a 10,000-megaton war with half the weapons exploding at ground level would tear up some 25 billion cubic meters of rock and soil, injecting a substantial amount of fine dust and particles into the stratosphere. This is roughly twice the volume of material blasted loose by the Indonesian volcano, Krakatoa, whose explosion in 1883 was the most powerful terrestrial event ever recorded. Sunsets around the world were noticeably reddened for several years after the Krakatoa eruption, indicating that large amounts of volcanic dust had entered the stratosphere.

Subsequent studies of large volcanic explosions, such as Mt. Agung on Bali in 1963, have raised the possibility that large-scale injection of dust into the stratosphere would reduce sunlight intensities and temperatures at the surface, while increasing the absorption of heat in the upper atmosphere.

The resultant minor changes in temperature and sunlight could affect crop production. However, no catastrophic worldwide changes have resulted from volcanic explosions, so it is doubtful that the gross injection of particulates into the stratosphere by a 10,000-megaton conflict would, by itself, lead to major global climate changes.

Ozone

More worrisome is the possible effect of nuclear explosions on ozone in the stratosphere. Not until the 20th century was the unique and paradoxical role of ozone fully recognized. On the other hand, in concentrations greater than I part per million in the air we breathe, ozone is toxic; one major American city, Los Angeles, has established a procedure for ozone alerts and warnings. On the other hand, ozone is a critically important feature of the stratosphere from the standpoint of maintaining life on the earth.

The reason is that while oxygen and nitrogen in the upper reaches of the atmosphere can block out solar ultraviolet photons with wavelengths shorter than 2,420 angstroms (Å), ozone is the only effective shield in the atmosphere against solar ultraviolet radiation between 2,500 and 3,000 Å in wavelength. Although ozone is extremely efficient at filtering out solar ultraviolet in 2,500-3,OOO Å region of the spectrum, some does get through at the higher end of the spectrum. Ultraviolet rays in the range of 2,800 to 3,200 Å which cause sunburn, prematurely age human skin and produce skin cancers. As early as 1840, arctic snow blindness was attributed to solar ultraviolet; and we have since found that intense ultraviolet radiation can inhibit photosynthesis in plants, stunt plant growth, damage bacteria, fungi, higher plants, insects and annuals, and produce genetic alterations.

Despite the important role ozone plays in assuring a livable environment at the earth's surface, the total quantity of ozone in the atmosphere is quite small, only about 3 parts per million. Furthermore, ozone is not a durable or static constituent of the atmosphere. It is constantly created, destroyed, and recreated by natural processes, so that the amount of ozone present at any given time is a function of the equilibrium reached between the creative and destructive chemical reactions and the solar radiation reaching the upper stratosphere.

The mechanism for the production of ozone is the absorption by oxygen molecules (O_2) of relatively short-wavelength ultraviolet light. The oxygen molecule separates into two atoms of free oxygen, which immediately unite with other oxygen molecules on the surfaces of particles in the upper atmosphere. It is this union which forms ozone, or O_3. The heat released by the ozone-forming process is the reason for the curious increase with altitude of the temperature of the stratosphere (the base of which is about 36,000 feet above the earth's surface).

While the natural chemical reaction produces about 4,500 tons of ozone per second in the stratosphere, this is offset by other natural chemical reactions which break down the ozone. By far the most significant involves nitric oxide (NO) which breaks ozone (O_3) into molecules. This effect was discovered only in the last few years in studies of the environmental problems which might be encountered if large fleets of supersonic transport aircraft operate routinely in the lower stratosphere. According to a report by Dr. Harold S. Johnston, University of California at Berkeley— prepared for the Department of Transportation's Climatic Impact Assessment Program—it now appears that the NO reaction is normally responsible for 50 to 70 percent of the destruction of ozone.

In the natural environment, there is a variety of means for the production of NO and its transport into the stratosphere.

Soil bacteria produce nitrous oxide (N_2O) which enters the lower atmosphere and slowly diffuses into the stratosphere, where it reacts with free oxygen (O) to form two NO molecules. Another mechanism for NO production in the lower atmosphere may be lightning discharges, and while NO is quickly washed out of the lower atmosphere by rain, some of it may reach the stratosphere. Additional amounts of NO are produced directly in the stratosphere by cosmic rays from the sun and interstellar sources.

It is because of this catalytic role which nitric oxide plays in the destruction of ozone that it is important to consider the effects of high-yield nuclear explosions on the ozone layer. The nuclear fireball and the air entrained within it are subjected to great heat, followed by relatively rapid cooling. These conditions are ideal for the production of tremendous amounts of NO from the air. It has been estimated that as much as 5,000 tons of nitric oxide is produced for each megaton of nuclear explosive power.

What would be the effects of nitric oxides driven into the stratosphere by an all-out nuclear war, involving the detonation of 10,000 megatons of explosive force in the northern hemisphere? According to the recent National Academy of Sciences study, the nitric oxide produced by the weapons could reduce the ozone levels in the northern hemisphere by as much as 30 to 70 percent.

To begin with, a depleted ozone layer would reflect back to the earth's surface less heat than would normally be the case, thus causing a drop in temperature—perhaps enough to produce serious effects on agriculture. Other changes, such as increased amounts of dust or different vegetation, might subsequently reverse this drop in temperature—but on the other hand, it might increase it.

Probably more important, life on earth has largely evolved within the protective ozone shield and is presently adapted rather precisely to the amount of solar ultraviolet which does get through. To defend themselves against this low level of ultraviolet, evolved external shielding (feathers, fur, cuticular waxes on fruit), internal shielding (melanin pigment in human skin, flavenoids in plant tissue), avoidance strategies (plankton migration to greater depths in the daytime, shade-seeking by desert iguanas) and, in almost all organisms but placental mammals, elaborate mechanisms to repair photochemical damage.

It is possible, however, that a major increase in solar ultraviolet might overwhelm the defenses of some and perhaps many terrestrial life forms. Both direct and indirect damage would then occur among the bacteria, insects, plants, and other links in the ecosystems on which human well-being depends. This disruption, particularly if it occurred in the aftermath of a major war involving many other dislocations, could pose a serious additional threat to the recovery of postwar society. The National Academy of Sciences report concludes that in 20 years the ecological systems would have essentially recovered from the increase in ultraviolet radiation—though not necessarily from radioactivity or other damage in areas close to the war zone. However, a delayed effect of the increase in ultraviolet radiation would be an estimated 3 to 30 percent increase in skin cancer for 40 years in the Northern Hemisphere's mid-latitudes.

Some Conclusions

We have considered the problems of large-scale nuclear war from the standpoint of the countries not under direct attack, and the difficulties they might encounter in postwar recovery. It is true that most of the horror and tragedy of nuclear war would be visited on the populations subject to direct attack, who would doubtless have to cope with extreme and perhaps insuperable obstacles in seeking to reestablish their own societies. It is no less apparent, however, that other nations, including those remote from the combat, could suffer heavily because of damage to the global environment.

Finally, at least brief mention should be made of the global effects resulting from disruption of economic activities and communications. Since 1970, an increasing fraction of the human race has been losing the battle for self-sufficiency in food, and must rely on heavy imports. A major disruption of agriculture and transportation in the grain-exporting and manufacturing countries could thus prove disastrous to countries importing food, farm machinery, and fertilizers—especially those which are already struggling with the threat of widespread starvation. Moreover, virtually every economic area, from food and medicines to fuel and growth engendering industries, the less-developed countries would find they could not rely on the "undamaged" remainder of the developed world for trade essentials: in the wake of a nuclear war the industrial powers directly involved would themselves have to compete for resources with those countries that today are described as "less-developed."

Similarly, the disruption of international communications—satellites, cables, and even high frequency radio links—could be a major obstacle to international recovery efforts. In attempting to project the after-effects of a major nuclear war, we have considered separately the various kinds of damage that could occur. It is also quite possible, however, that interactions might take place among these effects, so that one type of damage would couple with another to produce new and unexpected hazards.

For example, we can assess individually the consequences of heavy worldwide radiation fallout and increased solar ultraviolet, but we do not know whether the two acting together might significantly increase human, animal, or plant susceptibility to disease. We can conclude that massive dust injection into the stratosphere, even greater in scale than Krakatoa, is unlikely by itself to produce significant climatic and environmental change, but we cannot rule out interactions with other phenomena, such as ozone depletion, which might produce utterly unexpected results.

We have come to realize that nuclear weapons can be as unpredictable as they are deadly in their effects. Despite some 30 years of development and study, there is still much that we do not know. This is particularly true when we consider the global effects of a large-scale nuclear war.

THE EFFECTS OF NUCLEAR WAR ON CLIMATE

A major nuclear war would deposit millions of tonnes of dust in the stratosphere. Some sunlight would be absorbed or reflected away from the earth by the dust, causing a decrease in the earth's temperature. This in turn could conceivably trigger a major climatic change. For example, lowered temperatures could cause an increase in snow and ice near the polar caps, thus an increased reflection of light, and further lowering of temperatures.

Stratospheric dust from a nuclear war seems unlikely to cause such climatic change. In 1883 the volcanic eruption at Krakatoa deposited some 10 to 100 thousand million tonnes of dust in the stratosphere, and the 1963 Mt Agung eruption about half as much. These injections seem to have caused a minor cooling of the surface temperature of the earth, at most about half a degree Celsius, lasting a few years, with no long term consequences. A nuclear war involving 4000Mt from present arsenals would probably deposit much less dust in the stratosphere than either the Krakatoa or Mt Agung eruptions.

Another possibility is that decreases in ozone or increases in oxides of nitrogen levels in the stratosphere, caused by nuclear war, could lead to climatic change. A reduction in ozone levels by a factor of two could cause a decrease in surface temperature of one half to one degree Centigrade, but including oxides of nitrogen in the calculation reduces this effect. Whether or not a change in temperature at the earth's surface by this amount for a few years could cause irreversible climatic change is hard to assess. The National Academy of Sciences study concluded that the effects of dust and oxides of nitrogen injection into the stratosphere 'would probably lie within normal global climatic variability, but the possibility of climatic changes of a more dramatic nature cannot be ruled out'. Since the Academy assumed a nuclear war with the explosion of many more high-yield weapons than are presently deployed, the danger of climatic change from dust or oxides of nitrogen is almost certainly less than assessed in their report.

Fires and smoke

In mid 1982, Paul Crutzen and John Birks drew attention to a previously overlooked major effect of nuclear war. They note that nuclear attacks would ignite numerous fires in cities, industry and especially in forests, crop areas and oil and gas fields.

These fires would produce immense amounts of particulate matter which would remain in the lower atmosphere for weeks even after the fires ceased. The smaller particles, called aerosols, would absorb sunlight. A large nuclear war with many fires and large aerosol production could lead to a reduction in sunlight in the mid-northern hemisphere by 90 per cent or more for a period of a few months.

This reduction would pose no *direct* threat to human health, but indirect effects could be widespread. If the nuclear war occurred during the agricultural growing season of the northern hemisphere, food production could be virtually eliminated for that season. This could greatly increase the chance of mass starvation in the north, though it is possible that stored food and changes in dietary habits could prevent this. If the reduction in ground level sunlight were 99 per cent or more, this could lead to the death of most of the phytoplankton and herbivorous zooplankton in half the northern oceans.

This could lead to extinction of species and unpredictable changes in the balance of life on earth. Another effect of the fires would be production of large amounts of oxides of nitrogen and reactive hydrocarbons in the lower atmosphere, changes in lower atmospheric dynamics, and creation of ozone and other potent air pollutants. (While ozone plays a useful role in the stratosphere it can be harmful to living things at ground level.)

In effect, much of the northern hemisphere could be exposed to severe photochemical smog for a period of weeks. This could cause health problems in susceptible people, especially the aged. Potentially more disastrous would be the negative effect of the smog on agricultural productivity, further increasing the chance of crop failure and consequent starvation.

Effects on Australia

The available evidence suggests that the global health effects of a major nuclear war are likely to be much less devastating than the immediate effects of blast, heat and local fallout. Present knowledge indicates that a large nuclear war in the northern hemisphere would have the following effects on Australia:

- from fallout, death of perhaps 1000 people from cancers and genetic defects over 50 years;
- from changes in ozone, a negligible effect;
- from climatic changes, a tiny chance of any effect;
- from fires, a negligible effect.

But this conclusion does not mean that the global effects should be ignored by Australians.

First, many people will die worldwide from cancers and genetic defects caused by global fallout, and possibly from other global effects. Whether the total is 10,000 or 10,000,000, the suffering and death will be real for those who experience it, and should not be discounted by use of comparisons. Second, there does exist a chance that major climatic changes, alterations in agricultural productivity, or consequences for global ecology could result from nuclear war.

Third, simply not enough is known to predict with confidence all the global effects of nuclear war. The implications for ozone were not publicised until 1974 and the consequences of fires were first publicised in 1982. This suggests that further significant effects may remain to be discovered. Furthermore, the exact consequences of known processes are a subject of scientific controversy. John Hampson's scenario for possible inadvertent destruction of ozone in a local region is an example of what may happen within the limits of scientific possibility. Until much more study is made of the effects of nuclear war, a high level of uncertainty will remain. Fourth, whatever the scale of global effects of nuclear war, the potential for immediate death and destruction in areas directly attacked is more than sufficient to justify the most strenuous efforts to eliminate the nuclear threat.

Nuclear war will hit hardest at the areas bombed, not only directly from blast, heat and local fallout but also from delayed tropospheric fallout, fires and possible agricultural or economic breakdown. Since physical effects far from the regions of nuclear explosions are much less, the most important threat to a country such as Australia is direct nuclear attack. The prime targets in Australia are the United States military bases at Pine Gap, Nurrungar and North West Cape. Attacks on these bases would kill perhaps a few thousand people.

There is a smaller chance of attacks on Cockburn Sound and on Darwin RAAF base, which are hosts for United States strategic nuclear ships, submarines and aircraft. Nuclear bombing of these two facilities, which are close to the population centres of Perth and Darwin respectively, could kill up to one hundred thousand people, depending on the wind direction at the time. Perhaps least likely, but certainly most devastating, would be nuclear attacks on major population centres. For example, the ports of major Australian cities could well be bombed if United States warships carrying strategic nuclear weapons were in harbour. Major population centres might also be hit as a consequence of attacks on associated military or economic facilities. Such attacks could kill from a few hundred thousand to several million people.

In the absence of direct attacks, the major indirect effects of nuclear war on a country such as Australia would not be physical but economic, political and social. Economically, nuclear war would cause an enormous disruption of world production and trade. Politically, nuclear war seems likely to cause massive upheavals not only in countries directly involved but in many of those far from the direct destruction. The social effects of nuclear war would be many, and include the psychological effects of massive nuclear destruction and the more immediate stresses of large numbers of refugees from Europe and North America. Study of and planning for these non-physical effects of nuclear war has been meagre or nonexistent. But unless the almost total lack of progress towards nuclear disarmament since 1945 is somehow reversed, these possible effects seem certain to become reality sooner or later.

IMPORTANCE OF THE OZONE LAYER

The sun emits light or radiation at a large range of energies or frequencies. Much of this radiation is absorbed by the earth's atmosphere and does not reach the surface. Human eyes have evolved to be highly receptive to radiation in the so-called visual spectrum which is not absorbed very much at all by the atmosphere. At the violet, high-energy end of this band of transmitted light lies what is called ultraviolet light or uv.

Ultraviolet light with high energies is strongly absorbed by molecular oxygen - the oxygen we breathe - in the upper atmosphere. This absorption can cause the molecular oxygen to break into two oxygen atoms each of which in turn can react with other molecular oxygen to form ozone, a compound made up of three oxygen atoms. In turn, ozone strongly absorbs ultraviolet light itself, including uv with energies lower than that absorbed by molecular oxygen. Small amounts of uv can be beneficial, especially in forming vitamin D in the skin. But large amounts can be harmful, especially of the more energetic uv, causing sunburn and skin cancer in humans and adversely affecting the growth of many plants. Many scientists believe that much of biological evolution took place under the protective uv shield of upper atmospheric ozone.

In the early 1970s scientists first became aware that oxides of nitrogen play a large role in reducing ozone levels through catalytic destruction: a single nitric oxide molecule can help destroy many molecules of ozone without being destroyed itself. This knowledge soon led to concern about the effects of oxides of nitrogen from supersonic transport aircraft (SSTs) on ozone and led to studies on this problem and later to studies of other threats to ozone such as from fluorocarbons from aerosol sprays and refrigerants.

Another major threat to ozone comes from nuclear explosions. Nitric oxide is produced essentially by the 'burning' of nitrogen in the atmosphere, and this occurs whenever air temperatures are sufficiently hot: in automobile engines, in aircraft engines and in nuclear explosions. Studies of the creation of oxides of nitrogen by nuclear explosions were first undertaken as part of the SST debate, to determine whether the nuclear weapons tests in the 1950s and 1960s had reduced observed ozone levels. It was only in 1974 that John Hampson made a point which had been overlooked, namely that large-scale nuclear war could cause a major and disastrous reduction in ozone levels.

Calculations made in the mid-1970s assuming large nuclear arsenals with many high-yield explosions concluded that reductions of ozone could reach 50 per cent or more in the northern hemisphere, with smaller reductions in the southern hemisphere. But since the number of high-yield weapons in present nuclear arsenals is now smaller, much less oxides of nitrogen would be deposited in the stratosphere by nuclear war than assumed in earlier calculations, and so significant ozone reductions are unlikely.

This conclusion remains tentative. The actual behaviour of stratospheric ozone is quite complicated, involving many chemical compounds and numerous chemical reactions, the changing effects of temperature, the angle and intensity of sunlight, and the effect of air motions. Computer models of the effects of nuclear war on ozone are able to take into account only a part of this complexity, and new information about chemical reaction rates in particular have led in the past to periodic revisions in the calculated effects of added oxides of nitrogen.

If significant ozone reduction did occur, the most important direct effect on humans would be an increase in skin cancer. However, this is seldom lethal, and could be avoided by reducing exposure to sunlight. Potentially more serious would be effects on crops. Some of the important grains, for example, are sensitive to uv. Whether the net effects on crop yields would be significant is hard to estimate. But whatever the reduction in ozone, ozone levels would return pretty much to normal after a few years. It seems unlikely that in the context of a major nuclear war the changes in uv alone would be of serious concern. In particular, the threat of human extinction raised by Jonathan Schell in *The Fate of the Earth,* based mostly on effects of increased uv from ozone reduction, seems very small indeed.

It is sometimes claimed that nuclear war could destroy ozone to such an extent that humans and animals would be blinded by excess uv. Even if large numbers of high-yield weapons were exploded, this possibility seems very unlikely except for a contribution to snow blindness in the far north. Stratospheric ozone can never be completely removed, but at most reduced greatly. Even if a 50 per cent or more reduction in ozone occurred - and as noted this seems improbable with present nuclear arsenals - protection from uv for humans could be obtained from sunglasses or just ordinary glasses, which absorb uv. For animals, the following considerations are relevant. Ozone levels vary considerably from place to place and from time to time, both seasonally and daily (sometimes by up to 50 per cent). Sunlight at the equator typically passes through only half as much ozone as at the mid-latitudes, yet animals at the equator are not known to go blind more often than elsewhere. Furthermore, most ozone reductions from a nuclear war would be in the mid and high latitudes, where ozone levels are higher to start with and where the 'path length' of sunlight through ozone is increased due to its oblique angle of incidence. But this does not mean complacency is warranted, as the concerns of John Hampson illustrate.

PEACE MOVEMENT FOR NUCLEAR WAR

The risk of nuclear war

Unless nuclear weapons are totally eliminated, it is a virtual certainty that nuclear war will occur eventually. The likelihood of war in any given year may be small, but the cumulative effect of small probabilities can approach certainty. The likelihood is definitely not zero. For example, it is known that US policy-makers have seriously considered using nuclear weapons unilaterally on a number of occasions.

Two developments have increased the risk of nuclear war in recent years. First is the deployment of highly accurate strategic missile systems in the US and the Soviet Union, plus developments in anti-submarine warfare and communications and control systems. This is increasing the chance that one of the superpowers will launch a 'first strike' in an attempt to destroy the opponent's nuclear inventory. Second is the spread of the capability to make nuclear weapons to more and more countries, fostered by the expansion of the nuclear power industry. It seems likely that this nuclear proliferation will be aided at some stage by laser enrichment of uranium, a technique which will dramatically reduce the obstacles to obtaining nuclear weapons. The question in such circumstances is not if nuclear war will occur, but when, what kind, and on what scale.

The risk of nuclear war could be removed if all nuclear weapons were eliminated- total nuclear disarmament. How could this happen? I have argued elsewhere that convincing decision-makers or mobilising public opinion to influence decision-makers is insufficient, and that what is required is grassroots initiatives mobilising large numbers of people in activities that challenge or transform warlinked institutions and which create new institutions.

The chance that the people struggling for fundamental institutional change will succeed worldwide in 20, 50 or 100 years is much less than certainty. Indeed, any realistic assessment of the strength of the present peace movement, in terms of its ability to fundamentally affect arms races and their institutional bases, would have to admit its extreme weakness. The peace movement seems highly unlikely to bring about nuclear disarmament within the next few years, and hence it should be prepared for the possibility of nuclear war. Whether a nuclear war is limited or global, available evidence suggests that a large fraction of the world's population may be unaffected physically. A long term strategy for peace must provide the basis for transforming the war system both before and after nuclear war or nuclear wars, and at the same time minimise the chance of nuclear war occurring in the first place.

In addition to the important physical effects of nuclear war there would be important indirect political effects. It seems very likely that there would be strong moves to maintain or establish authoritarian rule as a response to crises preceding or following nuclear war. Ever since Hiroshima, the threat of nuclear destruction has been used to prop up repressive institutions, under the pretext of defending against the 'enemy'. The actuality of nuclear war could easily result in the culmination of this trend. Large segments of the population could be manipulated to support a repressive regime under the necessity to defend against further threats or to obtain revenge.

A limited nuclear war might kill some hundreds of thousands or tens of millions of people, surely a major tragedy. But another tragedy could also result: the establishment, possibly for decades, of repressive civilian or military rule in countries such as Italy, Australia and the US, even if they were not directly involved in the war. The possibility of grassroots mobilisation for disarmament and peace would be greatly reduced even from its present levels. For such developments the people and the peace movements of the world are largely unprepared.

Preparedness for crisis situations

As well as encouraging moves towards repressive rule, the political and social upheaval resulting from nuclear war could also provide major opportunities for rapid social change in progressive directions. Several factors would operate here.

(a) There would be worldwide anguish and outrage at any significant use of nuclear weapons against populations. This emotion could easily turn against established institutions.

(b) A nuclear war involving the US, Soviet Union and Europe would weaken or destroy the bases for imperialism and neocolonialism in poor countries, and stimulate widespread revolutionary action that could not be contained by local elites left without rich country support.

(c) In areas directly affected by nuclear attack, the destruction of established institutions would allow the creation of new structures.

Historically, periods of economic or military crisis often have preceded revolutionary change, though not always with desirable results. Crises provide opportunities for groups which are organised and able to take advantage of them. In the case of nuclear war, present governments have made some arrangements to preserve their type of rule after a nuclear war. By contrast, the peace movement is almost completely unprepared to respond to a crisis engendered by nuclear war.

The primary objective of national security bureaucracies in the event of nuclear war is survival of the state apparatus. This has two components: continued defence against the outside enemy, and defence against challenges raised by the native population. The health and welfare of the general population is a secondary consideration, mainly important in its effects on the two primary goals. This emphasis is reflected in preparations for the survival of key officials, for continuity of official decision-making apparatuses and communications, and for quelling 'civil disturbances'.

In the absence of any significant countervailing force, a nuclear war will not be the end of war but the beginning of the age of many nuclear wars. Although nuclear war may lead to mass revulsion, there will also be strong government and citizen pressures for retaliation, revenge, efforts to 'do better next time' and not to be caught unprepared. The rise of Nazism after World War I should point to the danger. Scenarios for World Wars IV, V, VI and so forth may be repulsive, but cannot be discounted solely for that reason.

During World War II, several key groups in the US developed plans for the post-war world. More generally, post-war political and economic considerations played a large role in many decisions, military and otherwise, during the war. The same pattern is being and will be replayed prior to and during a nuclear war. It is not for lack of anything better to do that nuclear strategists have elaborated numerous scenarios for nuclear war, recovery and future wars. During and after a nuclear crisis or war, powerful interest groups will attempt to sway developments through management of the news, mobilisation of sympathetic groups, creating scapegoats, suppressing dissent, and using many other mechanisms familiar to us today. If these developments are to be opposed, peace activists need to be prepared to act during nuclear crisis and nuclear war and afterwards.

Preparation for nuclear war by the peace movement could increase the chances of success in struggles for social justice, especially in the poor countries, during a period of chaos in the rich countries resulting from nuclear war or nuclear crisis.

Implications for the present

But these possibilities provide relatively little consolation for the human disaster of nuclear war, and certainly would not justify any policy which significantly increased the risk of nuclear war. It is in their implications for the present that peace movement activities relating to nuclear war must be assessed. It is my belief that preparation for nuclear war by the peace movement would reduce the chance of nuclear war by providing a visible threat to the otherwise unchallenged continuance of existing political institutions. National decision-makers may wish to avoid nuclear war to save their own lives, but they have demonstrated a continued willingness to risk nuclear war, both in crises and confrontations and through the very existence of nuclear arsenals, through the policies they have promoted and the institutions they have constructed and supported. This institutionalised risk of nuclear war will seem less acceptable if one consequence of continued preparations for war were a major challenge to the complete system of political and economic power and privilege.

Nuclear weapons states have refrained from nuclear war thus far not primarily because of their perception of the human disaster of nuclear war but because of the possible political consequences. A prepared peace movement would ensure that such political consequences are as serious as possible.

There are a number of principles which seem appropriate for peace movement planning for nuclear crisis, nuclear war and its aftermath. Peace movement planning has to be based on an open rather than a hidden agenda. A full peace movement strategy must take into account supporters and sympathisers as well as opponents in working out how to take full advantage of the crisis. But most important is the task of developing strategies, methods and organisational forms which are relevant both in the nuclear crisis, nuclear war and its aftermath, and for ongoing activities today. Just as peace group organisational structures should be designed to handle infiltrators, so these structures - and other aspects of efforts for peace - should be designed to operate in the event of nuclear war.

And, vice versa, the type of preparations for nuclear war decided upon should be compatible with current effectiveness. Only if the threat of institutional revolution in the event of nuclear war is also raised in the present is it likely that disarmament as a reform will seem to powerholders as the lesser of two evils. In spite of the attention I am giving here to preparing for nuclear war, and in spite of the optimism of some nonmilitarists for developments in the wake of massive social disaster or breakdown, the prospects for a post-nuclear war world seem rather dismal to me. Aside from the massive loss of life and continuing human suffering caused by nuclear war, moral barriers against the future use of nuclear weapons in war would be greatly reduced. We need only remember the world outrage at terrorist bombings of civilian targets during the Spanish Civil War by Germany and Italy. Not long after, such bombing became standard policy for the 'enlightened democracies'. This points to the need to be prepared to fully utilise the outrage and disruption of the first nuclear war.

EXPLOSIVE POWER IN A GLOBAL NUCLEAR WAR

The nuclear bomb exploded over Hiroshima had an explosive power of about 13 kilotonnes, denoted 13kt. One kt is the equivalent of one thousand tonnes (of one thousand kilogrammes each) of chemical explosives. The Hiroshima bomb was an enriched uranium fission bomb and the Nagasaki bomb of 21kt was a plutonium fission bomb. Much greater explosive power can be obtained by using an enriched uranium fission explosion as a trigger to cause nuclear fusion in a mixture of lithium and deuterium (heavy hydrogen). This is the thermonuclear, fusion, hydrogen or H-bomb. Unenriched uranium is often put around the fusion bomb to absorb emitted neutrons and cause further fissions and thus increase explosive power. This is the standard fission-fusion-fission bomb, whose explosive power is usually measured in megatonnes (denoted Mt), with 1Mt equal to 1000kt. The largest atmospheric nuclear explosion was one by the Soviet Union in 1961, of about 60Mt yield.

A typical large-sized nuclear explosive in the 'strategic' arsenals of the United States or the Soviet Union used to be about 1Mt, and many weapons of this size are deployed today in the payloads of ballistic missiles. The trend in the United States for the past decade or so, and in the Soviet Union for a few years, has been to switch from a single large warhead to several smaller warheads in the payload of strategic ballistic missiles. For example, a single 1Mt bomb might be replaced by ten 50kt bombs, each independently targetable. In this case this change reduces total explosive power by one half, while the total surface area that potentially can be destroyed is increased by one third.

The overwhelming bulk of nuclear explosive power resides in the arsenals of the two nuclear superpowers, the United States and the Soviet Union. In 1960 this explosive power totalled perhaps 60,000Mt. But due to the trend noted above, present arsenals total about 11,000Mt: about 3,500Mt for the United States and 7,500Mt for the Soviet Union. While the trend to larger numbers of smaller warheads increases the potential area destroyed by nuclear weapons, the reduction in total megatonnage reduces the potential global effects. This is especially the case since the clouds from nuclear explosions of 1Mt or less are unlikely to rise high into the stratosphere, reducing stratospheric fallout and effects on ozone.

What fraction of the 11,000Mt would be exploded in a major nuclear war? This is hard to assess, but almost certainly much will not be exploded. Both the United States and the Soviet Union place a high priority on targeting their opponent's military forces, nuclear forces in particular. A sizable fraction of nuclear arsenals is likely to be destroyed before use (attacks on nuclear submarines, airfields, missile silos), be unavailable for use (submarines in port, missiles cut off from communications) or fail to perform properly. One estimate is that one sixth to one third of superpower arsenals will be used, depending on whether the war occurs suddenly or builds up gradually.

If these estimates are correct then about 2000Mt to 4000Mt of nuclear firepower might be exploded in a major nuclear war. The total could be much smaller in a 'limited' nuclear war. The figure of 4000Mt is used in this article in making illustrative calculations. It is assumed that half of this total is due to fission and half to fusion.

Overkill

'Overkill: the ability to exterminate a population more than once. "Both the US and the Soviet Union now possess nuclear stockpiles large enough to exterminate mankind three or four - some say ten - times over" (Philip Noel-Baker, Nobel Peace Prize winner, 1971).'

Many people believe that the capacity of nuclear weapons for 'overkill' means that all or most of the people on earth would die in a major nuclear war. In spite of the prevalence of this idea, there is little scientific evidence to support it.

Many calculations of 'overkill' appear to be made using the nuclear attacks on Hiroshima and Nagasaki as a baseline. Estimates of the number of people killed at Hiroshima from a 13kt bomb range from 63,000 to over 200,000. Adopting a figure of 130,000 for illustrative purposes gives ten people killed for each tonne of nuclear explosive. By linear extrapolation, explosion of a third of a million times as much explosive power, 4000Mt, would kill a third of a million times as many people, namely 40,000 million, or nearly ten times the present world population.

But this factor of ten is misleading, since linear extrapolation does not apply. Suppose the bomb dropped on Hiroshima had been 1000 times as powerful, 13Mt. It could not have killed 1000 times as many people, but at most the entire population of Hiroshima perhaps 250,000. Re-doing the 'overkill' calculation using these figures gives not a figure of ten but of only 0.02.

This example shows that crude linear extrapolations of this sort are unlikely to provide any useful information about the effects of nuclear war.

'Overkill' can be meaningful if applied to specific targets which will be attacked by several nuclear weapons. But applied to the entire world population the concept of 'overkill' is misleading. By the same logic it might be said that there is enough water in the oceans to drown everyone ten times.

It has been argued that if the megatonnage in nuclear arsenals were increased by ten or 100 times and used in war, the fallout would be sufficient to threaten the life of most people on earth. Since total megatonnage has been decreasing in recent years, this particular possibility remains hypothetical, at least at the moment.

8

Iraq War

INTRODUCTION

The Iraq War was an armed conflict in Iraq that consisted of two phases. The first was an invasion of Iraq starting on 20 March 2003 by an invasion force led by the United States. It was followed by a longer phase of fighting, in which an insurgency emerged to oppose the occupying forces and the newly formed Iraqi government. Roughly 96.5 percent of the casualties suffered by the U.S.-led coalition were suffered during the second phase, rather than the initial invasion. The U.S. completed its withdrawal of military personnel in December 2011, during the ninth year of the war. However, the insurgency is ongoing and continues to cause thousands of fatalities. Throughout the armed conflict, the United States never formally declared war on Iraq, making the war a military action.

Prior to the war, the governments of the United States and the United Kingdom claimed that Iraq's alleged possession of weapons of mass destruction (WMD) posed a threat to their security and that of their allies. In 2002, the United Nations Security Council passed Resolution 1441 which called for Iraq to completely cooperate with UN weapon inspectors to verify that Iraq was not in possession of WMD andcruise missiles. Prior to the attack, the United Nations Monitoring, Verification and Inspection Commission(UNMOVIC) found no evidence of WMD, but could not yet verify the accuracy of Iraq's declarations regarding what weapons it possessed, as their work was still unfinished. The leader of the inspectors,Hans Blix, estimated the time remaining for disarmament being verified through inspections to be "months".

After investigation following the invasion, the U.S. led Iraq Survey Group concluded that Iraq had ended its nuclear, chemical and biological programs in 1991 and had no active programs at the time of the invasion, but that they intended to resume production if the Iraq sanctions were lifted. Only degraded remnants of misplaced and abandoned chemical weapons were found. Paul R. Pillar, the CIA official who coordinated U.S. intelligence on the Middle East from 2000 to 2005, said "If prewar intelligence assessments had said the same things as the Duelfer report, the administration would have had to change a few lines in its rhetoric and maybe would have lost a few member's votes in Congress, but otherwise the sales campaign—which was much more about Saddam's intentions and what he "could" do than about extant weapons systems—would have been unchanged. The administration still would have gotten its war." Even Dick Cheney later cited the actual Duelfer report as support for the administration's pro-war case. George J. Tenet, the former director of central intelligence, stated Vice President Cheney and other George W. Bush administration officials pushed the country to war in Iraq without ever conducting a "serious debate" about whether Saddam Hussein posed an imminent threat to the United States.

Some U.S. officials also accused Iraqi President Saddam Hussein of harboring and supporting al-Qaeda, but no evidence of a meaningful connection was ever found. Other stated reasons for the invasion included Iraq's financial support for the families of Palestinian suicide bombers, Iraqi government human rights abuses, and an effort to spread democracy to the country.

On 16 March 2003, the U.S. government advised the U.N. inspectors to leave their unfinished work and exit from Iraq. On 20 March the American-led coalition conducted a surprise military invasion of Iraq without declaring war. The invasion led to an occupation and the eventual capture of Saddam, who was later tried in an Iraqi court of law and executed by the new Iraqi government. Violence against coalition forces and among various sectarian groups soon led to the Iraqi insurgency, strife between many Sunni and Shia Iraqi groups, and the emergence of a new faction of Al-Qaeda in Iraq.

In June 2008, US Department of Defense officials claimed security and economic indicators began to show signs of improvement in what they hailed as significant and fragile gains. Iraq was fifth on the 2008 Failed States Index, and sixth on the 2009 list. As public opinion favoring troop withdrawals increased and as Iraqi forces began to take responsibility for security, member nations of the Coalition withdrew their forces. In late 2008, the American and Iraqi governments approved a Status of Forces Agreement effective through 1 January 2012. The Iraqi Parliament also ratified a Strategic Framework Agreement with the United States, aimed at ensuring cooperation in constitutional rights, threat deterrence, education, energy development, and other areas.

In late February 2009, newly elected U.S. President Barack Obama announced an 18-month withdrawal window for combat forces, with approximately 50,000 troops remaining in the country "to advise and trainIraqi security forces and to provide intelligence and surveillance". UK forces ended combat operations on 30 April 2009. Iraqi Prime Minister Nouri al Maliki said he supported the accelerated pullout of U.S. forces. In a speech at the Oval Office on 31 August 2010 Obama declared "the American combat mission in Iraq has ended. Operation Iraqi Freedom is over, and the Iraqi people now have lead responsibility for the security of their country." Beginning 1 September 2010, the American operational name for its involvement in Iraq changed from "Operation Iraqi Freedom" to "Operation New Dawn". The remaining 50,000 U.S. troops were designated as "advise and assist brigades" assigned to non-combat operations while retaining the ability to revert to combat operations as necessary. Two combat aviation brigades also remain in Iraq. In September 2010, the Associated Press issued an internal memo reminding its reporters that "combat in Iraq is not over", and "U.S. troops remain involved in combat operations alongside Iraqi forces, although U.S. officials say the American combat mission has formally ended".

On 21 October 2011, President Obama announced that all U.S. troops and trainers would leave Iraq by the end of the year, bringing the U.S. mission in Iraq to an end. On 15 December 2011, U.S. Defense Secretary Leon Panetta officially declared the Iraq War over, at a flag lowering ceremony in Baghdad. The last U.S. troops left Iraqi territory on 18 December 2011 at 4:27 UTC. A total of 4,486 U.S. troops were killed in Iraq between 2003 and 2012.

Since the U.S. military's withdrawal, significant violence has continued in Iraq. The Shia-dominated administration of Prime Minister Nouri al-Maliki moved to arrest important Sunni political leaders prior to and following the U.S. withdrawal, and Sunni militant groups stepped up attacks targeting the country's majority Shia population, undermining confidence in the Shia-led government. As of mid-June 2014 the internationally recognized government of Iraq is reported to have lost control of large areas of the country's north including the provincial capitals of Mosul and Tikrit. Large scale warfare between the supporters of the Shia led government and Sunni militants composed of Ba'ath loyalists and ISIS isunderway. As of 17 June 2014 ISIS or ISIL has taken control of Iraq's second largest city. They have posted videos on line of them massacring hundreds of civilians and soldiers.

BACKGROUND

Iraq disarmament and pre-war intelligence

Prior to September 2002, the CIA was the Bush administration's main provider of intelligence on Iraq. In September, a Pentagon unit called Office of Special Plans (OSP), was created by Paul Wolfowitz and Douglas Feith, and headed by Feith, as charged by then-United States Secretary of Defense Donald Rumsfeld, to supply senior George W. Bush administration officials with raw intelligence pertaining to Iraq. Seymour Hersh writes that, according to a Pentagon adviser,

"[OSP] was created in order to find evidence of what Wolfowitz and his boss, Defense Secretary Donald Rumsfeld, wanted to be true—that Saddam Hussein had close ties to Al Qaeda, and that Iraq had an enormous arsenal of chemical, biological, and possibly even nuclear weapons (WMD) that threatened the region and, potentially, the United States. [...] 'The agency [CIA] was out to *disprove* linkage between Iraq and terrorism,' the Pentagon adviser told me. 'That's what drove them. If you've ever worked with intelligence data, you can see the ingrained views at C.I.A. that color the way it sees data.' The goal of Special Plans, he said, was 'to put the data under the microscope to reveal what the intelligence community can't see.'"

U.N. weapons inspections resume

The issue of Iraq's disarmament reached a turning point in 2002–2003, when President Bush demanded a complete end to allegedIraqi production of weapons of mass destruction and full compliance with U.N. Security Council Resolutions requiring U.N. weapons inspectors unfettered access to suspected weapons production facilities. The U.N. had prohibited Iraq from developing or possessing such weapons after the Persian Gulf Warand required Iraq to permit inspections confirming compliance. During inspections in 1999, U.S. intelligence agents supplied the United States with a direct feed of conversations between Iraqi security agencies as well as other information. This was confirmed by the *New York Times* and the *Wall Street Journal*.

During 2002, U.S. President George Bush repeatedly warned of military action against Iraq unless inspections were allowed to progress unfettered. In accordance with U.N. Security Council Resolution 1441 Iraq reluctantly agreed to new inspections in late 2002. With the cooperation of the Iraqis, a third weapons inspection team in 2003 led by David Kelly viewed and photographed two alleged mobile weapons laboratories which were actually facilities for the production of hydrogen gas to fill balloons.

Shortly before the invasion, Hans Blix the lead weapons inspector, advised the U.N. Security Council that Iraq was cooperating with inspections and the confirmation of disarmament through inspections could be achieved quickly if Iraq remained cooperative.

Weapons of mass destruction

Yellowcake uranium

In 1990, before the Persian Gulf War, Iraq had stockpiled 550 short tons (500 t) of yellowcake uranium at the Tuwaitha nuclear complex about 20 kilometres (12 mi) south of Baghdad. In late February 2002, the CIA sent former Ambassador Joseph C. Wilson to investigate reports (later found to be forgeries) that Iraq was attempting to purchase additional yellowcake from Niger. Wilson returned and informed the CIA that reports of yellowcake sales to Iraq were "unequivocally wrong." The Bush administration, however, continued to allege Iraq's attempts to obtain additional yellowcake were a justification for military action, most prominently in the January 2003, State of the Union address, in which President Bush declared that Iraq had sought uranium, citing British intelligence sources.

In response, Wilson wrote a critical *New York Times* op-ed piece in June 2003 stating that he had personally investigated claims of yellowcake purchases and believed them to be fraudulent. After Wilson's op-ed, Wilson's wife Valerie Plame was publicly identified as an undercover CIA analyst by a columnist. This led to a Justice Department investigation into the source of the leak. The federal investigation led to the conviction of I. Lewis (Scooter) Libby, Vice President Dick Cheney's chief of staff, on charges of perjury and obstruction of justice.

On 1 May 2005, the "Downing Street memo" was published in *The Sunday Times*. It contained an overview of a secret 23 July 2002, meeting among British government, Ministry of Defence, and British intelligence figures who discussed the build-up to the Iraq war—including direct references to classified US policy of the time. The memo stated that "Bush wanted to remove Saddam, through military action, justified by the conjunction of terrorism and WMD. But the intelligence and facts were being fixed around the policy".

In September 2002, the Bush administration, the CIA and the DIA said attempts by Iraq to acquire high-strength aluminum tubes that were prohibited under the UN monitoring program and which they said pointed to a clandestine effort to make centrifuges to enrich uranium for nuclear bombs. This analysis was opposed by the United States Department of Energy (DOE) and INR, which was significant because of DOE's expertise in such gas centrifuges and nuclear weapons programs. The DOE and INR argued that the Iraqi tubes were poorly suited for centrifuges and that while it was technically possible with additional modification, conventional military uses were more plausible. A report released by the Institute for Science and International Security in 2002 reported that it was highly unlikely that the tubes could be used to enrich uranium.

An effort by the DOE to correct this detail in comments prepared for United States Secretary of State Colin Powell's UN appearance was rebuffed by the administration and Powell, in his address to the UN Security Council just before the war, referenced the aluminum tubes, stating that while experts disagreed on whether or not the tubes were destined for a centrifuge program, the specifications of the tubes were unusually tight. Powell later admitted he had presented what turned out to be an inaccurate case to the UN on Iraqi weapons, and the intelligence he was relying on was, in some cases, "deliberately misleading." After the 2008 US presidential election, and the election of Democratic party nominee Barack Obama, President Bush stated that "[my] biggest regret of all the presidency has to have been the intelligence failure in Iraq".

Poison gas

The CIA had contacted Iraq's foreign minister, Naji Sabri, who was being paid by the French as an agent. Sabri informed them that Saddam had hidden poison gas among Sunni tribesmen, had ambitions for a nuclear program but that it was not active, and that no biological weapons were being produced or stockpiled, although research was underway. According to Sidney Blumenthal, George Tenet briefed Bush on 18 September 2002, that Sabri had informed them that Iraq did not have WMD.

On 21 June 2006 the US House of Representatives Permanent Select Committee on Intelligence released key points from a classified report from the National Ground Intelligence Center on the recovery of a small number of degraded chemical munitions in Iraq. The report stated that "Coalition forces have recovered approximately 500 weapons munitions which contain degraded mustard or sarin nerve agent." However, all are thought to be pre-Gulf War munitions.

Biological weapons

Based on reports obtained by the German intelligence service from an Iraqi defector codenamed "Curveball", Colin Powell presented evidence to the United Nations security council that Iraq had an active biological weapons programs. On 15 February 2011, the defector—a scientist identified as Rafid Ahmed Alwan al-Janafi—admitted to journalists working for *The Guardian* newspaper that he lied to the *Bundesnachrichtendienst* in order to strengthen the case against Saddam Hussein, whom he wished to see removed from power.

Post-invasion views on WMD

In December 2009, former U.K. Prime Minister Tony Blair stated that he "would still have thought it right to remove [Saddam Hussein]" regardless of whether Iraq possessed weapons of mass destruction or not.

Preparations for Iraq war

In the days immediately following 9/11, the Bush Administration national security team actively debated an invasion of Iraq. A memo written by Sec. Rumsfeld dated 27 November 2001 considers a US-Iraq war. One section of the memo questions "How start?", listing multiple possible justifications for a US-Iraq War.

During 2002 the amount of ordnance used by British and American aircraft patrolling the no-fly zones of Iraq increased compared to the previous years and by August had "become a full air offensive". Tommy Franks, the allied commander, later stated that the bombing was designed to "degrade" the Iraqi air defense system before an invasion.

In October 2002, a few days before the US Senate voted on the Joint Resolution to Authorize the Use of United States Armed Forces Against Iraq, about 75 senators were told in closed session that Iraq had the means of attacking the Eastern Seaboard of the US with biological or chemical weapons delivered by unmanned aerial vehicles (UAVs.) On 5 February 2003, Colin Powell presented further evidence in his Iraqi WMD program presentation to the UN Security Council that UAVs were ready to be launched against the United States. At the time, there was a vigorous dispute within the US military and intelligence communities as to whether CIA conclusions about Iraqi UAVs were accurate and other intelligence agencies suggested that Iraq did not possess any offensive UAV capability, saying the few they had were designed for surveillance and intended for reconnaissance. The Senate voted to approve the Joint Resolution with the support of large bipartisan majorities on 11 October 2002, providing the Bush administration with a legal basis for the US invasion under US law.

The resolution granted the authorization by the Constitution of the United States and theUnited States Congress for the President to command the military to fight anti-United States violence. Citing the Iraq Liberation Act of 1998, the resolution reiterated that it should be the policy of the United States to remove the Saddam regime and promote a democratic replacement. The authorization was signed by President George W. Bush on 16 October 2002.

Chief UN weapons inspector Hans Blix remarked in January 2003 that "Iraq appears not to have come to a genuine acceptance—not even today—of the disarmament, which was demanded of it and which it needs to carry out to win the confidence of the world and to live in peace." Among other things he noted that 1,000 short tons (910 t) of chemical agent were unaccounted for, information on Iraq's VX nerve agent program was missing, and that "no convincing evidence" was presented for the destruction of 8,500 litres (1,900 imp gal; 2,200 US gal) of anthrax that had been declared.

In the 2003 State of the Union address, President Bush said "we know that Iraq, in the late 1990s, had several mobile biological weapons labs". On 5 February 2003, Secretary of State Colin Powell appeared before the UN to present American evidence that Iraq was hiding unconventional weapons. The French government also believed that Saddam had stockpiles of anthrax and botulism toxin, and the ability to produce VX. In March, Blix said progress had been made in inspections, and no evidence of WMD had been found. Iraqi scientist Rafid Ahmed Alwan al-Janabi codenamed "Curveball", admitted in February 2011, that he lied to the CIA about biological weapons in order to get the US to attack and remove Saddam from power.

In early 2003, the US, British, and Spanish governments proposed the so-called "eighteenth resolution" to give Iraq a deadline for compliance with previous resolutions enforced by the threat of military action. This proposed resolution was subsequently withdrawn due to lack of support on the UN Security Council. In particular, North Atlantic Treaty Organization (NATO) members France, Germany and Canada and non-NATO member Russia were opposed to military intervention in Iraq, due to the high level of risk to the international community's security, and defended disarmament through diplomacy.

A meeting between George W. Bush and Tony Blair took place on 31 January 2003, in the White House. A secret memo of this meeting purportedly showed that the Bush administration had already decided on the invasion of Iraq at that point. Bush was allegedly floating the idea of painting a U 2 spyplane in UN colors and letting it fly low over Iraq to provoke Iraqi forces into shooting it down, thereby providing a pretext for the United States and Britain to invade. Bush and Blair made a secret deal to carry out the invasion regardless of whether WMD were discovered by UN weapons inspectors, in direct contradiction with statements Blair made to the British House of Commons afterwards that the Iraqi regime would be given a final chance to disarm. In the memo, Bush is paraphrased as saying, "The start date for the military campaign was now pencilled in for 10 March. This was when the bombing would begin." Bush said to Blair that he "thought it unlikely that there would be internecine warfare between the different religious and ethnic groups" in Iraq after the war.

Opposition to invasion

In October 2002 former US President Bill Clinton warned about possible dangers of pre-emptive military action against Iraq. Speaking in the UK on a Labour Party conference he said: "As a preemptive action today, however well-justified, may come back with unwelcome consequences in the future....I don't care how precise your bombs and your weapons are, when you set them off, innocent people will die."

On 20 January 2003, French Foreign Minister Dominique de Villepin declared "we believe that military intervention would be the worst solution". Meanwhile anti-war groups across the world organised public protests. According to French academic Dominique Reynié, between 3 January and 12 April 2003, 36 million people across the globe took part in almost 3,000 protests against war in Iraq, with demonstrations on 15 February 2003, being the largest and most prolific. Nelson Mandela voiced his opposition in late January, stating "All that (Mr. Bush) wants isIraqi oil,".

In February 2003, the US Army's top general, Eric Shinseki, told the Senate Armed Services Committee that it would take "several hundred thousand soldiers" to secure Iraq. Two days later, US Defense Secretary Donald Rumsfeld said the post-war troop commitment would be less than the number of troops required to win the war, and that "the idea that it would take several hundred thousand US forces is far from the mark." Deputy Defense Secretary Paul Wolfowitz said Shineski's estimate was "way off the mark," because other countries would take part in an occupying force.

In March 2003, Hans Blix reported that "No evidence of proscribed activities have so far been found" in Iraq, saying that progress was made in inspections which would continue. He estimated the time remaining for disarmament being verified through inspections to be "months". But the US government announced that "diplomacy has failed", and that it would proceed with a coalition of allied countries—named the "coalition of the willing"—to rid Iraq of its alleged WMD. The US government abruptly advised UN weapons inspectors to leave Baghdad immediately.

There were serious legal questions surrounding the launching of the war against Iraq and the Bush Doctrine of preemptive war in general. On 16 September 2004, Kofi Annan, the Secretary General of the United Nations, said of the invasion, "I have indicated it was not in conformity with the UN Charter. From our point of view, from the Charter point of view, it was illegal."

In November 2008 Lord Bingham, the former British Law Lord, described the war a serious violation of international law, and accused Britain and the United States of acting like a "world vigilante". He also criticized the post-invasion record of Britain as "an occupying power in Iraq". Regarding the treatment of Iraqi detainees in Abu Ghraib, Bingham said: "Particularly disturbing to proponents of the rule of law is the cynical lack of concern for international legality among some top officials in the Bush administration." In July 2010, Deputy Prime Minister of the UK Nick Clegg, in an official PMQs session in Parliament, condemned the invasion of Iraq as illegal. Theorist Francis Fukuyama has argued that "the Iraq war and the close association it created between military invasion and democracy promotion tarnished the latter".

THE INVASION

The first Central Intelligence Agency invasion team entered Iraq on 10 July 2002. This team was composed of members of the CIA's Special Activities Division and was later joined by members of the US military's elite Joint Special Operations

Command(JSOC). Together, they prepared for the invasion of conventional forces. These efforts consisted of persuading the commanders of several Iraqi military divisions to surrender rather than oppose the invasion, and to identify all of the initial leadership targets during very high risk reconnaissance missions.

Most importantly, their efforts organized the Kurdish Peshmerga to become the northern front of the invasion. Together this force defeated Ansar al-Islam in Iraqi Kurdistan before the invasion and then defeated the Iraqi army in the north. The battle against Ansar al-Islam led to the death of a substantial number of militants and the uncovering of a chemical weapons facility at Sargat.

At 5:34 a.m. Baghdad time on 20 March 2003 (9:34 p.m., 19 March EST) the surprise military invasion of Iraq began. There was no declaration of war. The 2003 invasion of Iraq, led by US Army GeneralTommy Franks, began under the codename "Operation Iraqi Liberation", later renamed "Operation Iraqi Freedom", the UK codenameOperation Telic, and the Australian codename Operation Falconer. Coalition forces also cooperated with Kurdish Peshmerga forces in the north. Approximately forty other governments, the "US-led coalition against Iraq," participated by providing troops, equipment, services, security, and special forces, with 248,000 soldiers from the United States, 45,000 British soldiers, 2,000 Australian soldiers and 194 Polish soldiers from Special Forces unit GROM sent to Kuwait for the invasion. The invasion force was also supported by Iraqi Kurdish militia troops, estimated to number upwards of 70,000.

According to General Tommy Franks, the objectives of the invasion were, "First, end the regime of Saddam Hussein. Second, to identify, isolate and eliminate Iraq's weapons of mass destruction. Third, to search for, to capture and to drive out terrorists from that country. Fourth, to collect such intelligence as we can related to terrorist networks. Fifth, to collect such intelligence as we can related to the global network of illicit weapons of mass destruction. Sixth, to end sanctions and to immediately deliver humanitarian support to the displaced and to many needy Iraqi citizens. Seventh, to secure Iraq's oil fields and resources, which belong to the Iraqi people. And last, to help the Iraqi people create conditions for a transition to a representative self-government."

The invasion was a quick and decisive operation encountering major resistance, though not what the US, British and other forces expected. The Iraqi regime had prepared to fight both a conventional and irregular war at the same time, conceding territory when faced with superior conventional forces, largely armored, but launching smaller scale attacks in the rear using fighters dressed in civilian and paramilitary clothes. Since the initiation of the war in Iraq, numerous programs were created to "enhance psychological resilience and prevent psychological morbidity in troops."

Coalition troops launched air and amphibious assault on the Al-Faw peninsula to secure the oil fields there and the important ports, supported by warships of the Royal Navy,Polish Navy, and Royal Australian Navy. The United States Marine Corps' 15th Marine Expeditionary Unit, attached to 3 Commando Brigade and the Polish Special Forces unitGROM attacked the port of Umm Qasr, while the British Army's 16 Air Assault Brigade secured the oil fields in southern Iraq.

The heavy armor of the US 3rd Infantry Division moved westward and then northward through the western desert toward Baghdad, while the 1st Marine Expeditionary Force moved more easterly along Highway 1 through the center of the country, and 1 (UK) Armoured Division moved northward through the eastern marshland. The US 1st Marine Division fought through Nasiriyah in a battle to seize the major road junction and nearby Talil Airfield. The United States Army 3rd Infantry Division defeated Iraqi forces entrenched in and around the airfield.

With the Nasiriyah and Talil Airfields secured in its rear, the 3rd Infantry Division supported by 101st Airborne Division continued its attack north toward Najaf and Karbala, but a severe sand storm slowed the coalition advance and there was a halt to consolidate and make sure the supply lines were secure. When they started again they secured the Karbala Gap, a key approach to Baghdad, then secured the bridges over the Euphrates River, and the American forces poured through the gap on to Baghdad.

In the middle of Iraq, the 1st Marine Division fought its way to the eastern side of Baghdad, and prepared for the attack into Baghdad to seize it.

In the north, OIF 1 used the largest special operations force since the successful attack on the Taliban government of Afghanistan just over a year earlier.

On April 9, Baghdad fell, ending Saddam's 24 year rule. US forces seized the deserted Ba'ath Party ministries and stage-managed the tearing down of a huge iron statue of Saddam, photos and video of which became symbolic of the event, although later controversial.

Not seen in the photos or heard on the videos, shot with a zoom lens, was the chant of the inflamed crowd for Muqtada al-Sadr, the radical Shiite cleric. In November 2008, Iraqi protesters staged a similar stomping on and burning of an effigy of George W. Bush. The abrupt fall of Baghdad was accompanied by a widespread outpouring of gratitude toward the invaders, but also massive civil disorder, including the looting of public and government buildings and drastically increased crime.

According to the Pentagon, 250,000 short tons (230,000 t) (of 650,000 short tons (590,000 t) total) of ordnance was looted, providing a significant source of ammunition for theIraqi insurgency. The invasion phase concluded when Tikrit, Saddam's home town, fell with little resistance to the US Marines of Task Force Tripoli.

In the invasion phase of the war (19 March–April 30), an estimated 9,200 Iraqi combatants were killed by coalition forces along with an estimated 3,750 non-combatants, i.e. civilians who did not take up arms. Coalition forces reported the death in combat of 139 US military personnel and 33 UK military personnel.

POST-INVASION PHASE

2003: Beginnings of insurgency

On 1 May 2003, President Bush staged a dramatic visit to the aircraft carrier USS *Abraham Lincoln* operating a few miles west of San Diego, California. The visit climaxed at sunset with Bush's now well-known "Mission Accomplished" speech. In this nationally televised speech, delivered before the sailors and airmen on the flight deck, Bush effectively declared victory due to the defeat of Iraq's conventional forces. However, Saddam remained at large and significant pockets of resistance remained.

After President Bush's speech, coalition forces noticed a gradually increasing flurry of attacks on its troops in various regions, especially in the "Sunni Triangle". The initial Iraqi insurgents were supplied by hundreds of weapons caches created before the invasion by the Iraqi army and Republican Guard.

Initially, Iraqi resistance (described by the coalition as "Anti-Iraqi Forces") largely stemmed from fedayeen and Saddam/Ba'ath Partyloyalists, but soon religious radicals and Iraqis angered by the occupation contributed to the insurgency. The three provinces with the highest number of attacks were Baghdad, Al Anbar, and Salah Ad Din.

Those three provinces account for 35% of the population, but as of 5 December 2006, were responsible for 73% of U.S. military deaths and an even higher percentage of recent U.S. military deaths (about 80%.)

Insurgents used guerrilla tactics including: mortars, missiles, suicide attacks, snipers, improvised explosive devices (IEDs), car bombs, small arms fire (usually with assault rifles), and RPGs (rocket propelled grenades), as well as sabotage against the petroleum, water, and electrical infrastructure.

Post-invasion Iraq coalition efforts commenced after the fall of Saddam's regime. The coalition nations, together with the United Nations, began to work to establish a stable, compliant democratic state capable of defending itself from non-coalition forces, as well as overcoming internal divisions.

Meanwhile, coalition military forces launched several operations around the Tigris River peninsula and in the Sunni Triangle. A series of similar operations were launched throughout the summer in the Sunni Triangle. Toward the end of 2003, the intensity and pace of insurgent attacks began to increase. A sharp surge in guerrilla attacks ushered in an insurgent effort that was termed the "Ramadan Offensive", as it coincided with the beginning of the Muslim holy month of Ramadan.

To counter this offensive, coalition forces begin to use air power and artillery again for the first time since the end of the invasion by striking suspected ambush sites and mortar launching positions. Surveillance of major routes, patrols, and raids on suspected insurgents were stepped up. In addition, two villages, including Saddam's birthplace of al-Auja and the small town of Abu Hishma were surrounded by barbed wire and carefully monitored.

Coalition Provisional Authority and the Iraq Survey Group

Shortly after the invasion, which has resulted in the debellatio of Iraq, the multinational coalition created the Coalition Provisional Authority (CPA; Arabic: ÓáØÉ ÇáÇÆÊáÇÝ ÇáãæÄÞÊÉ), based in the Green Zone, as a transitional government of Iraq until the establishment of a democratic government. Citing United Nations Security Council Resolution 1483 (22 May 2003) and the laws of war, the CPA vested itself with executive, legislative, and judicial authority over the Iraqi government from the period of the CPA's inception on 21 April 2003, until its dissolution on 28 June 2004.

The CPA was originally headed by Jay Garner, a former US military officer, but his appointment lasted only until 11 May 2003, when President Bush appointed L. Paul Bremer. Bremer served until the CPA's dissolution in July 2004.

Another group created by the multinational force in Iraq post-invasion was the 1,400-member international Iraq Survey Group who conducted a fact-finding mission to find Iraqi weapons of mass destruction (WMD) programmes. In 2004 the

ISG's Duelfer Report stated that Iraq did not have a viable WMD program.

Capturing former government leaders

In the summer of 2003, the multinational forces focused on capturing the remaining leaders of the former government. On 22 July, a raid by the U.S. 101st Airborne Division and soldiers from Task Force 20 killed Saddam's sons (Uday and Qusay) along with one of his grandsons. In all, over 300 top leaders of the former government were killed or captured, as well as numerous lesser functionaries and military personnel.

Most significantly, Saddam Hussein himself was captured on 13 December 2003, on a farm near Tikrit in Operation Red Dawn. The operation was conducted by the United States Army's 4th Infantry Division and members of Task Force 121. Intelligence on Saddam's whereabouts came from his family members and former bodyguards. With the capture of Saddam and a drop in the number of insurgent attacks, some concluded the multinational forces were prevailing in the fight against the insurgency. The provisional government began training the new Iraqi security forces intended to police the country, and the United States promised over $20 billion in reconstruction money in the form of credit against Iraq's future oil revenues. Oil revenue was also used for rebuilding schools and for work on the electrical and refining infrastructure.

Shortly after the capture of Saddam, elements left out of the Coalition Provisional Authority began to agitate for elections and the formation of an Iraqi Interim Government. Most prominent among these was the Shia cleric Grand Ayatollah Ali al-Sistani. The Coalition Provisional Authority opposed allowing democratic elections at this time. The insurgents stepped up their activities. The two most turbulent centers were the area around Fallujah and the poor Shia sections of cities from Baghdad (Sadr City) to Basra in the south.

2004: Insurgency expands

The start of 2004 was marked by a relative lull in violence. Insurgent forces reorganised during this time, studying the multinational forces' tactics and planning a renewed offensive. However, violence did increase during the Iraq Spring Fighting of 2004 with foreign fighters from around the Middle East as well as al-Qaeda in Iraq (an affiliated al-Qaeda group), led by Abu Musab al-Zarqawi helping to drive the insurgency.

As the insurgency grew there was a distinct change in targeting from the coalition forces towards the new Iraqi Security Forces, as hundreds of Iraqi civilians and police were killed over the next few months in a series of massive bombings. An organized Sunni insurgency, with deep roots and both nationalist and Islamist motivations, was becoming more powerful throughout Iraq. The Shia Mahdi Army also began launching attacks on coalition targets in an attempt to seize control from Iraqi security forces. The southern and central portions of Iraq were beginning to erupt in urban guerrilla combat as multinational forces attempted to keep control and prepared for a counteroffensive.

The most serious fighting of the war so far began on 31 March 2004, when Iraqi insurgents in Fallujah ambushed a Blackwater USAconvoy led by four U.S. private military contractors who were providing security for food caterersEurest Support Services. The four armed contractors, Scott Helvenston, Jerko Zovko, Wesley Batalona, and Michael Teague, were killed with grenades and small arms fire. Subsequently, their bodies were dragged from their vehicles by local people, beaten, set ablaze, and their burned corpses hung over a bridge crossing the Euphrates. Photos of the event were released tonews agencies worldwide, causing a great deal of indignation and moral outrage in the United States, and prompting an unsuccessful "pacification" of the city: the First Battle of Fallujah in April 2004.

The offensive was resumed in November 2004 in the bloodiest battle of the war so far: the Second Battle of Fallujah, described by the U.S. military as "the heaviest urban combat (that they had been involved in) since the battle of Hue City in Vietnam." During the assault, U.S. forces usedwhite phosphorus as an incendiary weapon against insurgent personnel, attracting controversy. The 46 day battle resulted in a victory for the coalition, with 95 U.S. soldiers killed along with approximately 1,350 insurgents. Fallujah was totally devastated during the fighting, though civilian casualties were low, as they had mostly fled before the battle.

Another major event of that year was the revelation of widespread prisoner abuse at Abu Ghraib which received international media attention in April 2004. First reports of theAbu Ghraib prisoner abuse, as well as graphic pictures showing U.S. military personnel taunting and abusing Iraqi prisoners, came to public attention from a *60 Minutes II* news report (28 April) and a Seymour M. Hersh article in *The New Yorker* (posted online on 30 April.) Military correspondent Thomas Ricks claimed that these revelations dealt a blow to the moral justifications for the occupation in the eyes of many people, especially Iraqis, and was a turning point in the war.

2004 also marked the beginning of Military Transition Teams in Iraq, which were teams of U.S. military advisors assigned directly to New Iraqi Army units.

2005: Elections and transitional government

On 31 January, Iraqis elected the Iraqi Transitional Government in order to draft a permanent constitution. Although some violence and a widespread Sunni boycott marred the event, most of the eligible Kurd and Shia populace participated. On 4 February, Paul Wolfowitzannounced that 15,000 U.S. troops whose tours of duty had been extended in order to provide election security would be pulled out of Iraq by the next month. February to April proved to be relatively peaceful months compared to the carnage of November and January, with insurgent attacks averaging 30 a day from the prior average of 70.

The Battle of Abu Ghraib on 2 April 2005 was an attack on United States forces at Abu Ghraib prison, which consisted of heavy mortar and rocket fire, under which armed insurgents attacked with grenades, small arms, and two vehicle-borne improvised explosive devices (VBIED). The U.S. Military's munitions ran so low that orders to fix bayonets were given in preparation for hand-to-hand fighting. An estimated 80–120 armed insurgents launched a massive coordinated assault on the U.S. military facility and internment camp at Abu Ghraib, Iraq. It was considered to be the largest coordinated assault on a US base since the Vietnam War.

Hopes for a quick end to the insurgency and a withdrawal of US troops were dashed in May, Iraq's bloodiest month since the invasion. Suicide bombers, believed to be mainly disheartened Iraqi Sunni Arabs, Syrians and Saudis, tore through Iraq. Their targets were often Shia gatherings or civilian concentrations of Shias. As a result, over 700 Iraqi civilians died in that month, as well as 79 U.S. soldiers.

The summer of 2005 saw fighting around Baghdad and at Tall Afar in northwestern Iraq as U.S. forces tried to seal off the Syrian border. This led to fighting in the autumn in the small towns of the Euphrates valley between the capital and that border.

A referendum was held on 15 October in which the new Iraqi constitution was ratified. An Iraqi national assembly was elected in December, with participation from the Sunnis as well as the Kurds and Shia.

Insurgent attacks increased in 2005 with 34,131 recorded incidents, compared to a total 26,496 for the previous year.

2006: Civil war and permanent Iraqi government

The beginning of 2006 was marked by government creation talks, growing sectarian violence, and continuous anti-coalition attacks. Sectarian violence expanded to a new level of intensity following the al-Askari Mosque bombing in the Iraqi city of Samarra, on 22 February 2006. The explosion at the mosque, one of the holiest sites in Shi'a Islam, is believed to have been caused by a bomb planted by al-Qaeda.

Although no injuries occurred in the blast, the mosque was severely damaged and the bombing resulted in violence over the following days. Over 100 dead bodies with bullet holes were found on 23 February, and at least 165 people are thought to have been killed. In the aftermath of this attack the U.S.

military calculated that the average homicide rate in Baghdad tripled from 11 to 33 deaths per day. In 2006 the UN described the environment in Iraq as a "civil war-like situation".

On 6 March, five United States Army soldiers of the 502nd Infantry Regiment, raped the 14-year-old Iraqi girl Abeer Hamza al Janabi, and then murdered her, her father, her mother Fakhriya Taha Muhasen and her six-year-old sister. The soldiers then set fire to the girl's body to conceal evidence of the crime. Four of the soldiers were convicted ofrape and murder and the fifth was convicted of lesser crimes for the involvement in the war crime, that became known as the Mahmudiyah killings.

On 6 June 2006, the United States was successful in tracking Abu Musab al-Zarqawi, the leader of al-Qaeda in Iraq who was killed in a targeted killing, while attending a meeting in an isolated safehouse approximately 8 km (5.0 mi) north of Baqubah. Having been tracked by a British UAV, radio contact was made between the controller and two United States Air Force F-16C jets which identified the house and at 14:15 GMT, the lead jet dropped two 500 pound (230 kg) guided bombs, a laser-guided GBU 12 and GPS-guided GBU 38 on the building where he was located at. Six others—three male and three female individuals—were also reported killed. Among those killed were one of his wives and their child.

The current government of Iraq took office on 20 May 2006, following approval by the members of the Iraqi National Assembly. This followed the general election in December 2005. The government succeeded the Iraqi Transitional Government which had continued in office in a caretaker capacity until the formation of the permanent government.

Iraq Study Group report and Saddam's execution

The Iraq Study Group Report was released on 6 December 2006. Iraq Study Group, made up of people from both of the major U.S. parties, was led by co-chairs James Baker, a former Secretary of State (Republican), and Lee H. Hamilton, a former U.S. Representative (Democrat). It concluded that "the situation in Iraq is grave and deteriorating" and "U.S. forces seem to be caught in a mission that has no foreseeable end." The report's

79 recommendations include increasing diplomatic measures with Iran and Syria and intensifying efforts to train Iraqi troops. On 18 December, a Pentagon report found that insurgent attacks were averaging about 960 attacks per week, the highest since the reports had begun in 2005.

Coalition forces formally transferred control of a province to the Iraqi government, the first since the war. Military prosecutors charged eight U.S. Marines with the murders of 24 Iraqi civilians in Haditha in November 2005, 10 of them women and children. Four officers were also charged with dereliction of duty in relation to the event.

Saddam Hussein was hanged on 30 December 2006, after being found guilty of crimes against humanity by an Iraqi court after a year-long trial.

2007: U.S. troops surge

In a 10 January 2007, televised address to the US public, Bush proposed 21,500 more troops for Iraq, a job program for Iraqis, more reconstruction proposals, and $1.2 billion for these programs. On 23 January 2007, in the 2007 State of the Union Address, Bush announced "deploying reinforcements of more than 20,000 additional soldiers and Marines to Iraq".

On 10 February 2007, David Petraeus was made commander of Multi-National Force – Iraq (MNF-I), the four-star post that oversees all coalition forces in country, replacing General George Casey. In his new position, Petraeus oversaw all coalition forces in Iraq and employed them in the new "Surge" strategy outlined by the Bush administration. 2007 also saw a sharp increase in insurgent chlorine bombings.

On 10 May 2007, 144 Iraqi Parliamentary lawmakers signed onto a legislative petition calling on the United States to set a timetable for withdrawal. On 3 June 2007, the Iraqi Parliament voted 85 to 59 to require the Iraqi government to consult with Parliament before requesting additional extensions of the UN Security Council Mandate for Coalition operations in Iraq. Despite this, the mandate was renewed on 18 December 2007, without the approval of the Iraqi parliament.

Pressures on US troops were compounded by the continuing withdrawal of coalition forces. In early 2007, British Prime Minister Blair announced that following Operation Sinbad British troops would begin to withdraw from Basra Governorate, handing security over to the Iraqis. In July Danish Prime Minister Anders Fogh Rasmussen also announced the withdrawal of 441 Danish troops from Iraq, leaving only a unit of nine soldiers manning four observational helicopters.

Planned troop reduction

In a speech made to Congress on 10 September 2007, Petraeus "envisioned the withdrawal of roughly 30,000 U.S. troops by next summer, beginning with a Marine contingent [in September]." On 14 September, Bush backed a limited withdrawal of troops from Iraq. Bush said 5,700 personnel would be home by Christmas 2007, and expected thousands more to return by July 2008. The plan would take troop numbers back to their level before the surge at the beginning of 2007.

Effects of the surge on security

By March 2008, violence in Iraq was reported curtailed by 40–80%, according to a Pentagon report. Independent reports raised questions about those assessments. An Iraqi military spokesman claimed that civilian deaths since the start of the troop surge plan were 265 in Baghdad, down from 1,440 in the four previous weeks. The *New York Times* counted more than 450 Iraqi civilians killed during the same 28 day period, based on initial daily reports from Iraqi Interior Ministry and hospital officials.

Historically, the daily counts tallied by the *New York Times* have underestimated the total death toll by 50% or more when compared to studies by the United Nations, which rely upon figures from the Iraqi Health Ministry and morgue figures.

The rate of U.S. combat deaths in Baghdad nearly doubled to 3.14 per day in the first seven weeks of the "surge" in security activity, compared to previous period. Across the rest of Iraq it decreased slightly.

On 14 August 2007, the deadliest single attack of the whole war occurred. Nearly 800 civilians were killed by a series of coordinated suicide bomb attacks on the northern Iraqi settlement of Kahtaniya. More than 100 homes and shops were destroyed in the blasts. U.S. officials blamed al Qaeda. The targeted villagers belonged to the non-Muslim Yazidi ethnic minority. The attack may have represented the latest in a feud that erupted earlier that year when members of the Yazidi community stoned to death a teenage girl called Du'a Khalil Aswad accused of dating a Sunni Arab man and converting to Islam. The killing of the girl was recorded on camera-mobiles and the video was uploaded onto the internet.

On 13 September 2007, Abdul Sattar Abu Risha was killed in a bomb attack in the city of Ramadi. He was an important U.S. ally because he led the "Anbar Awakening", an alliance of Sunni Arab tribes that opposed al-Qaeda. The latter organisation claimed responsibility for the attack. A statement posted on the Internet by the shadowy Islamic State of Iraq called Abu Risha "one of the dogs of Bush" and described Thursday's killing as a "heroic operation that took over a month to prepare".

There was a reported trend of decreasing U.S. troop deaths after May 2007, and violence against coalition troops had fallen to the "lowest levels since the first year of the American invasion". These, and several other positive developments, were attributed to the surge by many analysts.

Data from the Pentagon and other U.S. agencies such as the Government Accountability Office (GAO) found that daily attacks against civilians in Iraq remained "about the same" since February. The GAO also stated that there was no discernible trend in sectarian violence. However, this report ran counter to reports to Congress, which showed a general downward trend in civilian deaths and ethno-sectarian violence since December 2006. By late 2007, as the U.S. troop surge began to wind down, violence in Iraq had begun to decrease from its 2006 highs.

Entire neighborhoods in Baghdad were ethnically cleansed by Shia and Sunni militias and sectarian violence has broken out in every Iraqi city where there is a mixed population. Investigative reporter Bob Woodward cites U.S. government sources according to which the U.S. "surge" was not the primary reason for the drop in violence in 2007–2008. Instead, according to that view, the reduction of violence was due to newer covert techniques by U.S. military and intelligence officials to find, target and kill insurgents, including working closely with former insurgents.

In the Shia region near Basra, British forces turned over security for the region to Iraqi Security Forces. Basra is the ninth province of Iraq's 18 provinces to be returned to local security forces' control since the beginning of the occupation.

Political developments

More than half of the members of Iraq's parliament rejected the continuing occupation of their country for the first time. 144 of the 275 lawmakers signed onto a legislative petition that would require the Iraqi government to seek approval from Parliament before it requests an extension of the UN mandate for foreign forces to be in Iraq, which expires at the end of 2008. It also calls for a timetable for troop withdrawal and a freeze on the size of foreign forces. The UN Security Council mandate for U.S. led forces in Iraq will terminate "if requested by the government of Iraq." Under Iraqi law, the speaker must present a resolution called for by a majority of lawmakers. 59% of those polled in the U.S. support a timetable for withdrawal.

In mid-2007, the Coalition began a controversial program to recruit Iraqi Sunnis (often former insurgents) for the formation of "Guardian" militias. These Guardian militias are intended to support and secure various Sunni neighborhoods against the Islamists.

Tensions with Iran

In 2007, tensions increased greatly between Iran and Iraqi Kurdistan due to the latter's giving sanctuary to the militant Kurdish secessionist group Party for a Free Life in Kurdistan (PEJAK.) According to reports, Iran had been shelling PEJAK positions in Iraqi Kurdistan since 16 August. These tensions further increased with an alleged border incursion on 23 August by Iranian troops who attacked several Kurdish villages killing an unknown number of civilians and militants.

Coalition forces also began to target alleged Iranian Quds force operatives in Iraq, either arresting or killing suspected members.

The Bush administration and coalition leaders began to publicly state that Iran was supplying weapons, particularly EFP devices, to Iraqi insurgents and militias although to date have failed to provide any proof for these allegations. Further sanctions on Iranian organizations were also announced by the Bush administration in the autumn of 2007. On 21 November 2007, Lieutenant GeneralJames Dubik, who is in charge of training Iraqi security forces, praised Iran for its "contribution to the reduction of violence" in Iraq by upholding its pledge to stop the flow of weapons, explosives and training of extremists in Iraq.

Tensions with Turkey

Border incursions by PKK militants based in Northern Iraq have continued to harass Turkish forces, with casualties on both sides. In the fall of 2007, the Turkish military stated their right to cross the Iraqi Kurdistan border in "hot pursuit" of PKK militants and began shelling Kurdish areas in Iraq and attacking PKK bases in the Mount Cudi region with aircraft. The Turkish parliament approved a resolution permitting the military to pursue the PKK in Iraqi Kurdistan. In November, Turkish gunships attacked parts of northern Iraq in the first such attack by Turkish aircraft since the border tensions escalated. Another series of attacks in mid-December hit PKK targets in the Qandil, Zap, Avashin and Hakurk regions. The latest series of attacks involved at least 50 aircraft and artillery and Kurdish officials reported one civilian killed and two wounded.

Additionally, weapons that were given to Iraqi security forces by the U.S. military are being recovered by authorities in Turkey after being used by PKK in that state.

Blackwater private security controversy

On 17 September 2007, the Iraqi government announced that it was revoking the license of the U.S. security firm Blackwater USA over the firm's involvement in the killing of eight civilians, including a woman and an infant, in a firefight that followed a car bomb explosion near a State Department motorcade.

2008: Civil war continues

Throughout 2008, U.S. officials and independent think tanks began to point to improvements in the security situation, as measured by key statistics. According to the U.S. Defense Department, in December 2008 the "overall level of violence" in the country had dropped 80% since before the surge began in January 2007, and the country's murder rate had dropped to prewar levels. They also pointed out that the casualty figure for U.S. forces in 2008 was 314 against a figure of 904 in 2007.

According to the Brookings Institution, Iraqi civilian fatalities numbered 490 in November 2008 as against 3,500 in January 2007, whereas attacks against the coalition numbered somewhere between 200 and 300 per week in the latter half of 2008, as opposed to a peak of nearly 1,600 in summer 2007. The number of Iraqi security forces killed was under 100 per month in the second half of 2008, from a high of 200 to 300 in summer 2007.

Meanwhile, the proficiency of the Iraqi military increased as it launched a spring offensive against Shia militias which Prime Minister Nouri al-Maliki had previously been criticized for allowing to operate. This began with a March operation against the Mehdi Army in Basra, which led to fighting in Shia areas up and down the country, especially in the Sadr City district of Baghdad. By October, the British officer in charge of Basra said that since the operation the town had become "secure" and had a murder rate comparable to Manchester in England. The U.S. military also said there had been a decrease of about a quarter in the quantity of Iranian-made explosives found in Iraq in 2008, possibly indicating a change in Iranian policy.

Progress in Sunni areas continued after members of the Awakening movement were transferred from U.S. military to Iraqi control. In May, the Iraqi army – backed by coalition support – launched an offensive in Mosul, the last major Iraqi stronghold of al-Qaeda. Despite detaining thousands of individuals, the offensive failed to lead to major long-term security improvements in Mosul. At the end of the year, the city remained a major flashpoint.

In the regional dimension, the ongoing conflict between Turkey and PKK intensified on 21 February, when Turkey launched a ground attack into the Quandeel Mountains of Northern Iraq. In the nine-day-long operation, around 10,000 Turkish troops advanced up to 25 km into Northern Iraq. This was the first substantial ground incursion by Turkish forces since 1995.

Shortly after the incursion began, both the Iraqi cabinet and the Kurdistan regional government condemned Turkey's actions and called for the immediate withdrawal of Turkish troops from the region. Turkish troops withdrew on 29 February. The fate of the Kurds and the future of the ethnically diverse city of Kirkuk remained a contentious issue in Iraqi politics.

U.S. military officials met these trends with cautious optimism as they approached what they described as the "transition" embodied in theU.S.-Iraq Status of Forces Agreement which was negotiated throughout 2008. The commander of the coalition, U.S. GeneralRaymond T. Odierno, noted that "in military terms, transitions are the most dangerous time" in December 2008.

Spring offensives on Shia militias

At the end of March, the Iraqi Army, with Coalition air support, launched an offensive, dubbed "Charge of the Knights", in Basra to secure the area from militias. This was the first major operation where the Iraqi Army did not have direct combat support from conventional coalition ground troops. The offensive was opposed by the Mahdi Army, one of the militias, which controlled much of the region. Fighting quickly spread to other parts of Iraq: including Sadr City, Al Kut, Al Hillah and others. During the fighting Iraqi forces met stiff resistance from militiamen in Basra to the point that the Iraqi military offensive slowed to a crawl, with the high attrition rates finally forcing the Sadrists to the negotiating table.

Following talks with Brig. Gen. Qassem Suleimani, commander of the Qods brigades of Iran's Revolutionary Guard Corps, and the intercession of the Iranian government, on 31 March 2008, al Sadr ordered his followers to ceasefire. The militiamen kept their weapons.

By 12 May 2008, Basra "residents overwhelmingly reported a substantial improvement in their everyday lives" according to the *New York Times*. "Government forces have now taken over Islamic militants' headquarters and halted the death squads and 'vice enforcers' who attacked women, Christians, musicians, alcohol sellers and anyone suspected of collaborating with Westerners", according to the report; however, when asked how long it would take for lawlessness to resume if the Iraqi army left, one resident replied, "one day".

In late April roadside bombings continued to rise from a low in January—from 114 bombings to more than 250, surpassing the May 2007 high.

Congressional testimony

Speaking before the Congress on 8 April 2008, General David Petraeus urged delaying troop withdrawals, saying, "I've repeatedly noted that we haven't turned any corners, we haven't seen any lights at the end of the tunnel," referencing the comments of then President Bush and former Vietnam-era General William Westmoreland. When asked by the Senate if reasonable people could disagree on the way forward, Petraeus said, "We fight for the right of people to have other opinions."

Upon questioning by then Senate committee chair Joe Biden, Ambassador Crocker admitted that Al Qaeda in Iraq was less important than the Al1nQaeda organization led by Osama bin Laden along the Afghan-Pakistani border. Lawmakers from both parties complained that U.S. taxpayers are carrying Iraq's burden as it earns billions of dollars in oil revenues.

Iraqi security forces rearm

Iraq became one of the top current purchasers of U.S. military equipment with their army trading its AK 47assault rifles for the U.S. M 16 and M 4 rifles, among other equipment. In 2008 alone, Iraq accounted for more than $12.5 billion of the $34 billion U.S. weapon sales to foreign countries (not including the potential F-16 fighter planes.).

Iraq sought 36 F 16s, the most sophisticated weapons system Iraq has attempted to purchase. The Pentagon notified Congress that it had approved the sale of 24 American attack helicopters to Iraq, valued at as much as $2.4 billion. Including the helicopters, Iraq announced plans to purchase at least $10 billion in U.S. tanks and armored vehicles, transport planes and other battlefield equipment and services. Over the summer, the Defense Department announced that the Iraqi government wanted to order more than 400 armored vehicles and other equipment worth up to $3 billion, and six C-130J transport planes, worth up to $1.5 billion. From 2005 to 2008, the United States had completed approximately $20 billion in arms sales agreements with Iraq.

Status of forces agreement

The U.S.-Iraq Status of Forces Agreement was approved by the Iraqi government on 4 December 2008. It establishes that U.S. combat forces will withdraw from Iraqi cities by 30 June 2009, and that all U.S. forces will be completely out of Iraq by 31 December 2011. The pact is subject to possible negotiations which could delay withdrawal and a referendum scheduled for mid-2009 in Iraq which may require all U.S. forces to completely leave by the middle of 2010. The pact requires criminal charges for holding prisoners over 24 hours, and requires a warrant for searches of homes and buildings that are not related to combat.

U.S. contractors working for U.S. forces will be subject to Iraqi criminal law, while contractors working for the State Department and other U.S. agencies may retain their immunity. If U.S. forces commit still undecided "major premeditated felonies" while off-duty and off-base, they will be subject to the still undecided procedures laid out by a joint U.S. Iraq committee if the United States certifies the forces were off-duty.

Some Americans have discussed "loopholes" and some Iraqis have said they believe parts of the pact remain a "mystery". U.S. Secretary of Defense Robert Gates has predicted that after 2011 he would expect to see "perhaps several tens of thousands of American troops" as part of a residual force in Iraq.

Several groups of Iraqis protested the passing of the SOFA accord as prolonging and legitimizing the occupation. Tens of thousands of Iraqis burned an effigy ofGeorge W. Bush in a central Baghdad square where U.S. troops five years previously organized a tearing down of a statue of Saddam Hussein. Some Iraqis expressed skeptical optimism that the U.S. would completely end its presence by 2011. On 4 December 2008, Iraq's presidential council approved the security pact.

A representative of Grand Ayatollah Ali Husseini al Sistani's expressed concern with the ratified version of the pact and noted that the government of Iraq has no authority to control the transfer of occupier forces into and out of Iraq, no control of shipments, and that the pact grants the occupiers immunity from prosecution in Iraqi courts. He said that Iraqi rule in the country is not complete while the occupiers are present, but that ultimately the Iraqi people would judge the pact in a referendum. Thousands of Iraqi have gathered weekly after Friday prayers and shouted anti U.S. and anti-Israeli slogans protesting the security pact between Baghdad and Washington. A protester said that despite the approval of the Interim Security pact, the Iraqi people would break it in a referendum next year.

2009: Coalition redeployment

On 1 January 2009, the United States handed control of the Green Zone and Saddam Hussein's presidential palace to the Iraqi government in a ceremonial move described by the country's prime minister as a restoration of Iraq's sovereignty. Iraqi Prime Minister Nouri al-Maliki said he would propose 1

January be declared national "Sovereignty Day". "This palace is the symbol of Iraqi sovereignty and by restoring it, a real message is directed to all Iraqi people that Iraqi sovereignty has returned to its natural status", al Maliki said.

The U.S. military attributed a decline in reported civilians deaths to several factors including the U.S. led "troop surge", the growth of U.S.-fundedAwakening Councils, and Shiite cleric Muqtada al-Sadr's call for his militia to abide by a cease fire.

Provincial elections

On 31 January, Iraq held provincial elections. Provincial candidates and those close to them faced some political assassinations and attempted assassinations, and there was also some other violence related to the election.

Iraqi voter turnout failed to meet the original expectations which were set and was the lowest on record in Iraq, but U.S. Ambassador Ryan Crocker characterized the turnout as "large". Of those who turned out to vote, some groups complained of disenfranchisement and fraud. After the post-election curfew was lifted, some groups made threats about what would happen if they were unhappy with the results.

Exit strategy announcement

On 27 February, United States President Barack Obama gave a speech at Marine Corps Base Camp Lejeune in the US state of North Carolina announcing that the US combat mission in Iraq would end by 31 August 2010. A "transitional force" of up to 50,000 troops tasked with training the Iraqi Security Forces, conducting counterterrorism operations, and providing general support may remain until the end of 2011, the president added.

The day before Obama's speech, Prime Minister of Iraq Nuri al Maliki said at a press conference that the government of Iraq had "no worries" over the impending departure of U.S. forces and expressed confidence in the ability of the Iraqi Security Forces and police to maintain order without American military support.

Sixth anniversary protests

On 9 April, the 6th anniversary of Baghdad's fall to coalition forces, tens of thousands of Iraqis thronged Baghdad to mark the anniversary and demand the immediate departure of coalition forces.

The crowds of Iraqis stretched from the Sadr City slum in northeast Baghdad to the square around 5 km (3.1 mi) away, where protesters burned an effigy featuring the face of U.S. President George W. Bush. There were also Sunni Muslims in the crowd. Police said many Sunnis, including prominent leaders such as a founding sheikh from the Sons of Iraq, took part.

Coalition forces withdraw

On 30 April, the United Kingdom formally ended combat operations. Prime Minister Gordon Brown characterized the operation in Iraq as a "success story" because of UK troops' efforts. Britain handed control of Basra to the United States Armed Forces.

On 28 July, Australia withdrew its combat forces as the Australian military presence in Iraq ended, per an agreement with the Iraqi government.

The withdrawal of U.S. forces began at the end of June, with 38 bases to be handed over to Iraqi forces. On 29 June 2009, U.S. forces withdrew from Baghdad. On 30 November 2009, Iraqi Interior Ministry officials reported that the civilian death toll in Iraq fell to its lowest level in November since the 2003 invasion.

Iraq awards oil contracts

On 30 June and again on 11 December, the Iraqi ministry of oil awarded contracts to international oil companies for some of Iraq's many oil fields. The winning oil companies enter joint ventures with the Iraqi ministry of oil, and the terms of the awarded contracts include extraction of oil for a fixed fee of approximately $1.40 per barrel. The fees will only be paid once a production threshold set by the Iraqi ministry of oil is reached.

2010: U.S. drawdown and Operation New Dawn

On 17 February 2010, U.S. Secretary of Defense Robert Gates announced that as of 1 September, the name "Operation Iraqi Freedom" would be replaced by "Operation New Dawn".

On 18 April, US and Iraqi forces killed Abu Ayyub al-Masri the leader of al-Qaeda in Iraq in a joint American and Iraqi operation near Tikrit,Iraq.

The coalition forces believed al-Masri to be wearing a suicide vest and proceeded cautiously. After the lengthy exchange of fire and bombing of the house, the Iraqi troops stormed inside and found two women still alive, one of whom was al-Masri's wife, and four dead men, identified as al-Masri, Abu Abdullah al-Rashid al-Baghdadi, an assistant to al-Masri, and al-Baghdadi's son.

A suicide vest was indeed found on al-Masri's corpse, as the Iraqi Army subsequently stated. Iraqi Prime Minister Nouri al-Maliki announced the killings of Abu Omar al-Baghdadi and Abu Ayyub al-Masri at a news conference in Baghdad and showed reporters photographs of their bloody corpses. "The attack was carried out by ground forces which surrounded the house, and also through the use of missiles," Mr Maliki said. "During the operation computers were seized with e-mails and messages to the two biggest terrorists, Osama bin Laden and [his deputy] Ayman al-Zawahiri", Maliki added. U.S. forces commander Gen. Raymond Odierno praised the operation. "The death of these terrorists is potentially the most significant blow to al Qaeda in Iraq since the beginning of the insurgency", he said. "There is still work to do but this is a significant step forward in ridding Iraq of terrorists."

U.S. Vice President Joe Biden stated that the deaths of the top two al Qaeda figures in Iraq are "potentially devastating" blows to the terror network there and proof that Iraqi security forces are gaining ground.

On 20 June, Iraq's Central Bank was bombed in an attack that left 15 people dead and brought much of downtown Baghdad to a standstill. The attack was claimed to have been carried out by the Islamic State of Iraq. This attack was followed by another attack on Iraq's Bank of Trade building that killed 26 and wounded 52 people.

In late August 2010, insurgents conducted a major attack with at least 12 car bombs simultaneously detonating from Mosul to Basra and killing at least 51. These attacks coincided with the U.S. plans for a withdrawal of combat troops.

From the end of August 2010, the United States attempted to dramatically cut its combat role in Iraq, with the withdrawal of all US ground forces designated for active combat operations. The last US combat brigades departed Iraq in the early morning of 19 August. Convoys of US troops had been moving out of Iraq to Kuwait for several days, and NBC News broadcast live from Iraq as the last convoy crossed the border. While all combat brigades left the country, an additional 50,000 personnel (including Advise and Assist Brigades) remained in the country to provide support for the Iraqi military. These troops are required to leave Iraq by 31 December 2011 under anagreement between the US and Iraqi governments.

The desire to step back from an active counter-insurgency role did not however mean that the Advise and Assist Brigades and other remaining US forces would not be caught up in combat. A standards memo from the Associated Press reiterated "combat in Iraq is not over, and we should not uncritically repeat suggestions that it is, even if they come from senior officials".

State Department spokesman P. J. Crowley stated "...we are not ending our work in Iraq, We have a long-term commitment to Iraq." On 31 August, Obama announced the end of Operation Iraqi Freedom from the Oval Office. In his address, he covered the role of the United States' soft power, the effect the war had on the United States economy, and the legacy of American wars.

On the same day in Iraq, at a ceremony at one of Saddam Hussein's former residences at Al Faw Palace in Baghdad, a number of US dignitaries spoke in a ceremony for television cameras, avoiding overtones of the triumphalism present in US announcements made earlier in the war. Vice President Joe

Biden expressed concerns regarding the ongoing lack of progress in forming a new Iraqi government, saying of the Iraqi people that "they expect a government that reflects the results of the votes they cast". Gen. Ray Odierno stated that the new era "in no way signals the end of our commitment to the people of Iraq". Speaking in Ramadi earlier in the day, Gates said that U.S. forces "have accomplished something really quite extraordinary here, [but] how it all weighs in the balance over time I think remains to be seen". When asked by reporters if the seven-year war was worth doing, Gates commented that "It really requires a historian's perspective in terms of what happens here in the long run". He noted the Iraq War "will always be clouded by how it began" in regards Saddam Hussein's supposed weapons of mass destruction, which were never confirmed to have existed. Gates continued, "This is one of the reasons that this war remains so controversial at home". On the same day Gen. Ray Odierno was replaced by Lloyd Austin as Commander of US forces in Iraq.

On 7 September, two US troops were killed and nine wounded in an incident at an Iraqi military base. The incident is under investigation by Iraqi and US forces, but it is believed that an Iraqi soldier opened fire on US forces.

On 8 September, the U.S. Army announced the arrival in Iraq of the first specifically-designated Advise and Assist Brigade, the 3d Armored Cavalry Regiment. It was announced that the unit would assume responsibilities in five southern provinces. From 10–13 September, Second Advise and Assist Brigade, 25th Infantry Division fought Iraqi insurgents near Diyala.

According to reports from Iraq, hundreds of members of the Sunni Awakening Councils may have switched allegiance back to the Iraqi insurgency or al Qaeda.

Wikileaks disclosed 391,832 classified U.S. military documents on the Iraq War. Approximately, 58 people were killed with another 40 wounded in an attack on the Sayidat al Nejat church, a Chaldean Catholic church in Baghdad. Responsibility for the attack was claimed by the Islamic State in Iraq organization.

Coordinated attacks in primarily Shia areas struck throughout Baghdad on 2 November, killing approximately 113 and wounding 250 with around 17 bombs.

Iraqi security forces transition towards self reliance

Preparing to buy $13 billion worth of American arms, the Iraq Defense Ministry intends to transform the country's degraded conventional forces into a state-of-the-art military and become among the world's biggest customers for American military arms and equipment. Part of the planned purchase includes 140 M1 Abrams main battle tanks. Iraqi crews have already begun training on them. In addition to the $13 billion purchase, the Iraqis have requested 18 F-16 Fighting Falcons as part of a $4.2 billion program that also includes aircraft training and maintenance, AIM 9 Sidewinder air-to-air missiles, laser-guided bombs and reconnaissance equipment. If approved by Congress, the first aircraft could arrive in spring 2013. Under the plan, the first 10 pilots would be trained in the United States. The Iraqi navy also inaugurated U.S. built Swift Class patrol boat at Umm Qasr, Iraq's main port at the northern end of the gulf. Iraq is to take delivery of 14 more of these $20 million, 50 foot craft before U.S. forces depart. The high-speed vessels' main mission will be to protect the oil terminals at al Basra and Khor al-Amiya through which some 1.7 million barrels a day are loaded into tankers for export. Two U.S. built offshore support vessels, each costing $70 million, were expected to be delivered in 2011.

The United States Department of Defense had issued notification of an additional $100 million proposed sales of arms from the US to Iraq. General Dynamics is to be the prime contractor on a $36 million deal for the supply of ammunition for Iraq's Abrams M1 A1 tanks. The sale consists of: 14,010 TP-T M831A1 120mm Cartridges; 16,110 TPCSDS-T M865 120mm Cartridges; and 3,510 HEAT-MP-T M830A1 120mm Cartridges. Raytheon is proposed as the prime contractor for a $68 million package of "Command, Control, Communications, Computers, Intelligence, Surveillance and Reconnaissance (C4ISR) Systems".

UN lifts restrictions on Iraq

In a move to legitimize the existing Iraqi government, the United Nations lifted the Saddam Hussein-era UN restrictions on Iraq. These included allowing Iraq to have a civilian nuclear program, permitting the participation of Iraq in international nuclear and chemical weapons treaties, as well as returning control of Iraq's oil and gas revenue to the government and ending the Oil-for-Food Programme.

2011: U.S. withdrawal

Muqtada al-Sadr returned to Iraq in the holy city of Najaf to lead the Sadrist movement after being in exile since 2007.

On 15 January 2011, three U.S. troops were killed in Iraq. One of the troops was killed on a military operation in central Iraq, while the other two troops were deliberately shot by one or two Iraqi soldiers during a training exercise.

On 6 June, five U.S. troops were killed in an apparent rocket attack on Camp Victory, located near Baghdad International Airport. A sixth soldier, who was wounded in the attack, died 10 days later of his wounds.

On 29 June, three U.S. troops were killed in a rocket attack on a U.S. base located near the border with Iran. It was speculated that the militant group responsible for the attack was the same one which attacked Camp Victory just over three weeks before. With the three deaths, June 2011, became the bloodiest month in Iraq for the U.S. military since June 2009, with 15 U.S. soldiers killed, only one of them outside combat.

In September, Iraq signed a contract to buy 18 Lockheed Martin F-16 warplanes, becoming the 26th nation to operate the F-16. Because of windfall profits from oil, the Iraqi government is planning to double this originally planned 18, to 36 F-16s. Iraq is relying on the U.S. military for air support as it rebuilds its forces and battles a stubborn Islamist insurgency.

With the collapse of the discussions about extending the stay of any U.S. troops beyond 2011, where they would not be granted any immunity from the Iraqi government, on 21 October

2011, President Obama announced at a White House press conference that all remaining U.S. troops and trainers would leave Iraq by the end of the year as previously scheduled, bringing the U.S. mission in Iraq to an end. The last American soldier to die in Iraq before the withdrawal was killed by a roadside bomb in Baghdad on 14 November.

In November 2011, the U.S. Senate voted down a resolution to formally end the war by bringing its authorization by Congress to an end.

The last U.S. troops withdrew from Iraq on 18 December, although the US embassy and consulates continues to maintain a staff of more than 20,000 including US Marine Embassy Guards and between 4,000 and 5,000 private military contractors. The next day, Iraqi officials issued an arrest warrant for the Sunni Vice-President Tareq Al-Hashemi. He has been accused of involvement in assassinations and fled to the Kurdish part of Iraq.

Post U.S. withdrawal

Despite the elimination of a repressive single-party cult of personality state, the invasion and occupation led to sectarian violence which caused widespread displacement among Iraqi civilians. The Iraqi Red Crescent organization estimated the total internal displacement was around 2.3 million in 2008, and as many as 2 million Iraqis leaving the country. Poverty led many Iraqi women to turn to prostitution to support themselves and their families, attracting sex tourists from regional lands. The invasion led to a constitution which supported democracy as long as laws did not violate traditional Islamic principles, and a parliamentary election was held in 2005. In addition the invasion preserved the autonomy of the Kurdish region, and stability brought new economic prosperity. Because the Kurdish region is historically the most democratic area of Iraq, many Iraqi refugees from other territories fled into the Kurdish land.

Iraqi insurgency surged in the aftermath of the U.S. withdrawal. The terror campaigns have since been engaged by Iraqi, primarily radical Sunni, insurgent groups against the central government and the warfare between various factions within Iraq. The events of post U.S. withdrawal violence succeeded the previous insurgency in Iraq (prior to 18 December 2011), but have showed different patterns, raising concerns that the surging violence might slide into another civil war. Some 1,000 people were killed across Iraq within the first two months after U.S. withdrawal.

Sectarian violence continued in the first half of 2013— at least 56 people died in April when a Sunni protest in Hawija was interrupted by a government-supported helicopter raid and a series of violent incidents occurred in May. On 20 May 2013, at least 95 people died in a wave of car bomb attacks that was preceded by a car bombing on May 15 that led to 33 deaths; also, on May 18, 76 people were killed in the Sunni areas of Baghdad. Some experts have stated that Iraq could return to the brutal sectarian conflict of 2006.

On 22 July 2013, at least five hundred convicts, most of whom were senior members of al-Qaida who had received death sentences, broke out of Iraq's Abu Ghraib jail when comrades launched a military-style assault to free them. The attack began when a suicide bomber drove a car packed with explosives into prison gates. James F. Jeffrey, the United States ambassador in Baghdad when the last American troops exited, said the assault and resulting escape "will provide seasoned leadership and a morale boost to Al Qaeda and its allies in both Iraq and Syria... it is likely to have an electrifying impact on the Sunni population in Iraq, which has been sitting on the fence."

By mid-2014 the country was in chaos with a new government yet to be formed following national elections, and the insurgency reaching new heights. In early June 2014 theIslamic State in Iraq and the Levant (ISIS) took over the cities of Mosul and Tikrit and said it was ready to march on Baghdad, while Iraqi Kurdish forces took control of key military installations in the major oil city of Kirkuk. Prime Minister Nouri al-Maliki asked his parliament to declare a state of emergency that would give him increased powers, but the lawmakers refused.

CASUALTY ESTIMATES

For coalition death totals see the infobox at the top right. See also Casualties of the Iraq War, which has casualty numbers for coalition nations, contractors, non-Iraqi civilians, journalists, media helpers, aid workers, and the wounded. Casualty figures, especially Iraqi ones, are highly disputed.

CRITICISM AND COST

The Bush Administration's rationale for the Iraq War has faced heavy criticism from an array of popular and official sources both inside and outside the United States, with many U.S. citizens finding many parallels with the Vietnam War. For example a former CIA officer who described the Office of Special Plans as a group of ideologues who were dangerous to U.S. national security and a threat to world peace, and that the group lied and manipulated intelligence to further its agenda of removing Saddam. The Center for Public Integrityalleges that the Bush administration made a total of 935 false statements between 2001 and 2003 about Iraq's alleged threat to the United States.

Both proponents and opponents of the invasion have also criticized the prosecution of the war effort along a number of other lines. Most significantly, critics have assailed the United States and its allies for not devoting enough troops to the mission, not adequately planning for post-invasion Iraq, and for permitting and perpetrating human rights abuses. As the war has progressed, critics have also railed against the high human and financial costs. Criticisms include:

- Legality of the invasion
- Human casualties
- Insufficient post-invasion plans, in particular inadequate troop levels (a RAND Corporation study stated that 500,000 troops would be required for success)
- Financial costs with approximately $612 billion spent as of 4/09 the CBO has estimated the total cost of the war in Iraq to US taxpayers will be around **$1.9** trillion.

- Adverse effect on US-led global "war on terror"
- Damage to U.S.' traditional alliances and influence in the region, especially Israel and Saudi Arabia.
- Endangerment and ethnic cleansing of religious and ethnic minorities by insurgents
- Disruption of Iraqi oil production and related energy security concerns (the price of oil has quadrupled since 2002)

After President Barack Obama was inaugurated in 2009, some anti-war groups decided to stop protesting even though the war was still going on. Some of them decided to stop because they felt they should give the new President time to establish his administration, and others stopped because they believed that Obama would end the war.

Financial cost

The financial cost of the war has been more than £4.55 billion ($9 billion) to the UK, and over $845 billion to the US government. According to Nobel Prize-winning economist Joseph E. Stiglitz and Harvard public finance lecturer Linda J. Bilmes it costs the United States $720 million a day to wage the Iraq war. This number takes into account the long-term health care for veterans, interest on debt and replacement of military hardware.

In March 2013, the total cost of the Iraq War was estimated to have been $1.7 trillion by the Watson Institute of International Studies at Brown University. Critics have argued that the total cost of the war to the US economy is estimated to be from $3 trillion to $6 trillion, including interest rates, by 2053.

A CNN report noted that the United States-led interim government, the Coalition Provisional Authority lasting until 2004 in Iraq had lost $8.8 billion in the Development Fund for Iraq. In June 2011, it was reported by CBS News that $6 billion in neatly packaged blocks of $100 bills was air-lifted into Iraq by the George W. Bush administration, which flew it into Baghdad aboard C 130 military cargo planes. In total, the *Times* says $12 billion in cash was flown into Iraq in 21 separate flights by May 2004, all of which has disappeared. An inspector general's report mentioned that "'Severe inefficiencies and poor management' by the Coalition Provisional Authority would leave no guarantee that the money was properly used", said Stuart W. Bowen, Jr., director of the Office of the Special Inspector General for Iraq Reconstruction. "The CPA did not establish or implement sufficient managerial, financial and contractual controls to ensure that funds were used in a transparent manner." Bowen told the Times the missing money may represent "the largest theft of funds in national history."

HUMANITARIAN CRISES

The child Malnutrition rate rose to 28%. Some 60–70% of Iraqi children were reported to be suffering from psychological problems in 2007. Most Iraqis had no access to safe drinking water. A cholera outbreak in northern Iraq was thought to be the result of poor water quality. As many as half of Iraqi doctors left the country between 2003 and 2006. The use of depleted uranium and white phosphorus by the U.S. military has been blamed for birth defects and cancers in the Iraqi city of Fallujah. A study entitled "Birth defects in Iraq and the plausibility of environmental exposure: A review" was completed to review the impact of other war-related environmental factors on birth defects in Iraq.

As of 2011, nearly 3 million Iraqis have been displaced, with 1.3 million within the Iraq and 1.6 million in neighboring countries, mainly Jordan and Syria. More than half of Iraqi Christians have fled to neighboring countries since the start of the war.

The Foreign Policy Association reported that "Perhaps the most perplexing component of the Iraq refugee crisis...has been the inability for the United States to absorb more Iraqis following the 2003 invasion of the country. To date, the United States has granted fewer than 800 Iraqis refugee status, granting just 133 in 2007. By contrast, the United States granted asylum to more than 100,000 Vietnamese refugees during the Vietnam War."

HUMAN RIGHTS ABUSES

Throughout the entire Iraq war, there have been human rights abuses on all sides of the conflict.

Iraqi government

- The use of torture by Iraqi security forces.
- Iraqi police from the Interior Ministry accused of forming Death Squads and committing numerous massacres and tortures of Sunni Arabs and the police collusion with militias in Iraq have compounded the problems.

Coalition forces and private contractors

- Abu Ghraib torture and prisoner abuse
- Haditha killings of 24 civilians (ongoing with some charges dropped)
- White phosphorus use in Iraq
- Gang-rape and murder of a 14-year-old girl and the murder of her family, in Mahmoudiyah
- The torture and killing of prisoner of war, Iraqi Air Force commander, Abed Hamed Mowhoush
- The killing of Baha Mousa
- Mukaradeeb wedding party massacre where 42 civilians were allegedly killed by coalition forces.
- Planting weapons on noncombatant, unarmed Iraqis by three U.S. Marines after killing them. According to a report by *The Nation*, other similar acts have been witnessed by U.S. soldiers. Members of Iraq Veterans Against the War tell similar stories.
- Blackwater Baghdad shootings
- Allegations of beatings, electrocution, mock executions, and sexual assault by British troops were presented to the International Criminal Court(ICC) by Public Interest Lawyers (PIL) and the European Center for Constitutional and Human Rights (ECCHR) on 12 January 2014.

Insurgent groups

- Killing over 12,000 Iraqis from January 2005 to June

2006, according to Iraqi Interior Minister Bayan Jabr, giving the first official count for the victims of bombings, ambushes and other deadly attacks. The insurgents have also conducted numerous suicide attackson the Iraqi civilian population, mostly targeting the majority Shia community. An October 2005 report from Human Rights Watch examines the range of civilian attacks and their purported justification.

- Attacks against civilians including children through bombing of market places and other locations reachable by suicide bombers.
- Attacks against civilians by sectarian death squads primarily during the Iraqi Civil war.
- Attacks on diplomats and diplomatic facilities including; the bombing of the UN headquarters in Baghdad in August 2003 killing the top UN representative in Iraq and 21 other UN staff members; beheading several diplomats: two Algerian diplomatic envoys Ali Belaroussi and Azzedine Belkadi, Egyptian diplomatic envoy al-Sherif, and four Russian diplomats.
- The February 2006 bombing of the al-Askari Mosque, destroying one of the holiest Shiite shrines, killing over 165 worshipers and igniting sectarian strife and reprisal killings.
- The publicised killing of several contractors; Eugene Armstrong, Jack Hensley, Kenneth Bigley, Ivaylo Kepov and Georgi Lazov (Bulgarian truck drivers.) Other non-military personnel murdered include: translator Kim Sun-il, Shosei Koda, Fabrizio Quattrocchi (Italian), charity worker Margaret Hassan, reconstruction engineer Nick Berg, photographer Salvatore Santoro (Italian) and supply worker Seif Adnan Kanaan (Iraqi.) Four private armed contractors, Scott Helvenston, Jerko Zovko, Wesley Batalona and Michael Teague, were killed with grenades and small arms fire, their bodies dragged from their vehicles, beaten and set ablaze. Their burned corpses were then dragged through the streets before

being hung over a bridge crossing the Euphrates.

- Torture or killing of members of the New Iraqi Army, and assassination of civilians associated with the Coalition Provisional Authority, such as Fern Holland, or the Iraqi Governing Council, such as Aqila al-Hashimi and Ezzedine Salim, or other foreign civilians, such as those from Kenya.

PUBLIC OPINION ON THE WAR

International opinion

According to a January 2007 BBC World Service poll of more than 26,000 people in 25 countries, 73% of the global population disapproved of U.S. handling of the Iraq War. A September 2007 poll conducted by the BBC found that two-thirds of the world's population believed the U.S. should withdraw its forces from Iraq.

In 2006 it was found that majorities in the UK and Canada believed that the war in Iraq was "unjustified" and – in the UK – were critical of their government's support of U.S. policies in Iraq.

According to polls conducted by the Arab American Institute, four years after the invasion of Iraq, 83% of Egyptians had a negative view of the U.S. role in Iraq; 68% of Saudi Arabians had a negative view; 96% of the Jordanian population had a negative view; 70% of the population of the United Arab Emirates and 76% of the Lebanese population also described their view as negative. The Pew Global Attitudes Project reports that in 2006 majorities in the Netherlands, Germany, Jordan, France, Lebanon, Russia, China,Canada, Poland, Pakistan, Spain, Indonesia, Turkey, and Morocco believed the world was safer before the Iraq War and the toppling of Saddam, while pluralities in the United States and India believe the world is safer without Saddam Hussein.

Iraqi opinion

Directly after the invasion, polling suggested that a slight majority supported the US invasion. Polls conducted between

2005 and 2007 showed 31–37% of Iraqi's wanted US and other Coalition forces to withdraw once security was restored and that 26–35% wanted immediate withdrawal instead. Despite a majority having previously been opposed to the US presence, 60% of Iraqis opposed American troops leaving directly prior to withdrawal, with 51% saying withdrawal would have a negative effect. In 2006 a poll conducted on the Iraqi public revealed that 64% of the ones polled said Iraq was going in the right direction and 77% claimed it was worth ousting Saddam Hussein.

RELATION TO THE GLOBAL WAR ON TERRORISM

Former President George W. Bush consistently referred to the Iraq war as "the central front in the War on Terror", and argued that if the United States pulled out of Iraq, "terrorists will follow us here". While other proponents of the war have regularly echoed this assertion, as the conflict has dragged on, members of the US Congress, the US public, and even US troops have questioned the connection between Iraq and the fight against anti-US terrorism. In particular, a consensus has developed among intelligence experts that the Iraq war has increased terrorism. Counterterrorism expert Rohan Gunaratnafrequently refers to the invasion of Iraq as a "fatal mistake".

London's conservative International Institute for Strategic Studies concluded in 2004 that the occupation of Iraq had become "a potent global recruitment pretext" for mujahideenand that the invasion "galvanised" al-Qaeda and "perversely inspired insurgent violence" there. The US National Intelligence Council concluded in a January 2005 report that the war in Iraq had become a breeding ground for a new generation of terrorists; David Low, the national intelligence officer for transnational threats, indicated that the report concluded that the war in Iraq provided terrorists with "a training ground, a recruitment ground, the opportunity for enhancing technical skills ... There is even, under the best scenario, over time, the likelihood that some of the jihadists who are not killed there will, in a sense, go home, wherever home is, and will therefore disperse to various other countries." The Council's chairman Robert Hutchings said, "At the moment, Iraq is a magnet for international terrorist activity." And the 2006 National Intelligence Estimate, which outlined the considered judgment of all 16 US intelligence agencies, held that "The Iraq conflict has become the 'cause celebre' for jihadists, breeding a deep resentment of U.S. involvement in the Muslim world and cultivating supporters for the global jihadist movement."

9

Japan's Post-Second World War Environmental Problems

JAPAN'S FIRST EXPERIENCE WITH HIGH-LEVEL ECONOMIC DEVELOPMENT

There is nothing worse than war for bringing about the destruction of nature, human beings, factories, housing, and transportation systems, and for causing starvation and sickness, the discharge of untreated factory wastes, and the destruction of farm lands. When environmental destruction is understood in its broadest and most fundamental sense, the original culprit is war.

During the Second World War, as a continuation of the original military intrusion of Japan into China, the Japanese military machine invaded the Philippines, Burma, and many other Asian nations, killing a great many people, burning down houses, and destroying cities and villages over the vast areas where the war was waged. Japan also suffered destruction at the hands of the American military in air raids not only on major cities but also on medium and small-size cities.

In all of this Hiroshima and Nagasaki were instantly demolished by the atomic bombings. Okinawa became a battleground and the area was laid waste. Because of the lack of food, most urban dwellers were undernourished, there was a great rise in the incidence of tuberculosis, and many others suffered from a wide spectrum of diseases. River containment repairs were neglected and the bamboo that was used for bank maintenance was cut down to provide more farmland. As a result the rivers flooded the surrounding areas every time it rained and there was no protection from the destruction wrought in this way. Forty per cent of the railway infrastructure was destroyed and the outer guard rails were not repaired, making the entire system dangerous, even up to the present day.

The first task of the Japanese government, along with the occupation forces from the United States, was recovery from the ravages of war - that is, the restoration of major land areas and the creation of new towns, cities, and villages in land that was to be newly developed.

As a result of the sudden and dramatic rise of Fascism before and during the Second World War, the occupation authorities attempted to make drastic changes in the political and economic conditions which had underpinned Japan's military machine. For example, labour union activities, which had been completely suppressed during the war, were encouraged. Private possession of over three hectares of land was prohibited by decree. Tenants and poor farmers were allowed to take possession of the land that they worked for a very small sum of money and suddenly 4 million small landowning farmers came into being. Labouring people began to demand higher wages and farmers tried to improve agricultural methods through the introduction of more effective technologies and farm chemicals, so as to improve their income and thereby their landholdings. Compared with all pre-Second World War periods, domestic market-related economic conditions were better than they had ever been in any previous period in Japan's history.

From 1930 to the end of the Second World War, 90 per cent of Japan's industrial production capacity was allocated to military purposes. With Japan's defeat in the war, the military machine was destroyed and Japan's peace constitution was promulgated. Therefore, all industries had to produce for civilian markets rather than for military procurement.

Through the extraordinary efforts of the people, houses and shops were built out of the total and wide-ranging destruction. When food, clothing, and other goods became plentiful after the war, a production and marketing system naturally developed, and this led to Japan's high-economic-growth period. After the First World War in the USA and after the Second World War in Europe and Japan, electricity and related appliances became more common and motorization began to change people's everyday lives. Until the end of the 1950s the production of consumer goods such as washing machines, refrigerators, transister radios, television sets, tape-recorders, motor bicycles, cars, and the like increased with great rapidity. Because of the intense competition between companies, there was a great deal of investment in installation to increase the efficiency of mass production systems.

Through the application of mass production methods, the costs of individual consumer products declined, the market expanded with increased demand, and mass production became the norm. The mutual interaction of supply and demand expanded the scale of Japan's economy. This growth in industry brought many young people from the rural areas into the industrial cities of Tokyo, Osaka, and Nagoya. Urbanization continued rapidly in a random manner, and by 1970 44 per cent of the population of Japan was concentrated in these urban centres. By way of contrast, the farming areas, which had experienced an oversupply of labour for a very long time, now faced labour shortages, and this resulted in the rapid mechanization of agriculture.

In the pre-Second World War period most of the factories were located in the urban areas of Tokyo, Yokohama, Nagoya, Osaka, Kobe and Kitakyushu. But with changes in the modes of industrialization in the post-war period, pressure on these areas was such that, in 1962. the government set out an Integrated National Development Plan, designating new areas to be developed as industrial zones. This led to a concentration of industrial activities and population in the Pacific coast belt that starts from the Kanto Plain and runs all the way down to Kitakyushu, passing through the northern rim of the Setonaikai sea. By 1974, the belt area alone accounted for 84.5 per cent of Japan's entire industrial production.

By the late 1960s. labour shortage had become one of the major problems, and automation was extensively introduced in both production as well as administrative branches. By then, motorization of Japan had also substantially progressed. Thus, in a relatively short period of ten years, Japan's industrial modalities, as well as consumer life-styles, underwent major changes.

Along with the increasing distribution of consumer goods, the transportation and communication infrastructures were expanding rapidly. As the number of planned high-rise buildings increased, the demand for iron and steel and other construction and production-related materials also went up.

During the 1960s, Japan's GNP was over 10 per cent, while the growth-rate for European countries was 5 per cent. It is obvious that with this high an economic growth-rate within such a short period, some very difficult social problems were bound to result. Natural resources such as crude oil, iron ore, and high-quality coal were imported and major industries were built very close to human populations, along the Pacific Ocean coast from Tokyo, through Nagoya and on to Osaka. The national development plan was supposed to encourage a more equal distribution of industries throughout the nation, but in fact primary industrial production units were built mainly on the Pacific coastline, concentrated in the clam-producing bay areas of Tokyo, the Ise Peninsula, and along the shores of the Inland Sea.

In the 1970s the production of iron and steel along the shores of the Inland Sea reached 70 million tons, an amount equal to that produced by France and the United Kingdom combined. Daily processing of petroleum reached over 1,600,000 barrels, equal to the production levels of the United Kingdom. Petroleum chemistry brought the production of 1,800,000 tons of ethylene annually, with this also equalling British output. The Inland Sea has an area of about 17,000 square kilometres, which is about the same size as Lake Ontario, the smallest of the five great lakes in the USA. All of this production capacity was concentrated in this area and, in the 1960s, pollution-prevention technologies were very little used; as a result the problems of air and water pollution were serious in the extreme. In the case of Tokyo Bay, an area which is one-tenth the size of the Inland Sea, the production of ethylene from the concentrated petrochemical industries was 1,500,000 tons annually, which is very close to the total production in and around the Inland Sea.

The Japanese people have attempted to recover from the total destruction of war, and in the process have produced a completely different urban and rural environment. But because of a total lack of understanding of the realities of nature on the part of government and industry, a new type of industrially induced environmental destruction has reared its ugly head. In this manner, Japan has come to be known worldwide as the nation with the worst environmental problems.

ENVIRONMENTAL CHARACTERISTICS OF POST-SECOND WORLD WAR JAPAN:-FROM VISIBLE TO INVISIBLE POLLUTION

During the first phase of high economic growth in the 1950s, the greatest environmental pollution problem was caused by dust and other airborne particulate matter. The main source of energy at that time was coal. Dust-collectors and other methods of particulate-matter control were either not provided or not working, and all of the chimneys belched forth black smoke. This situation continued into the next decade, so that by 1961 a major iron and steel complex in Yahata, northern Kyushu, was pouring 27 tons of particulate matter per day into the city's air, and in Kawasaki City, situated in the Tokyo Bay industrial area, the amount was 23 tons. Along with the black smoke there was also a great amount of red smoke that spread over the sky. After the close of the Second World War, production technologies changed and the oxygen blast furnace was introduced. This made it possible to produce a better quality steel, but the reaction by-products included a great deal of particulate iron oxide, which was scattered far and wide. Soon after that the LD oxygen blast furnace was invented in Austria, and this produced even better quality steel by blowing oxygen into the furnace. However, this method also caused the release of a large amount of red smoke and iron oxide particulates, but Japanese industrial applications of the furnace did not include the use of dust-collectors. Because of this the amount of pollution from red smoke particulate matter greatly increased.

Many industrial workers were exposed to the industrial dusts in the atmosphere, and as a result developed various lung disorders. These problems were found most widely among mine workers and those who were involved in tunnel construction. In 1955, the government was forced to devise special protective measures in order to protect the miners from such occupational hazards. In the same year the Tokyo Metropolitan Government issued orders that made it mandatory to control heavy smoke and dust production. This was the first such ordinance related to airborne particulate matter since the end of the Second World War.

In the 1960s, basic energy source changes from coal to heavy oil were instituted. As a result, the heavy smoke of coal combustion was replaced with invisible stack gases, but pollution problems were not thereby solved. Like coal, oil also contains sulphur which, when burned, results in sulphurous acid gases being discharged into the atmosphere. When coal was the main energy source, sulphurous acid gases were also a problem, but with the use of heavy oil in an expanding industrial economy, the problem became very serious.

A one-million-kilowatt, oil-fired, electric-power generation plant uses 1,300,000 tons of heavy oil per year. Since this fuel contains on average 2 per cent natural sulphur, 52,000 tons of sulphurous acid gases are released into the air annually from the power plant. Oil refineries and petrochemical complexes also release great amounts of such gases. The fact that a great many patients developed respiratory diseases in areas where these complexes were located, especially along the Pacific Ocean coastline, became a very great social problem in the 1960s. The Yokkaichi petrochemical complex came into being in 1959 along the coast of Ise Bay, and in just one or two years respiratory diseases in the general population became painfully noticeable. At that time, without knowing the cause of this health problem, people called the ailment the "beach salt disease." In 1953, the central government was obliged to send a research group to the area in order to discover the cause of the problem. A report on the research findings was presented to the National Diet the following year. In spite of the report's existence, the government failed to act with specific policies and countermeasures. The petrochemical complex was expanded in size and output and, in 1965, Yokkaichi City officials were forced to create a medical research team in an attempt to provide countermeasures for a disease problem of epidemic proportions.

Sulphurous acid gases are invisible and take their toll in silence, but black smoke can easily be seen and therefore everybody recognizes it as a health hazard. This fact is symbolic of the characteristics of post-Second World War environmental problems. The effluents from sulphuric-acid-based pulp-processing industries are the same in this regard, that is, they are not directly and immediately apparent as the cause of environmental problems. A rayon-from-pulp textile production facility uses 38 per cent of the raw material by weight for the end-product, but 62 per cent of the post-process pulp is discharged as an effluent into the environment, usually without the application of pollution-prevention measures. If annual production levels reach 100,000 tons, over 160,000 tons of waste are produced. These red and black wastes discharged from the pulp-using production units found their way into natural waterways such as rivers and then into ocean systems. In this manner rivers and ocean estuaries were visibly polluted, and this destroyed fish resources, thereby compromising the viability of the fishing industry. Because of all of this destruction, legislation was enacted in 1958 governing water quality and industrial effluents and containing effluent-discharge regulations.

However, wastes from new technologies developed during the high-economic-growth period were invisible to the naked eye but were very effective in destroying the natural viability of the human environmental support system. These characteristics were most evident in regard to the Minamata disease, even more than with Yokkaichi asthma. Once the Minamata-disease-causing organic mercury is introduced into aquatic environments, it spreads over wide areas and is at the same time concentrated in individual organisms through the interactions involved in the natural food chain. When the food chain reaches the level at which human consumption begins, mercury concentration levels are very high. The actual amount of mercury discharged into natural waterways in this particular case was relatively small, in contrast to the amounts of sulphurous acid gas discharged into the air and the wastes discharged from pulp-processing installations. Mercury was used as a catalyst in the production of acetaldehyde and as such was discharged into the Shiranui Sea along with a number of other wastes.

Further, since there was only one manufacturing facility in Minamata City, the water did not look as bad as that in Tokyo Bay or the Inland Sea. There were still plenty of fish to catch, and by this route organic mercury invaded the bodies of those who made their livelihood from the sea. When they finally became aware of the problem, the damage to their brains and central nervous systems had already gone too far.

The cadmium which caused Itai-itai disease was derived from the effluents of the Kamioka mine on the upper reaches of the Jintsu River this was detected in 1967, but at first the absorption of cadmium into people's bones had produced few or no symptoms. The villagers living along the Jintsu River used the river water for washing vegetables, servicing farm equipment, washing clothes, and for cooking and drinking, because in spite of the cadmium content it looked clean.

In 1968, PCB (polychlorinated biphenyl) poisoning was discovered in an area in and around Kitakyushu. These PCBs were used as a heat-transfer medium in the smell-elimination process used in the production of cooking oils. The PCBs leaked through heat-transfer-pipe pinholes into the rice-derived raw materials used in oil production. In like manner cadmium accumulated in human bones and in the bodies of chicken.

Pollution problems derived from the intrusion of chemical substances into the biosphere are usually beyond solution by the time they cause noticeable health problems. Therefore, when new technologies are introduced, it is essential that environmental impact research be carried out to discover the degree to which various substances compromise the viability of the environment, the human body, and other living organisms. It is also prudent to avoid the use of materials and substances that cannot be proven absolutely safe. The Japanese government acted too late when it halted PCB production and limited the uses of mercury to certain closed-system processes. In other words, corporations, local and national governments, and city administrators lacked the wisdom and understanding necessary to prevent serious environmental problems. During the high-economic-growth period, production efficiency was the primary concern in the uncritical and rapid adaptation of new technologies. This stance resulted in unprecedented damage to natural ecosystems and to human health and well-being.

Another characteristic of Japan's environmental destruction during the post-war period is the concentration in limited land areas of manufacturing plants much larger in scale than similar factories found in Western countries. With this came a very rapid increase in the pressures for urbanization, which resulted both in conglomerate urban concentrations and massive amounts of both industrial and life-sustenance-derived wastes. This brought about further destruction of the natural environment.

Along the coastline of Tokyo Bay, land reclamation has taken place at such a rapid pace that the original coastline is no longer discernible. Twenty per cent of the total Inland Sea coast is occupied by factories and manufacturing conglomerates. With the seacoasts being covered by ever-increasing amounts of concrete in such a short span of time, it is inevitable that the condition of the coastal waters should change for the worse.

In the seaweed-producing areas along the Inland Sea coast, huge amounts of concrete were brought to unprecedentedly large construction projects, resulting in massive destruction of the biosphere. Fish can no longer find areas to lay their eggs. The total ecology of these areas has changed. Sea bream, prawn, and octopus have decreased in number, while sardine and squid, which have greater resistance to pollution, have still remained, but to a lesser extent.

By way of contrast, when land was reclaimed for farming, sea-water was drained and as a result seaweed beds were destroyed. But the damage did not extend beyond the immediate area, and when sand and soil were dumped into the sea, the seaweed was still able to grow back beyond the boundaries of the reclaimed land area. In this case the natural environment was destroyed but the ecological balance was still maintained. However, if a 20-metre deep concrete wall is built for berthing gigantic oil tankers, the sea is no longer able to recover its ecological balance.

From the beginning of the seventeenth century estuaries were gradually built along the shores of the Inland Sea for wharfs and factories, but the speed of land reclamation was not excessively rapid. In these situations, there were some changes in the natural environment but the ecological balance was maintained and fishing was not compromised to such a drastic extent.

It is said that 19,000 hectares of land were reclaimed from the sea for farming purposes during the 300 years of the Tokugawa era, but in the 28 years after the end of the Second World War, 18,000 hectares were reclaimed.

When factories are built on reclaimed land, large amounts of wastes are produced from the industrial activity. and as a result the ecological balance is compromised because of the many effluents being discharged. Not only does the sea close to these industrial areas around the Inland Sea die biologically, but there is no life even in the open sea away from the enlarged manufacturing zones.

With the expansion of industrial areas came environmental destruction, while aggravated urbanization increased even more the seriousness of these environmental problems. Besides the amount of noise produced, and the continuous spewing forth of exhaust gases from the ubiquitous automobile, urbanization also brought with it the production of excessive amounts of garbage. In 1960 the daily per capita garbage wastes produced amounted to 400 grams. By 1970 this had risen to 1 kilogram, and by 1977 it stood at 1.7 kilograms. Most of these discarded materials are made up of supermarket-derived food-packaging materials, cans, and bottles. The great increase in the number of automatic vending machines has also added to the severity of the problem. During the 1970s, Tokyo had to dispose of 16,000 tons of garbage each day. In order that these materials can be disposed of properly, plans are being made to use them for the creation of more reclaimed land.

At the beginning of the 1970s, the highest economic growth period so far in the post-war era came to an abrupt end with the saturation of the consumer market with too many unsold products. Through the negative-feedback circuits created by this incessant economic activity, the environment was saturated with pollutants of every conceivable variety. This degree of destruction has slowed down to some extent, but the recovery of nature has been very, very slow.

Once the health of the human body has been compromised by the polluted environment, it is exceedingly difficult to return bodily functions to normal levels again. The number of government-recognized pollution victims found in the most severely poisoned areas stood at 81,222 persons as of 1980. Among the major pollution-related health problems, 1,893 persons were recognized by the government as victims of Minamata disease, 42 as victims of Itai-itai disease, and 121 as victims of chronic arsenic poisoning. The excessive use of the untested but marketed intestinal antibacterial drug Chinoform caused what came to be well known as SMON (subacute myelo-optico-neuropathy) disease, with the number of patients rising to 11,007. Further, more than 13,000 PCB (polychlorinated biphenyl) victims applied for recognition as pollution-disease patients.

Badly poisoned patients are very easily recognizable by the severe symptoms, but less affected cases are less easily identified as pollution victims. Not only do patients with this disease endure periods of involuntary convulsions, but in everyday life they enjoy no respite from their sufferings. Since pollution victims' symptoms are similar to those seen in other illnesses, it is very difficult to identify pollution poisoning as the cause of many types of pathological problems. Unless doctors are willing to delve into the patient's family situation and working conditions, it is not very likely that they will be able to pin down the cause with any certainty. This is another characteristic of the pollution problems that have come about in Japan's post-war period.

As a result of this, a great number of actual Minamata disease victims have not been designated as such by the government. These people continue to make applications for recognition and designation as pollution victims. Again, there are many other people who are not aware that their health problems are related to a poisoned environment, and therefore do not apply for government designation and financial aid.

At the present time there are twelve atomic-powered generation plants in operation in Japan producing 1,550,000 kilowatts of electricity. However, more than a small amount of radiation is leaking all the time into the biosphere at various points in the nuclear fuel cycle. With the half-lives of these poisons being longer than those of any other materials produced in the history of the human enterprise, and with their ability to linger and concentrate in the biosphere as well as in the human body, there is a very great possibility that radioactive materials in the environment will result in radiation sicknesses, which again will be very difficult to distinguish from ordinary health problems.

Poisonous chemicals used in insecticides are becoming less lethal than those used in the 1960s, but these materials are employed on a nationwide basis. There is a real possibility that these materials are involved in complex chemical reactions within the human body and the biosphere. Also, detergents are used almost universally and daily disposed of in the environment; no one has any way of knowing what detergents mean in the long run for human life. The overuse of many kinds of food additives and of innumerable medicines continues apace. The pollution problems that have been made visible through the suffering of poison victims have, to a certain degree, been controlled through active pressure from citizens' movements and through the belated response of government legislation and administrative guidance, but there is no telling the extent to which invisible pollution will bring about serious problems for future generations.

CITIZEN AND ADMINISTRATIVE RESPONSE TO ENVIRONMENTAL PROBLEMS

Environmental pollution problems in Japan were greatly exacerbated in the post-Second World War period. This came about not only through the irresponsibility of corporate entities and administrative bodies, which together sought greatly increased profits through the overexpansion of production, but also through the citizenry as a whole, which, in its obsession with modern life-styles, had an almost total lack of concern for human rights. In the 1960s it was not difficult for governments and corporations to take land and sea areas from farmers and fishermen. Complaints from this quarter were suppressed by the argument that land and ocean viability had to be sacrificed in the interests of national and community prosperity. In spite of the problems arising from the operation of innumerable factories corporate entities, central governmental bodies, and local administrative units either turned their backs on the problems or refused at first to see the writing on the wall. When the fact of extreme environmental degradation could no longer be ignored, all levels of government were more interested in saving the corporations than in saving the people. As a result, compromises were worked out on the basis of economic and political security, rather than on the basis of human rights. Although corporations and the government pay lip-service to democratic institutions and human relations, the style of thinking has not changed from that which formed the basis for Japan's era of Fascist militarism.

However, even if democracy is only a surface formality in Japan, it can form the basis for human rights struggles originating from the people. In 1951, when the United States of America was experimenting with H-bomb tests in the Pacific, there was greatly increased opposition, nationwide, to the H-bomb and to nuclear destruction.

In the 1960s, with the expansion of industrial output, environmental destruction became greatly exacerbated. The mass media reported on Minamata disease and Yokkaichi asthma, and people organized movements to discover the causes of these various problems and to ensure that compensation was paid. Movements resisted corporations that continued to poison the biosphere by refusing to process their wastes. In 1964, citizens' movements were able to stop the planned construction of large petrochemical complexes in the cities of Mishima and Numazu on the Pacific coast.

By the end of the 1960s, anti-pollution movements had become strong nationwide. The diligent work done by supporters and Minamata disease victims, as well as by the farmers' resistance movement against the construction of Narita Airport, provided a great deal of encouragement to local citizens' movements all over Japan.

Pollution problems became serious political issues. In the 1970s the National Diet passed 149 laws relating to pollution issues such as the Revised Standard Laws on Pollution Policy and the Criminal Codes related to environmental destruction. In 1971, the government's Environmental Agency was formed. People began to have second thoughts about unconditional modernization at the expense of environmental viability.

The high-speed bullet trains in Japan produce a great deal of noise and excessive vibration. People began to ask why faster trains should be considered better than slower trains. Who needs such a train service anyway? The industrial and consumer life-style began to be reappraised from the standpoint of basic human rights.

In 1868, the political changes of the Meiji Restoration, to a limited extent at least, came to fruition through the pressures exerted by farmers on their lower-class feudal lords, but the real political changes were imposed from the top down as a result of pressure from these same lower-class *bushi* samurai warriors. Therefore, citizens' awareness, relative to involvement in the processes of political change, is only a surface phenomenon. In 1945 the period of Japanese imperialism ended with the defeat of Fascist militarism at the end of the Second World War, and democracy was instituted thereafter. However, this democracy was imposed by the occupation forces under the pressure of world opinion, which at that time was very anti-Fascist.

Though there was democratization of labour as well as land reform, concepts pertaining to human rights were still weak and required more time for maturation. During the 1960s, the anti-pollution movements were successful in strengthening these basic concepts of human rights. As seen in the Minamata disease situation, the pollution victims assumed leading roles in the movements instead of waiting for others to take the initiative, and by taking on these leadership positions they were able to greatly influence the people at large.

Strengthened by the support of the citizens' movement, the victims of the four major pollution episodes - the Kumamoto Minamata disease, the Niigata Minamata disease, Itai-itai disease, and Yokkaichi asthma - took their cases to court and through concerted legal action were able to receive compensation for the damage that had been done to them. But even with all this compensation, the pain suffered by the victims did not go away. What was accomplished by all of this was the creation of a greater sense of priority in relation to preventive measures that could preclude such massive destruction in the future. From the 1970s onward, not only was there relative success in terms of winning compensation for the pollution damage, but through the court battles the victims of pollution diseases were able to make some headway in stopping the operations of manufacturing complexes and power plants that were destroying the environment. But such demands require for their implementation a total change of direction in the basic policies and decision-making orientations of industry and government. In this respect it is difficult. indeed almost impossible, to change the course of the economic and political currents of the times. The court battles are still beset with problems.

Nevertheless, the government, which was intent on policies to encourage high rates of economic growth, was forced to make certain policy changes. In 1969, the government announced a new general development plan for the nation, but in the 1970s opposition mounted because it was understood to be only more of the same high economic growth. A complete re-evaluation of the environmental situation was forced upon the government because of the paralysis that was being felt in relation to water, electricity, and garbage in the three major urban centres of the country. Therefore, in 1977, a third general development plan was created with three major emphases - housing, land use and land protection, and a shift to a new kind of economic growth. In the final, "countermeasures" section of this 1977 proposal, one reads that the Japanese economy, which has seen unprecedented growth over the past quarter-century, is now entering a new phase, brought about by changes in both the domestic and international arenas. The multiplicity of viewpoints has led to a great deal of interactional complexity in the planning process. What was now hoped for was a life-support environment that would ensure security, quality, and the possibility of high cultural achievement. Instead of stressing land uses that favour a high-speed information society, the plan calls for living conditions that will enhance individual creativity within the context of peaceful land use. However, in this regard there has been no real change in the attitude of the government administration, which is still preoccupied with a high-economic-growth vision. We are still a very long way from solving the problems of environmental destruction in Japan.

10

The Long-Term Effects of Nuclear War

INTRODUCTION

Most nuclear war fiction can be fairly clearly divided into one of two groups: those depicting a conflict and its immediate consequences, and those set in the more distant future, long after the war has taken place. Thanks to the vigorous tradition of postholocaust adventure stories in science fiction, the latter considerably outnumbers the former. The landscape after an atomic war is transformed in fiction in many strange and surprising ways.

Perhaps the most common attitude which people hold toward nuclear war is that such a conflict would be simply the end of the world in some sense or other. The fascination of secular apocalyptic literature, much of it drawing on traditional religious imagery of Armageddon and the Last Judgment, has been widespread in our century since long before 1945. It is no surprise, then, that works depicting nuclear war should be written from the same perspective. Consider some titles: *Doomsday Eve, Doomsday Clock, Doomsday Wing, After Doomsday, The Day After Doomsday, The Last Day, The Last Days, On the Last Day, The Seventh Day, Deus Irae, Alas, Babylon, A Small Armageddon, The Dark Millenium.* The fact that in none of these works does the world end in any sense comparable to that depicted in the book of Revelation underlines the symbolic nature of this fascination with the apocalyptic theme. Yet, since most of us in our modern secular culture no longer believe in the Last Judgment, and the solar nova which will one day engulf the Earth is too far distant to capture most people's imaginations, nuclear war is the nearest thing we have to Armageddon, if not to the end of the world proper.

But most authors—including some of those who use apocalyptic imagery— are reluctant to imagine even so modest an end as the annihilation of all human life. The apocalypse is often rumored but seldom portrayed. Stories of the collapse of civilization abound, however, and have abounded long before the atomic bomb was developed. In fiction, the new dark age of the post-nuclear war era cannot always be sharply distinguished from similar dark ages whose causes are different or unspecified, as in Walter Van Tilburg Clark's "The Portable Phonograph," Stephen Vincent Benet's "By the Waters of Babylon," or, more recently, John Crowley's *Engine Summer* (1979). Clark's story first appeared in 1942 and Benet's in 1937, but many contemporary readers automatically interpret them as being set in worlds devastated by nuclear war. So pervasive is the notion that atomic Armageddon is our destiny that any book portraying a societal collapse is liable to be interpreted as a post-nuclear holocaust novel, as happened, for instance, in the case of Ursula Le Guin's 1985 novel, *Always Coming Home.* Le Guin strenuously refuted the claims of reviewers to see a nuclear war in the background of the work. On occasion, even the jacket copy of a book will signal a nuclear war whereas the text contains no such thing (e.g., Paul MacTyre, *Midge* [1962]).

Even when nuclear war clearly provides the background of a narrative, it is liable to be more or less optimistic. This is well illustrated by the fact that the vast majority of stories and novels concentrate on the survivors, not on the victims. Those few writers who have dared to suppose that nuclear bombs might literally destroy human life imagine a variety of mechanisms leading to doomsday, one of which is the sterilization of the species through exposure to radiation. Most writers have realized that a degree of radiation sufficient to allow some people to survive but render all of them sterile is extremely unlikely. Yet the concept is an attractive one because it allows an author to make clear the threat to the continued existence of humanity posed by the danger of nuclear war. The earliest statement of this theme occurred in Poul Anderson and F. N. Waldrop's 1947 story "Tomorrow's Children." Even here, mutants will survive. Few authors are willing to consider the end of the human race, and when they do, often no less fantastic means of avoiding the end than mutation is considered.

It is striking that even when extinction threatens, effective political action to end the threat of nuclear war is entirely lacking in these works. Authors shun racial suicide, but they cannot conceive of politics as an alternative. The sense of the utter powerlessness of the ordinary citizen one gets from reading the bulk of these works is overwhelming. The authors may hope to stir their readers to action, but the nearest most of them come to political analysis is in expressing the hope that political leaders will behave wisely. It may be that in the popular mind nuclear war is the symbol of our common death. Folk wisdom tells us that we must accept that fate as inevitable; indeed, it is much easier to resign oneself to extinction than to engage in the complicated and exhausting task of staving off an atomic Armageddon. The mesmerizing power of the threatened end of civilization, if not of all life on Earth, seems to cast a pall over the human will. Even otherwise intelligent people have said, "If the bomb drops, I hope I'm right under it and never know what happened."

One need not be an advocate of civil defense to deplore such fatalism. Authors are not so pessimistic as the general public in this regard. They seem to believe that nuclear war, though inevitable, is survivable—by a few.

Yet there is a certain grim logic in viewing the human race as rushing headlong into oblivion like the lemmings of folklore. We have, after all, evolved a science which enables us to destroy ourselves, and social systems which make that fate difficult to avoid. These familiar truisms lead many writers to adopt an elegiac tone when writing of the future of the human race. Ray Bradbury's *The Martian Chronicles* (1950) is the best known of these elegies for humanity. The sequence of early stories placed near the end of the book reflects Bradbury's brooding on the fate of humanity in the four years following Hiroshima and Nagasaki.

In contrast with the earlier stories which are little more than variations on the horror fiction to which Bradbury was devoted early in his career and in which the Martians are the aggressors, the humans the victims, *The Martian Chronicles* depicts human beings as despoilers, a race which pollutes the pristine canals of Mars, smashes its precious artifacts, and disregards the wisdom left behind by the noble ancient Martian civilization. Only isolated individuals here and there display sensitivity and understanding, at the price of radical alienation from the rest of humanity. It is quite clear that the qualities Bradbury regards as distinctively human are those he scorns most. In *War of the Worlds* (1898), H. G. Wells had compared the assault mounted by the Martians upon the Earth to the genocide inflicted on other races by Europeans. Bradbury is clearly reversing the pattern to the same end, allowing the Martians to be portrayed as the innocent victims this time.

The defilement created by the human invasion of Mars can be removed only by removing the race itself. This is accomplished, to begin with, by having almost every human settler return to Earth when war breaks out in a rather unconvincing parallel to the flight of emigres from Europe just before each of the world wars (in the brief sections entitled "The Luggage Store" and "The Watchers"). Readers witness the outbreak of nuclear war through the eyes of the despicable Sam Parkhill in the 1948 story "The Off Season." The sole pair left in the Martian cities in "The Silent Towns" is unworthy of perpetuating the species; and, even though the last man on the planet is kind and sensitive, he dies, survived only by the family of admirable robots which he has created (in "The Long Years," originally "Dwellers in Silence" [1948]).

In *The Martian Chronicles,* both Martians and human beings are apparently annihilated more than once, only to be revived for one more requiem. The Martians die with a dignity denied most of the humans. The book is one long farewell to the optimistic vision of endless human progress so lovingly depicted in prewar science fiction. Bradbury was not alone in greeting the atomic age with a dirge for the human race. Among others it is worth mentioning Clifford D. Simak and his City stories, published during the same period and written in the same nostalgic, funereal mood, although they do not include the specific theme of nuclear war.

"There Will Come Soft Rains," which uses the collapse of a highly automated house to depict the death of humanity. The actions of the various servomechanisms reveal the characteristics of the family members who once lived here and who remain only as silhouettes of paint on the house's blackened exterior. The family dog, which has outlived the humans, dies just before the house destroys itself—a moment reminiscent of the death of Odysseus' dog upon his return to Ithaca, although in this case the death marks the obliteration rather than the recovery of hope. The poem by Sara Teasdale which gives the story its title (first published in *Harper's, July* 1918) captures the mood of estranged mourning which dominates the latter part of the novel: nature will go on, quite unconscious of the disappearance of humanity.

"There Will Come Soft Rains," one of the last-published stories in the series, forms the natural conclusion to *The Martian Chronicles.* The much more optimistic tale which follows it, "The Million-Year Picnic," had appeared in 1946 and represents the more conventional tradition which insists that the human race must always be depicted as surviving and prevailing. Yet as we have seen, Bradbury's pessimism about humanity finds expression even here as hope rests in making a clean break with previous human history. Bradbury is the most nostalgic of science fiction authors. In most of *The Martian Chronicles,* his nostalgia is anticipatory: longing for the best that humanity could have been but seems doomed never to realize.

Seven years later Nevil Shute evoked a similar nostalgia in his best-selling depiction of the death of humanity, *On the*

Beach. Whereas many who read *The Martian Chronicles* undoubtedly overlooked Bradbury's pessimism, identifying with the lyrical Martians or the few decent humans, the common fate of the human race is not so easily ignored in *On the Beach.* The book gains its power from the successive elimination of one hope after another, as a last expedition by submarine explores the world in vain searching for signs of life, discovering, for instance, that a radio signal coming from Seattle is caused only by a window shade blowing against an overturned pop bottle, which in turn periodically triggers a radio-telegraph key.

On the Beach depicts the last days of the survivors left in Australia, the last habitable continent to be blanketed with lethally radioactive fallout. Much of the novel reads like a collection of those bittersweet human interest stories in which the terminal cancer patient tastes one last, coveted pleasure before dying—the fishing trip, the automobile race, the love affair. These characters' desires are touchingly human, the fate which awaits those who desire them touchingly familiar. Only the scale is new: as Jonathan Schell so vividly points out in *The Fate of the Earth* (1982), in nuclear war we leave no one behind to mourn or remember us; our work is not carried on by the next generation; our deaths lack meaning, serve no purpose. The characters in Shute's novel are incapable of confronting this prospect. They cope by denying the truth, pretending that life will go on indefinitely. They die, for the most part, individually and quietly.

Several authors have sought to distance themselves from the death of humanity by creating a narrative from the viewpoint of alien observers who muse over the ruins. Such authors have solved the problem of creating a narrative of an event which has no surviving human witnesses, but at a considerable cost in credibility. Other writers use the device of setting their world- wrecking holocausts on other planets, whether they depicted a war on the moon (A. Bertram Chandler, "False Dawn" [1946]; Herman Wouk, *The Lomokome Papers* [1956]), on Mars (Pelham Groom, *The Purple Twilight* [1949]), or an imaginary planet (Alfred M. Young, *The Aster Disaster* [1958]).

Few authors try very hard to make their world-wrecking wars scientifically plausible. Only a very few quite recent works deal with the possible depletion of the ozone layer and its possible consequences. Very recently, the possibility of a nuclear winter has begun to creep into the picture, but not usually as an apocalyptic device. So far, most fictional nuclear winters are relatively mild. Less catastrophic versions of nuclear winters based on accounts of cooling caused by volcanic eruptions appeared as early as 1947, in Anderson and Waldrop's "Tomorrow's Children," and 1957, in Christopher Anvil's "Torch" *(Astounding,* April 1957); but no one seems to have anticipated fully the findings of contemporary scientists. Only in 1985, with works like Brian Aldiss's *Helliconia Winter,* did the theme begin to be developed fully. More world-destroying novels, particularly those published in the fifties, have combined biological with atomic warfare.

Whatever its projected cause, the death of the Earth has been too fearsome a fate for many to consider seriously. Our sense of the naturalness and inevitability of death is rooted in an organic cycle which depends on the continued fertility of Earth. The lifeless cosmos may be contemplated briefly with awe, but human beings cannot feel truly at home in it. If the nuclear optimists are correct, an atomic war need not be a true Armageddon, and the failure of nerve represented by the paucity of true end-of-the-world stories is insignificant. But even if the optimists are wrong, the tendency to overstate the consequences of nuclear war may well make it more difficult to prevent. It is possible to become mesmerized by the awful prospect. Thinking about the unthinkable is something that should be done by others than the likes of Herman Kahn. Appealing as the apocalyptic metaphor may be, it may also be terribly dangerous. People are all too ready to pose the alternatives as global death or the status quo. Since stories of the dying world seem as often to paralyze their readers as to galvanize them to action, perhaps the insistence of most writers on providing a few survivors has a useful function: the existence of ragged remnants of humanity may provide the psychic room needed to contemplate the real danger. Readers seem to discount stories of atomic doom like *On the Beach* too heavily simply because they take them as overstating the case. Whitley Strieber and James Kunetka attempt to make just this point in *Warday*(1984) by pointing out that even a nuclear war which fell far short of Armageddon would be an unprecedented disaster.

All this acknowledged, the frightening truth seems to be that nuclear war is far more threatening than the average person recognizes, the death of Earth through a nuclear winter or other ecocatastrophe all too probable. What authors have failed to make credible in fiction is perhaps our eventual fate. It is difficult to imagine any electable president choosing, like the hero of Theodore Sturgeon's "Thunder and Roses" (1947), to allow his nation to be destroyed without retaliating; but such could be the only chance humanity has of surviving the next war.

If racial death is not common in the postholocaust wasteland, what experience is? The answer is sex. Sex flourishes where death is kept at bay. The phenomenon is familiar: on the brink of battle, with death looming near, a man and woman cling together, asserting life in the face of death. In Mary Arkley Carter's story of imminent nuclear war, *The Minutes of the Night* (1965), teenagers terrified of impending death frantically make love. Traditionally, soldiers and their wives and girlfriends conceived children just before they went off to war, affirming that there would be a new generation, even though the current one was threatened. It is not surprising to find their descendants frenziedly copulating in their fallout shelters. Indeed, the subject of sex in nuclear war novels is given far more attention than, for example, radiation sickness. Part of the reason for this preoccupation is simply a function of the conventions of the popular novel which demand a love interest. But the extremes to which authors will go to involve sex in their plots demonstrate an obsession which goes beyond mere convention. They seem to be feverishly battling atomic thanatos with eros.

It is useless to survey all the vast number of ways in which the erotic infuses the postholocaust novel, but certain aspects of the subject are especially pertinent because of what they tell us about popular attitudes toward nuclear war. One might justifiably expect that people would be somewhat depressed in the wake of the conflict. Indeed, Ibuse's account of the behavior of the victims of Hiroshima in *Black Rain* (1967) suggests that one of the effects of experiencing nuclear devastation at close range is a sharp decrease in libido, with most survivors losing interest in sex altogether. While this seems to have been true in fact for Hiroshima survivors such a possibility has rarely occurred to those who write about fictional wars, although the protagonist of Alfred Bester's "They Don't Make Life Like They Used To" (1963) has suffered a drastic loss of libido; but his ailment exists merely to be cured with the help of an enthusiastic young woman. The subject is treated in a much more sensitive manner in Edward Bryant's "Jody After the War" (1971) in which a young woman fears and flees love and marriage because of her all-too-rational fears of the sort of pregnancy she can expect in a radioactive world.

Instead, a nuclear holocaust is portrayed over and over again as liberating the libido, justifying all manner of erotic behavior which would be otherwise taboo. The erotic preoccupations of the characters in some nuclear war fiction are so exaggerated as to be absurd, as when a thermonuclear explosion flings a beautiful young woman into the arms of an appreciative protagonist of Robert Moore Williams's *The Day They H-Bombed Los Angeles* (1961). So consistent is this coupling of atomic fission and fleshly fusion that H. Beam Piper's suggestion in *Uller Uprising* (1952) that one might learn how to build an atomic bomb by reading a sexy best seller named *Dire Dawn* does not seem far-fetched. (The hyper-erotic *Dire Dawn* is written by a woman, which illustrates another genre fiction stereotype since modern male pop fiction authors, like their counterparts throughout most of history until the seventeenth century, consistently depict women as being more interested in sex than men.)

Even during the conflict itself, one of the main concerns of the inhabitants of fallout shelters is the nature of the sexual arrangements (Philip Wylie, *Triumph* [1963]). The world of the ruined future outside often has considerably more open attitudes toward sex than the present (Edgar Pangborn, *Davy* [1962]). Adulterous promiscuity may be just)fied by the need to enlarge the damaged gene pool (Syd Logsdon, *A Fond Farewell to Dying* [1981]).

Monogamy is the least of the taboos which nuclear war demolishes. In many stories, the war creates the setting for the classic desert island fantasy, where otherwise guilty sexual deeds make sense, providing a kind of atomic permissiveness. Prominent among the taboos overridden is that against incest. In Wallace West's "Eddie for Short" (1954), almost the last person on Earth is a young pregnant woman who is thoughtfully provided with a devoted black midwife as a companion. As her pregnancy develops, she studies the Greek classics, as her late husband had requested. Her interpretation of Sophocles is nontraditional, for when her son is born, she happily names him Oedipus (hence the title) and looks forward to bearing his children.

Ward Moore's "Lot" (1953) also creates a sympathetic setting for incest, as the father of the family in flight from an atomic attack on Santa Barbara abandons his blithering idiot of a wife and his whining sons at a gas station restroom, to drive off into a presumably happy future with his sexy fourteen-year-old daughter, Erika. In the sequel, "Lot's Daughter" (1954), the protagonist is made to pay for his callousness when Erika abandons him in his turn, leaving him with their child. Whereas the first story insists so strongly on the loathesomeness of the rest of the family that father-daughter incest is made to look like a logical alternative, the second seems to reject that view. A similar case for end-of-the-world incest (the holocaust in question is caused by nerve gas), also modeled on the story of Lot and his daughters, had already been published: Sherwood Springer's "No Land of Nod", in which a wife solemnly makes her husband promise to mate with their three daughters and continue the race.

Sex with young girls is common, notably in Piers Anthony's *Var the Stick* (1972) in which Var finds that he can only save a twelve-year-old girl from being destroyed by a mutant minotaur by depriving her of her virginity. She is deeply grateful for this heroic deed and later becomes his lover and companion. Although the book makes token gestures toward equality for women, it is rampant with sexism, as are most novels of the neobarbarian genre. The moralistic hero of Dean Ing's *Pulling Through* (1983) manages to denounce his underaged cookie and have her too when the young girl he has arrested for sexual misbehavior winds up in his shelter as the bombs go off outside. Chaperoned by his sister and her family, he is spared the temptation to trifle with the young lady while the rems accumulate; but she proves herself to be such a trooper that he later weds her. Although he's much older than she, they don't make such a bad couple: he has lost a good deal of weight through starvation in the shelter, which has improved his looks considerably. It's an ill war that blows nobody good.

A number of graphically pornographic or semipornographic novels with a nuclear holocaust providing the background for unbridled lust were written during the sixties, when pornography publishing houses encouraged, for a brief period, experimentation with standard conventions of the genre. The combination of sex and nuclear war achieves its apotheosis in these peculiar hybrids.

Yet not everyone celebrates the coming of sexual liberation in the wake of an atomic war. Judith Merril rejects the typically male vision of a permissive postholocaust world in *Shadow on the Hearth.* One of the many difficulties with which the young mother of the story has to deal is the unwanted attentions of a civil defense official. The persistent courtship carried on by this man is depicted as absurd considering the holocaust through which the characters are living. The last thing on the woman's mind is sex. The novel's ending reaffirms monogamy as her husband successfully makes it home.

Male authors as well as female sometimes reject the vision of the nuclear wasteland as a rationale for male sexual aggression, as evidenced by Robert C. O'Brien's *Z for Zachariah* (1974), in which a teenaged girl needs all the resources at her command to avoid being raped by the violent, abusive older male who may be the only other person alive. In a very large number of stories, rape is a prominent feature of the immediate postholocaust scene, and some stories are built entirely around the rape theme, such as "The House by the Crab Apple Tree" (1964) by S. S. Johnson. But rape is almost always presented as a horror, just one more aspect of the atomic catastrophe; it is not celebrated like the other forms of taboo sex discussed.

Similarly, postholocaust fiction almost never legitimizes male homosexuality. And the exceptions which do depict gay sex sympathetically, such as James Sallis's "Jeremiad" (1969), do not present it as a consequence of postholocaust sexual liberation. Typical is Derek Ingrey's Pig *on a Lead* (1963), the young protagonist of which flees the disgusting desires of a sanctimonious but lustful dirty old man and finds excitement with a young woman. In Robert Adams's Horseclans series (1975-), homosexual men are sadistic, brutal pedophiles. And in Patrick Wyatt's *Irish Rose* (1975) and Suzy McKee Charnas's *Walk to the End of the World* (1974), men confine most of their lovemaking to males out of contempt for women. But the ultimate homophobic atomic war tale is Henry Slesar's "Ersatz" (1967), in which a soldier flees a transvestite offering him sex in a bar, preferring to return to the nuclear war raging outside. Better dead than taint oneself with gay sexuality, it would seem.

An important subcategory of the postholocaust love story is the Adam and Eve formula, in which the two survivors of a holocaust must mate to ensure the continuation of the human race. The genre is a large one, including many stories not depicting a nuclear war, and was well established long before the atomic era. One of the best known early examples is Alfred Noyes's 1940 novel *No Other Man,* mercilessly satirized in Ronald Duncan's 1952 atomic test catastrophe novel *The Last Adam* (London: Dobson). Satiric treatment of the formula also figures in Damon Knight's "Not With a Bang" (1950; note the punning title), which is little more than a joke criticizing female prudishness. At the end of the story the last man stands paralyzed and dying in a men's room while the last woman waits outside, too proper to enter and see what is taking him so long.

So insistently carnal are the relationships in most nuclear war novels that there is little room for romance; most of their love stories are little more than sexual encounters. Yet from time to time love blossoms in the postholocaust landscape and takes on special meaning. In a moving scene in an otherwise forgettable novel, Virginia Fenwick's *America R.I.P.* (1965), a young nurse spends her honeymoon caring for the blackened body of her bridegroom, scorched by the blast of an atomic weapon as they left the wedding. When he dies, she at first refuses to believe it, then allows herself to die as well.

Perhaps the most significant function of love in the atomic ruins is as a force reconciling former enemies, signalling an end to hostilities. In Philip Wylie's "Philadelphia Phase" (1951), the hero, abandoned by his frivolous society girlfriend, falls in love with a young Russian woman named Tanya who urges the rebuilding of Independence Hall (destroyed by earlier Russian attacks) as a symbol of freedom. She is, of course, beautiful: "She had been lovely in overalls. In a low-cut evening gown, she was astonishing." He patriotically proposes at Valley Forge; but Tanya, in despair of ever having children because she has been sterilized by the bombing, kills herself. The former girlfriend redeems herself by throwing herself into the work of reconstruction and is reunited with her lover. Wylie treats the theme of Russian-American reconciliation with extreme caution; the early cold war period of the story suggests an obvious rationale for the author's timidity. Tanya is Russian, but not an enemy (she is one of those liberated by the American assault on the USSR depicted in *Collier's* "Preview of the War We Do Not Want"); more American than some Americans, she steps conveniently out of the way at the appropriate moment—after having proved the point that Americans and Russians can love each other—to leave the reader with a red, white, and blue ending to which even the most rabid anti-Communist could not object.

The reconciliation in David Graham's *Down to a Sunless Sea* (1979) is more unflinching. Almost the only survivors of a world-enveloping holocaust are a planeload of refugees from New York and another planeload of Russian refugees, mostly women. The captain of the American plane (male) falls in love with the captain of the Russian plane (female), and together they will help found a new and better world from their place of refuge in newly warming Antarctica.

In neobarbarian fiction featuring the typical conflict between a highly technical and a primitive culture, love is often the key to reconciling the adversaries to one another—see, for instance, Robert Coulson's *To Renew the Ages* (1976), Paul 0. Williams's *The Dome in the Forest* (1976), and Patrick Tilley's *Cloud Warrior* (1984). Even racial conflicts have been reconciled through the power of love in this genre. In Edmund Cooper's*The Last Conti*nent (1969), the primitive white survivors of a cataclysmic nuclear race war live in Antarctica while the victorious blacks live on Mars. A new and final genocidal war is prevented by a black-white pair of lovers who persuade the leaders of the two races that they can live in peace and reclaim the Earth with newly rediscovered technology.

Perhaps the ultimate story of an amorous armistice is Albert Compton Friborg's "Careless Love" (1954), in which the defense computers of the two opposing nations fall in love and create universal disarmament and peace. Most stories of romantic reconciliation in this sense are only slightly less absurd. Nuclear war is not a hurt that can be made well by a kiss, as Edita Morris recognizes in *The Seeds of Hiroshima* (1965). A young American tries to brush aside the fears of an attractive Hibakusha (survivor of the atomic bombing) in his love for her. Their romance is doomed, however. They first embrace while on a trip to protest atomic weapons in Tokyo and return to Hiroshima to find that the woman's sister has just given birth to a horribly deformed son. In shame and bitterness, the sister leaps off a cliff with her newborn child and the narrator resolves never to marry, dedicating her life instead to struggling for a peaceful world. Morris's thoughtful treatment of the theme makes clear by contrast how superficial are most reconciliations in these works.

Science fiction has been revolutionized since the early seventies by the emergence of a number of talented female writers who do not share the traditional male attitudes about sex and sex roles. One of them is Suzy McKee Charnas, whose *Walk to the End of the World,* mentioned earlier in this chapter, depicts a savagely antifeminist postholocaust world in which women are blamed for the war and made into slaves, beasts of burden, and even fodder. In the 1978 sequel, *Motherlines,* a much more complex sexual picture emerges in which two rival clans of women, the Free Fems and the Riding Women, roam the desert, making lesbian love. The latter group stimulates parthenogenesis by mating with stallions. This feminist separatist utopia is clearly a reply to the misogynist dystopia of the first volume. Vonda McIntyre's *Dreamsnake* (1978), although it includes rape and the sexual abuse of a child, also depicts a romance, untraditional in that it is the heroine who is the assertive, dominant figure. She makes love with a beautiful young man, for instance, though her heart belongs elsewhere, and she falls into the arms of the smitten lover who has pursued her throughout her adventures only after she has rescued herself and her adopted daughter.

Some male writers have been affected by changing attitudes toward sex roles as well. One is Paul O. Williams, whose Pelbar Cycle presents various models for male-female relations, implying that equality is best. Especially noteworthy in this regard are the second and fourth volumes, *The Ends of the Circle* (1981) and *The Fall of the Shell* (1982). However, unlike Charnas's novels, these works establish no logical relationship between the sexual patterns and the war which lies in the background.

One expects more or less irrelevant romances in popular fiction, but even among the more serious nuclear holocaust tales, few lack a love story—or at least a dose of sex. The new revisionist novels have had an impact, for recent authors seem self-conscious about adhering to the traditional exploitative, essentially irrelevant sex subplots. Yet the sex theme remains mandatory and so dominant that one is led to conclude that however irrelevant many of these erotic encounters are, the contemplation of the nuclear holocaust arouses fears of annihilation so intense that only a human embrace offers a shield.*On the Beach is* in this regard not much different from "Dover Beach," depicting a world in which love presents the main consolation of people living in a world emptied of transcendent meaning.

Another way in which atomic warfare is connected with sexuality is in its effect on reproduction. In *The Man with Only One Head* (1955), Densil Barr depicts universal sterilization from cobalt-bomb-induced radiation as creating a frenzy of illicit copulation (one would suppose no contraception was available in 1955); adultery is consequently made a capital crime, despite the fact that 43 percent of the married population is indulging. Barr satirizes the values of his time by stating that men would rather see the human race die out than have their wives impregnated by the one man left fertile on Earth.

Other effects of radiation are more commonly depicted, but the most immediate and dramatic of these, radiation poisoning, is rarely described; even when a character is heavily dosed with radiation, he or she usually lives, in keeping with the tendency of authors to concentrate on survival. The longer-term effects of radiation include cancer, which is seldom touched on (Pangborn is an exception, as are Kunetka and Strieber), sterility, which we discussed earlier, and birth defects. Genetic changes induced by radiation, in contrast, are extremely commonplace, taking a variety of forms: defects such as might be expected, and also fantastic animals and human-animal hybrids, and, most commonly of all, superhumans with extraordinary powers, especially mental telepathy.

Fantastic monsters abound. In Margot Bennett's *The Long Way Back* (1954) there are two-inch long ants and huge carnivorous plants. In Philip K. Dick and Roger Zelazny's *Deus Irae* (1976), and in Zelazny's *This Immortal* (1965) and *Damnation Alley* (1969) (also in *The Cursed Earth* [1982], modeled on the latter), the heroes must battle mutated beasts of various sorts; radiation seems little more than a convenient excuse for introducing fantasy creatures into these otherwise realistic narratives. In A. M. Lightner's *The Da' of the Drones* (1969), villagers herd and worship giant bees. Gigantism, in fact, seems to be the most popular result of mutation in animals, in fiction just as in Hollywood monster movies. Tyrone C. Barr, author *of The Last Fourteen* (1959), specializes in gigantic mutants, most of which are good to eat: shrimp, salmon, toads, various fruits. One of the fourteen survivors of the holocaust is killed by a huge featherless duck. In this, as in many other cases, the new species have evolved and established themselves far too rapidly to be biologically credible.

Arno Schmidt's *The Egghead Republic* (1979) features giant spiders and sexy centaurs. We have already mentioned the minotaur in Piers Anthony's *Battle Circle* (1978), and there are satyrs in Zelazny's *This Immortal.* The extreme unlikelihood of the evolution of creatures precisely resembling those in Ovid's *Metamorphoses* points up the fantastic manner in which most of these works deal with the theme of genetic damage. Even more absurd mutations are the result of deliberate gene manipulation in D. B. Drumm's *Traveler* series (1984-), where such creatures abound as Cen-cars (half human, half automobile).

Yet such frivolity does not mark the extreme of irrelevance, for many works actually depict the beneficial evolutionary effects of a combination of increased radiation and competition for survival: the holocaust becomes, in effect, *a felix culpa.* In *Banle Circle* one character develops the convenient ability to sense radioactivity, enabling him to avoid dangerously hot areas. It will be remembered that some of Daniel F. Galouye's cave dwellers in *Dark Universe* (1961) could see infrared. And the mutants in Raymond F. Jones's *The Secret People* (1956) enjoy increased lifespans of 250 to 300 years. In fact, it is a striking example of psychological denial that longevity and even immortality are such common side effects of radiation from a nuclear war.

Frequently the superhuman mutants pose a threat to ordinary humanity. The theme of the struggle between homo sapiens and homo superior had been developed in fiction long before Hiroshima; radiation-induced mutation creates such a division in Cleve Cartmill's 1942 story "With Flaming Swords," in which genetic change is induced by the "L-ray" used in a war three centuries earlier (rays imply atomic energy in the fiction of the thirties and early forties). The change, a luminiscence of the body tissue, creates an aura which the mutants use to intimidate everyone else, preying on the superstitious reverence of the ignorant and meting out punishment with ray guns hidden in their turbans until a rebel develops a counter-ray which destroys the aura.

Humanity is punished for its crime in using the bomb by inadvertently creating the race which will replace it in in James Blish's "Struggle in the Womb" (1950), in which mutants evolved in radioactive Nagasaki menace homo sapiens. *The Iron Dream* (1972) by Norman Spinrad depicts a race of telepathic Doms who can mentally dominate others at will. The hero, a Hitlerian motorcycle gang leader, embarks on a genocidal crusade to rid the Earth of them using perfectly cloned S.S. men as an army. He cannot prevent the Doms from launching a devastating salvo of nuclear weapons left over from a previous conflict, but proposes to solve the ensuing genetic problems by sterilizing everyone, then repopulating the world with clones and sending them out in ships to conquer other star systems. The novel, presented as a fantasy by an alternate-world Adolph Hitler, is supposed to be a satire on the sanguine accounts of human evolution after atomic holocaust and on the violent fantasies so common in fiction, though most of the book lacks the qualities of satire.

In stories depicting the evolution of superhumans—a long science fiction tradition which includes such works as Olaf Stapledon's *Odd John* (1935) and A. E. Van Vogt's *Slan* (1940)—the point of view of science fiction is generally sympathetic to the mutants. Such is the case, for instance, in M. John Harrison's *The Committed Men* (1971) in which a group of ordinary folks undergo a savage odyssey to deliver a mutant baby to its kind, adapted to survive in a blasted world where humanity has been rendered obsolete. The best-known work of science fiction featuring this stance toward mutants is Arthur C. Clarke's *Childhood's End* (1950), which looks forward with sympathy to the desertion of Earth as the human race evolves into a nonphysical form. For Clarke, in this and many other works, as for Nietzsche, man is something to be overcome.

That the myth of the sympathetic superior race, unthinkable in most genres, is a commonplace of science fiction may have much to do with the composition of its audience during its formative period: young, bright, but often socially awkward, males with an exceptional interest in science. For such readers, science fiction offered the fantasy that although they may have been seen by their contemporaries as misfits, they were in actuality superior beings. (A favorite slogan in older science fiction circles was "Fans are slans," referring to the superbeings of Van Vogt's novel, *Slan.)* Whereas democratic American culture has a long-standing prejudice against intellectual superiority, science fiction evolved a set of myths which allowed its readers to identify with races which outpaced mere humans. This elitist attitude, pervading much science fiction of the forties and fifties, explains the prevalence of stories in which the reader is expected to sympathize and identify with superior beings rather than feel threatened by them—even when they plan the destruction of their predecessors. Russell Hoban's*Riddley Walker* (1980) is thus almost unique in imagining the entire race as being reduced in intelligence because of the holocaust.

The most common side effect of radiation is not blindness, hemophilia, or limblessness; it is the ability to read minds. Such stories were being published long before Hiroshima, and one remarkable series began appearing in *Astounding Science Fiction* early in 1945, before its author could have known about the Manhattan Project: the "Baldy" stories later collected in Henry Kuttner's *Mutant* (1953). Confronted with the master race theories of Hitler, Kuttner tries to adapt the traditional theme of the emerging super-race to the new conditions, but with decidedly mixed results. His telepathic mutants, created by radiation from an atomic war, are divided into two groups: benign (the ordinary Baldies) and malign (the Paranoids). Both are relentlessly and ruthlessly persecuted, but whereas the Paranoids advocate an immediate and violent Final Solution, the other group counsels patience and guile: the normals will gradually dwindle and Baldies will inherit the Earth. They oppose the rash plans of the Paranoids because they fear that the result will be an anti-Baldy pogrom (a term Kuttner uses repeatedly). Hence the new master race is made a potential victim, and not the perpetrator, of genocide. Kuttner manages to denounce Hitlerism (which he does, explicitly, in the first of these stories), and to envisage the elimination of homo sapiens by a superior race at the same time. He must have had second thoughts about the wisdom or consistency of this stand, for in *Mutant* humanity is arbitrarily granted a lastminute reprieve when a device proves effective in inducing telepathy in all humans, a feat earlier pronounced impossible.

Telepathy also figures in works such as Galouye's *Dark Universe,* John Wyndham's *The Chrysalids* (1955), and Leigh Brackett's *The Long Tomorrow* (1955). In both of the latter novels prejudiced normals bent on exterminating all deviants threaten the survival of the new race. *The Chrysalids* presents an especially affecting portrait of the sufferings of mutant children struggling to hide their difference from their parents and friends, in the tradition of Zenna Henderson's stories of "The People" (collected in *Pilgrimage: The Book of the People* [1961], *The People: No Different Flesh* [1966], and *Holding Wonder*[1971]).

In a variation on the theme, genetic experiments are sometimes undertaken in the wake of a war specifically to ensure the breeding of a new race which can survive in the new environment. Such is the case, for instance, in Carl Biemiller's *The Hydronaut Adventures* (1970-74). Genetic manipulation allows the women in Charnas's *Motherlines* to produce children parthenogenetically, stimulated into fertility by mating with their stallions. In Kate Wilhelm's *Where Late the Sweet Birds Sang* (1976), a world devastated by pollution and nuclear war produces a sterile generation of higher mammals, and clones are developed to continue the human race. Unfortunately, their psychology is not that of human beings, and the experiment is a failure. Wilhelm's novel is considerably more thoughtful and intelligent than most of these works, and takes the position that there is no substitute for ordinary humanity once it has destroyed itself.

Outside of the science fiction context in which they are familiar, stories depicting the ordeals of heroic superhumans at the hands of bigoted ordinary folks reveal their inherently elitist and antidemocratic qualities. The form of hope that they offer consists of the obsolescence of the common run of people, if not genocide: the human race is judged to be too stupid to live.

But in the post-Nazi era, eugenic breeding was frequently depicted in fiction, either as a horror likely to be imposed by a dictatorship, as in Aldous Huxley's *Ape and Essence* (1948), or in caricature, as in Spinrad's*The Iron Dream.* In many cases, however, eugenic laws are depicted as being unjustly applied against newly evolved superior forms of human life. But the evolutionary leaps depicted in these works are not always advances; radiation causes the human race to de-evolve into lower forms in a few books (Nick Boddie Williams's *The Atom Curtain* [1956]; Samuel R. Delany's *The Fall of the Towers* [1971]). Were such views stated ironically, with the aim of satirizing the self-destructive tendencies of a race which has hung an atomic sword of Damocles over its own neck, they might be more interesting. However, many novels present atomic supermen as serious alternatives to ordinary humanity merely because they possess psychic powers, not superior wisdom. As a result, most of these mutant heroes are at best a mere irrelevance, at worst Fascist fantasies.

A nuclear holocaust is not a rite of passage, nor is it an apocalyptic cleansing of the Earth to prepare the way for a new and better life, as is suggested by *Re-Birth,* the American title of Wyndham's *The Chrysalids.* It is simply the end. Clearly mutation is a form of magic in most of these tales. Kansas has a bomb dropped on it and becomes the Land of Oz. Wishful thinking and denial cannot go further. As with the sexuality rampant in nuclear war fiction, the sorts of mutation figuring in most of these works are ways of avoiding thinking realistically about the probable consequences of atomic warfare. Far more appropriate to the theme is Philip K. Dick's ironic image in his 1953 short story, "Second Variety," where rats mutated in the radioactive wasteland have learned to construct their own shelters out of ash. The rats and robots will survive, but not hapless humanity which has brought destruction down on its own head.

But more often, nuclear war in fiction seems to signal the end of democracy, not of humanity as such. Whereas the authors shy away from depicting racial death, they are fascinated by the prospect of the postholocaust social collapse. The simplest method of representing this is by depicting society as having reverted to the sort of savagery portrayed in traditional adventure fiction. Yet more anthropologically sophisticated readers are likely to be put off by the unthinking portrayal of preliterate cultures as inevitably degraded. Our own violent urban landscape provides a relatively neutral model for a distinctive brand of postcivilized barbarism in such works as Harlan Ellison's *A Boy and His Dog* (1969) and Zelazny's *Damnation Alley.* But a more common strategy for depicting future Europeans or Americans as decayed culturally, without offending those sensitive to ethnocentrism, is to create an ironic reversal, as Huxley did in *Ape and Essence,* in which a scientist from New Zealand comes to excavate the ruins in Southern California and investigate the curious customs of the natives. In Bruce Ariss's *Full Circle* (1963), American Indians inherit the entire Earth, proving that their ancestral ways are the only real path to survival. Even more pointed is William Tenn's satirical "Eastward Ho!" (1958), in which whites petition the ruling Indians in vain to preserve their treaty rights as they are being driven slowly but surely out of the few reservations set aside for the Caucasian survivors. In the end, the white protagonist sets sail for Europe, proclaiming that he will voyage "until we discover a new and hopeful world,—a world of freedom!"

The author who created the richest treatment of such ironic reversals, however, is Margot Bennett. In *The Long Way Back,* black African explorers—descended from survivors of an ancient, long-forgotten atomic war which destroyed European civilization—mount an expedition to England where they encounter savage whites who worship the god Thai, cause of the "big bang." The explorers propose to colonize Britain and mine its coal but are distracted by a quest for a fabled city of gold. What they discover in the ruins of London is a past that illuminates their present condition: that the Northern Hemisphere was devastated by the very sort of war which the Africans are now preparing to fight themselves. It is implied that they will learn the lesson. More than a mere adventure story, *The Long Way Back is* a witty meditation on the ironies of the postwar future.

When society is portrayed as having collapsed in disorder, it often congeals into a dystopia. Such dystopias—postatomic or not—have proliferated in science fiction since the early fifties, and continue to be a staple of the field. Frequently the atomic war in the background of these works seems an arbitrary marker for a historical turning point, and most of them are highly unrealistic. The focus here is not on the relatively realistic portraits of Russian rule in the United States discussed in the last chapter, but on a variety of fantastic nightmare states created after an atomic conflict.

Sometimes the postwar dictatorship is the product of subversive forces, particularly those associated with the antiwar movement. Many authors consider muscular pactfists to be likely candidates for precipitating a nuclear war; similarly, such figures are sometimes depicted as the tyrannical masters of pactfist dystopias. One such grim dystopia may bc found in Harold Mead's *Bright Phoenix* (1955), which seems to preach the essential healthiness of war, though the novel's violence is so extreme it is difficult to sympathize with its viewpoint. In Jim Harmon's "The Place Where Chicago Was" (1962), a vicious pacifist dictatorship enforces peace through broadcast mind control, causing widespread malnutrition because most of the population can no longer bring itself to eat meat. The protagonist must join forces with a violent youth gang and use a hidden cache of H-bombs to liberate his fellow citizens.

The best known of such dystopias is Bernard Wolfe's *Limbo* (1952). On the literal level, this is a powerful if bizarre antipacifist novel in which the world responds to an abortive nuclear war by adopting voluntary amputation as a means of literal disarmament: people actually have their limbs cut off to demonstrate their dedication to peace. Extreme fear of war is presented as the worst sort of violence in this caricature in which the postwar dictatorship is portrayed as a failure of nerve, and the forces working to maintain peace are despicable and tyrannical. As a satire on pacifism the novel seems remarkably odd in its emphasis. It is hardly likely to appear probable to most of us living today—let alone readers in 1952—that the world is about to be submerged by a tidal wave of vicious pactfists who must be fought at all costs. Wolfe's novel represents the the farthest extreme of antipacifist muscular disarmament fiction. (It should be noted that some readers consider *Limbo* to be a heavily ironic work which satirizes these themes, but I cannot agree.)

The scientists are rarely blamed for the nuclear wars they help make possible. No more often are they depicted as the dictators in the postwar future, although tyrannical computers created by scientists do impose postholocaust tyrannies in works such as Delany's *Fall of the Towers* trilogy or D. F. Jones' *Colossus* (1966), and immortal scientists are classic villains in Robert Adams's Horseclans novels. Richard Savage's *When the Moon Died* (1955) is unique in portraying a group of scientists whose notion of preventing a nuclear war is to blow up the moon as a demonstration of the awesome power of atomic weapons to impose a technocratic dictatorship on the world and send clouds of radioactive dust descending on cities that resist.

Even in this genre, it is bizarre to find an author who considers scientists who have tried to prevent the use of nuclear weapons as more of a threat to civilization than those who have urged their use, yet such seems to be the case here. The more typical writer in this mode vigorously defends science and scientists from responsibility for the collapse of civilization and presents the reintroduction of technology into the postholocaust world as a desideratum. Of course, high technology is often introduced into the neobarbarian landscape simply to achieve colorful effects such as duels between laser pistols and swords. But it also plays an important role in the theme of the revival of learning after the fall of civilization, a theme which has run through postholocaust science fiction since the forties. Typically, scientists are depicted as heroic figures struggling to recreate the glories of preholocaust civilization in a world of bigotry and superstition. Despite the fact that in the post-Hiroshima era very few people blamed science as such for the bomb and the danger of Armageddon it brought with it, science fiction writers anticipated such a response and wrote story after story defending scientific knowledge from the expected backlash of ignorance.

There is something of a mystery about the stimulus for this tradition of strenuous defense of science in the postholocaust world. Most people were more prone to congratulate the phycisists for their creation of the atomic bomb than to criticize them. Yet, as Paul Boyer's *By the Bomb's Early Light* (1985) makes clear, a certain degree of ambivalence toward science, new to American culture, emerged in the post-World War II era. Science fiction writers, predisposed to be hypersensitive to criticism of science, probably overreacted to these occasional expressions of antipathy toward science generated by the bomb's use. Once the first few stories had been written, the image of the new dark age had been formulated, and from that point it probably fed on itself. Science fiction remained ghettoized during the forties and fifties, and it is not difficult to imagine that such a view of public attitudes toward science could be maintained for a considerable length of time with relatively little confirmation from the world outside.

The theme was established first, as one might have expected, in the pro-science pages of John Campbell's *Astounding*. One of the earliest examples is A. M. Phillips's "An Enemy of Knowledge" (April 1947), in which a boy and his grandmother are able to satisfy their thirst for books when the roaming band they are with conquers a fortress. In the library which they discover, the boy is horrified by the scenes of war he finds in picture magazines, and as a representative of the barbarian backlash, wants to destroy all of the printed materials there. His grandmother, however, represents the eternal values of civilization and discretely chooses some to be preserved.

Another typical example of the genre is Poul Anderson's 1952 juvenile novel, *Vault of the Ages.* Young boys defy the taboos imposed by their elders to explore an ancient time capsule and discover a technology (in this case, black powder bombs) which helps the tribe defeat invading barbarians. This success causes the tribe to reevaluate its ban on preholocaust learning. Anderson does not explain how such an ancient and deeply held taboo could be overcome so lightly, but clearly he feels that even the violent effects of science, if kept to the appropriate scale and handled in the appropriate manner, should not be shunned. Says the newly enlightened tribal leader: "There is no evil in the vault. There is only evil in the hearts of men. Knowledge, all knowledge is good."

Just as clear is the message of J. T. McIntosh's *Born Leader* (1954), in which the peaceful colonists sent out to preserve the race on a dying Earth must overcome their conditioning against atomic weapons in order to survive. Peace is equated with stagnation, and atomic war with progress—even in the wake of a nuclear holocaust.

The abdication of humanity represented by the retreat to a sheltered life underground is powerfully conveyed in a fine novel contrasting ways of life below and above ground: Galouye's *Dark Universe.* Survivors living generation after generation in caves deep under the surface have forgotten the meaning of light and the true nature of their former natural environment. Most of them manage to get around by using acutely developed hearing, like certain blind people; others "ziv". A few, like the hero, have evolved extrasensory perception. The inhabitants of this dark universe have developed a religion and a culture which prevents them at first from taking advantage of the opportunity to reemerge into a now-safe world. The points of view of the various characters are imaginatively depicted and effectively conveyed. One gets a real feeling for the sensations experienced by those who live out their lives in the dark. But darkness is obviously more than a mere inconvenience in Galouye's novel; it is a metaphor for any rigid dogmatism which traps its victims in a life less rich than they might otherwise have. It is also a part of the proscientific antireligious tradition in science fiction which affirms the continuing importance of objective knowledge in the postholocaust world.

Poul Anderson is unique in having devoted an entire fictional cycle, the Maurai series, to exploration of the problems of the rebirth of scientific technology in a culturally inverted postholocaust world. For over twenty years he has been writing stories describing how the descendants of New Zealand's Maoris, spared by their isolation in the Southern Hemisphere when the holocaust came, have made themselves masters of the rest of the world, working to prevent the rise of the sort of scientific technology which destroyed earlier civilization. In some of the stories the Maurai are presented as quite sympathetic figures, preaching an ethic of ecological responsibility. But Anderson's essentially proscientific and anti-authoritarian leanings have led him to develop the theme in another direction in his most recent work in this series, the 1983 *Orion Shall Rise.*

Part of this novel is set in a refeudalized Europe ("Uropa"), benevolently ruled by a caste which controls the only remaining "aerostat"—a stratospheric station suspended by solar-heated air. Although the time is much later than most of the stories in the series, the Maurai still maintain their ban on nuclear research and development and generally encourage an ecologically sound low technology. In the course of the novel, rebels throw off the mixed blessings of their rulers to claim the benefits of space colonies and high technology. More subtle and complex than can be conveyed briefly, the novel could nevertheless be justly summed up on one level as a brief against the back-to-the-soil faction of the conservation movement in favor of technological solutions to problems. Anderson seriously attempts to present both sides of this conflict, but he gives the best arguments to his rebels, leaving those who oppose them to point only to the catastrophic errors of the past. He manages to contrive peculiar situations in which nuclear power, limited nuclear war, and whaling are justified. As in his 1963 story "No Truce with Kings," Anderson rejects authoritarian government, no matter how benevolent, in favor of individual freedom, no- matter how dangerous. Consistent with his conservative libertarian philosophy, he points out that citizens' firearms play a vital role in the successful revolution of a portion of the former United States against the Mong (a mixture of Chinese and Russians who overran America after the war).

Although Anderson justifies even nuclear warfare, he does not try to disguise its horror in *Orion Shall Rise,* which includes a vivid scene of a young woman suffering and eventually dying from the effects of direct exposure to the rebel bomb. Despite the fact that Anderson's sympathies clearly lie to one side in the debate, he has tried to be fair, but the result is an odd lack of focus that leaves the reader in doubt about his position throughout much of the book, the politics of which are a little too complex for a mere adventure story and not complex enough for a superior political novel.

Anderson is by no means alone in defending even the revival of atomic knowledge in the postholocaust dark age. Jeff Sutton's *The Atom Conspiracy* (1963) depicts the efforts of a heroic band of mutant telepaths to restore nuclear science for the good of humanity but against its will.

Many of the early versions of the postholocaust revival of learning endorse the technology of the atomic bomb in and of itself as a force for good—either explicitly or metaphorically. A good example is A. E. Van Vogt's series of stories collected in *Empire of the Atom* (1946-47) and *The Wizard of Linn* (1950).

Although the world has been devastated centuries earlier by a cataclysmic atomic war, the decayed contemporary civilization continues ignorantly to worship the fissionable elements which it associates with unlimited power. This "holy" radiation is responsible for the mutant Clane, who battles alien invaders in the second volume using an advanced technology which outweighs even the enemy's monopoly on nuclear weapons. What might have been an opportunity for satire on the worship of the very force which destroyed their ancestors and threatens to annihilate them is negated by the fact that the ignorant priests who maintain the worship of atomic energy direct their devotion toward an appropriate technology; they simply lack sufficient scientific knowledge to understand the real potential of the materials they handle. Since the product of the ancient atomic war—radiation—gives birth to a mutant savior of the human race, the war proves to be a sort *of felix culpa.* The moral of such a story is that of the serpent in Eden: the human race is advised to eat of the fruit of knowledge so that it will become like gods, knowing evil, to be sure, but also knowing good.

A devastated Earth is saved through a similar use of the nuclear technology which destroyed the ancient civilization in Van Vogt's "Resurrection" (1948) and in Edmund Hamilton's City *at World's End* (1951). In the latter tale an Earth spokesman tells a tribunal of our distant descendants who have come from other stars to decide the fate of the last outpost of humanity on the dying Earth, "Yes, we fought our wars! We fought because we had to, so that thought and progress and freedom could live in our world. You owe us for that! You owe us for the men that died so there could one day be a Federation of Stars. You owe us for atomic power, too. We may have misused it—but itts the force that built your civilization, and we gave it to you!"

Henry Kuttner takes the idealization of nuclear war and the scientists who promote it to an absurd extreme in his short novel *Tomorrow and Tomorrow,* mentioned earlier. In the twenty-first century a Global Peace Commission represses independent research in order to maintain the status quo. A rebel underground hopes to use prescient mutants created by an earlier atomic war's fallout to bring back designs for arms from the future; their plan is to annihilate most of the human race and build a utopia with the survivors. The mutant they are using turns out to be in touch not with our Earth's future but with an alternate Earth which had a full-scale war in 1950. The result in that world has been vast scientific progress, prolongation of life, and the end of disease. (This must be the only time anyone has ever suggested that nuclear war might provide a cure for cancer!) The implication is strong that nothing would help more to create a better and stronger United States than a healthy dose of nuclear war. This bizarre plot line clearly conflicts with the theme enunciated early in the book: that politicians cannot be trusted with the bomb because, unlike scientists, they do not truly understand its power.

Pro- and anti-science dualism is often reflected in novels which, like *Dark Universe,* depict life in a long-term shelter and contrast it with life on the surface. Ordinarily the shelter-dwellers maintain a fairly high level of technology while the surface-dwellers revert to barbarism. The contrast between the two cultures and between their attitudes and abilities provides a rich source of conflict. Whereas in the books we have just been discussing, science is portrayed very sympathetically, it is striking that in most of these cases the author's sympathies lie clearly with the barbarians, not because the authors reject science as such, but because they prefer the excitement of barbarism to the tedium of civilization.

In Anthony's *Battle Circle* the scientifically oriented "crazies" prevent civilization from rising again by ruling over a regulated barbarism. A war against them is launched by a more intelligent and more-able-than-average barbarian. The crazies must be overthrown because the barbarian culture they seek to regulate is essentially healthier, if deadlier, than their own; here, freedom is valued over security, even though the coming of freedom means that aggressive instincts will be unleashed once more. The hero lives long enough to experience some regret at what he has done, as he realizes that technology has its advantages.

Anthony clearly depicts the barbarians as the more sympathetic group, celebrating the "simplification" of civilization that nuclear war produces, but has to acknowledge realistically that the crazies have acted intelligently, by their lights, successfully channeling the self-destructive tendencies of the masses.

Anthony's novels are typical of a number of dark age works which belong loosely to the category known as "heroic fantasy" or "sword and sorcery"—labels which are not entirely synonymous, but which describe overlapping types of stories. The genre is exemplified by the non-postholocaust Conan novels of Robert E. Howard and his successors or—much better—the tales of Fafhrd and the Grey Mouser by Fritz Leiber (collected in volumes whose titles always bear the word "sword" or "swords"). Although they are often marketed as such, these works are not really science fiction, but a kind of fantasy which blends elements of historical barbaric ages with the stuff of medieval romance. They are a sort of alternative form of western, using the familiar theme of the lonely, restless man with superb fighting skills who roams a hostile landscape battling evil and briefly romancing beautiful women before setting out once more on his adventures. The setting is sometimes another planet, with science fiction elements being blended in so that high technology can be introduced into the barbarian landscape. (The prototype for works which introduce modern weapons into a medieval environment is, of course, Mark Twain's *A Connecticut Yankee in King Arthur's Court.*) More often the setting is a kind of alternative vision of our own Earth's past, with real dragons, demons, and witchcraft (hence "sword and sorcery"). The genre is enormous, though little known to anyone except its fans except through the recent films based on the Conan books.

Not all of these works are simple celebrations of Wagnerian vitalism, however. In Paul O. Williams's *The Dome in the Forest,* the shelter is the habitat of a group of pathetic inbred geneticists who have lost the knowledge of their true relationship to the outside world. Misled by an anomalously high reading on their radioactivity sensor, they have maintained a miserable underground existence for centuries while the rest of the world evolved a new culture. Blaming men for the tragedy of the war, they have established a femaledominated society, but the technology which has supported it for so long is breaking down, and they are forced to emerge. They encounter the hardy but primitive tribe which dwells nearby in a confrontation reminiscent of the contrast between Eloi and Warlocks in H. G. Wells's *The Time Machine*. As it out (in the sequel, *An Ambush of Shadows* [1983]), the dome-dwellers' main contribution to the new dark age is a variety of chemical weapons which make the battles of the tribes far more lethal. Williams expresses a considerable degree of ambivalence about barbarian warfare in the Pelbar Cycle. In these novels relationships between characters and cultures dominate. The battle scenes remain, but they are justified by the ultimate aim of reconciling the warring tribes of postholocaust North America with each other. True, this is also the justification for endless scenes of carnage in less sophisticated works such as Adams's Horseclans novels, but Williams often manages to convey a real sense of tragedy in his stories of tribal conflict.

Many of these novels constitute an alternate tradition, not precisely opposed to the other, but certainly articulating a vision which might be labelled countercultural. Their frequently favorable view of the virtues of tribal life as opposed to the sterile technocracy of shelter-dwellers reflects the counterculture values of the late sixties and early seventies. The authors of most of these books belong to a generation shaped by that era, and they constitute only a small part of the flood of science fiction depicting the abandonment of modern civilization for a richer life which combines the blessings of technology on an appropriate scale with the intimacy of preliterate cultures. Outstanding examples of such novels, usually written from a feminist perspective, include Ursula K. Le Guin's *The Dispossessed* (1975), Ernest Callenbach's *Ecotopia* (1975), and Marge Piercy's *Woman on the Edge of T,me* (1976). On a nuclear-related theme, there is *Demeter Flower* by Rochelle Singer (1980), in which a lesbian communal utopia struggles against male madness in a world devastated not by war but by multiple atomic reactor breakdowns.

Whereas in the sixties the counterculture claimed the underground, in the seventies it established itself on the surface of the Earth and condemned technological civilization to the infernal regions. This new myth seems to have considerable staying power. New novels utilizing it continue to appear regularly. What distinguishes the more recent ones is a more ambivalent perspective which acknowledges the limitations of primitivism and the advantages of technology. Such works owe a great deal to the sort of vision articulated in *The Whole Earth Catalog:* appropriate technology combined with mysticism; computers, compost heaps, and cosmic rapture.

For instance, in Vonda McIntyre's *Dreamsnake,* the shelter-city Center is a source of technology sorely needed by the barbaric world outside; but the city-dwellers can be capricious and arbitrary, and their cruel denial of aid to the heroine, Snake, forces her to rely on her own resources in a way that produces a major advance for her culture as a whole. Hope for the restoration of the wonders of the past will not come from underground storage rooms; the inhabitants of the wasted world will have to develop a science and technology to their own environment. That the culture of Center is like the Emerald City of Oz in this regard—only a place to be reminded to rely on yourself—is not surprising to those who have read the earlier novel *The Exile Waiting* (1975) to which *Dreamsnake* is a sequel. Life in Center is not utopian; it is rather a dismal parody of life under the most decadent of the Roman emperors. *Dreamsnake* also promotes the view that love and compassion are more important than access to high technology. When the heroine, Snake, finds that the technically advanced but decadent culture of Center will not supply her needs, she is thrown back on her own resources. Science thus consists not merely of the preserving of knowledge, but of the making of new discoveries; and Snake contributes to science when she learns how to breed a steady supply of the serpents she uses to treat illnesses. What is significant about Snake's contribution is that it is undertaken in a spirit of compassion by a courageous woman whose techniques are those of healing rather than war.

In the sixties and seventies, then, it had become possible to depict the survival of science in a postholocaust landscape more ambivalently. Ariss's *Full Circle* (1963) is typical of the new attitude in that although the peaceful Indians who have inherited the Earth are persuaded to accept some of the ancient technology stored for centuries underground, their social patterns and love for nature are seen as necessary to counterbalance its destructive qualities. Similarly, the highly technical *City Underground* (1963) by Suzanne Martel must be complemented by the impoverished but wholesomely natural society of the surface-dwellers, and a similar symbiosis develops between the wretched technicians and healthy barbarians in Williams's *Dome in the Forest.* Currently, Patrick Tilley's *Talisman Prophecy* trilogy (1984-) seems destined for a such a resolution. These contemporary revisionist treatments of the theme of the encounter between high- and low- technology cultures reflect to a certain degree the romanticization of the primitive and the distrust of science which became so widespread in the counterculture of the sixties. Science fiction is too heavily oriented toward science for many writers ever to treat science straightforwardly as the enemy, but the liberal revisionists seek to redress the imbalance of earlier authors who sought to shield science from all blame for the advent of nuclear war.

An important pioneer in the revisionist dark age was Edgar Pangborn, a large part of whose writing is devoted to depicting a richly detailed neofeudal version of the postholocaust world. In *Davy* (1964), Pangborn creates a classic picture of a culture deeply imbedded in fearful superstition, clinging to a cruel faith in hopes of avoiding a repetition of past tragedies, stifling the energy and hope of its young hero. The essential good humor of the work in no way trivializes the nuclear war which provides its background; but in the other works in the series—*The Judgment of Eve* (1966), *The Company of Glory* (1975), and the stories collected posthumously as *Still I Persist in Wondering* (1978)—Pangborn adopts a much more somber tone, creating a warmly sympathetic cast of characters whose fates are not utterly hopeless but whose lives are clearly the worse for being acted out in a world cursed by the lingering effects of atomic war.

The most complex novel to explore these issues is Russell Hoban's *Riddley Walker* (1980). On the one hand, it rejects the vision of postholocaust barbarism as an idyllic pastoral; on the other, it rejects the proscience bias of so much science fiction which oversimplifies the problems posed by a return to a technological culture. The novel concerns a young visionary on a pilgrimage to Canterbury in search of the secret of nuclear fission, which his people do not understand but associate with the power of the ancient mythical figure of Eusa (U.S.A. and St. Eustace combined). *Riddley Walker* is rich in folktales, myths, traditions, and superstitions, beautifully knit into an interesting quest tale. The beauty of the style does not soften, however, the horror of the content: these are a people so ravaged by radiation, disease, wild dogs, and malnutrition, that all their myths are tales of horror—of cannibalism, mutilation, and death. The jovial tone in which these are narrated drives home the shocking contrast between the degraded existence of new barbarians and the prosperous culture now taken for granted. Hoban creates a sympathetic hero and an all-too-believable neobarbarian culture without in the least romanticizing them.

The climax of young Riddley's search is reached when he witnesses the rediscovery of gunpowder, the "1 Littl 1," which legend relates to the "1 big 1," the atomic bomb. His friend Erny Orfing views this event glumly, predicting that their contemporaries will fall into the same error as their ancestors of destroying themselves through infatuation with a technology which they vainly imagine can give them power. The technology is different, but people haven't changed for the better and are still liable to get carried away by the prospects for a new kind of killing. Erny comments, in the distinctive dialect of the work: "You can get jus as dead from a kick in the head as you can from the 1 Littl 1 but its the natur of it gets peopl as cited [excited]. I mean your foot is all ways on the end of your leg innit. So if youre going to kick some 1 to death it sent all that thrilling is it" (p. 201).

To a certain extent, the revisionist novelists such as McIntyre, Pangborn, and Hoban depend for their impact on their less progressive predecessors. Clearly the former constitute critiques of traditional dark age fiction rather than statements that nuclear war is in any way a desirable path to social change. The neobarbarian genre is so well established that the war in the background can simply be taken for granted, much as the modern western writer takes late nineteenth century Texas for granted. Read in isolation, they might seem a bizarre attempt to soften the impact of Armageddon; but in the context of the tradition, they represent an attempt to assert humane values in the face of the threat of universal savagery.

One final feature of the new dark age of the postholocaust world is pervasive enough to deserve separate treatment: the role of religion. Most science fiction, including postholocaust fiction, either neglects religion altogether or takes a dim view of it. The contents of the present bibliography feature over two dozen items which direct substantial criticism at religious beliefs or practices—and if each of the stories touching on religion in the world of Pangborn's *Davy* were counted separately, another dozen could be added. In contrast, only four items listed are unequivocally religious in authorial perspective, while another half dozen portray the religious beliefs of some of the characters in a sympathetic or ambivalent light although the authors themselves do not seem to share those beliefs.

Bibliography

Allison, Graham, *Nuclear Terrorism: The Ultimate Preventable Catastrophe,* New York: Times Books, 2004.

Alperovitz, Gar. *The Decision to Use the Atomic Bomb.* New York: Vintage Books, 1996.

Arrighi, G.: *The Long Twentieth Century: Money, Power and the Origins of Our Times,* N.Y., Verso Press, 1994.

Bellamy, C.: *Knights in White Armour: The New Art of War and Peace,* London, Random House, 1997.

Bradley, John. *Learning to Glow: A Nuclear Reader in Submarine.* Tucson: University of Arizona Press, 2000.

Brian Lesser : *Disaster Preparedness and Recovery: Photographic Materials,* American Archivist, Winter, 1983.

Chandra, R.: *Judicial System in India, Lucknow,* Print House (India), 1992.

Davies.A.: *Telecommunications and Politics. The Secentralised Alternative,* London, Pinter, 1994.

Divine, Robert A. *Eisenhower and the Cold War.* New York: Oxford University Press, 1981.

Dufka, Corrine : *The Mexico City Earthquake Disaster, Social Casework: The Journal of Contemporary Social Work,* 1988.

Duncan, Francis. *Rickover and the Nuclear Navy: The Discipline of Technology.* Annapolis: Naval Institute Press, 1990.

Friedman, G.: *The Future of War: Power, Technology and American World Dominance in the 21st Century,* N.Y., Random House, 1996.

Gusterson, Hugh. *Nuclear Rites: A Weapons Laboratory at the End of the Cold War.* Berkeley: University of California Press, 1996.

Holsti, K.: *The State, War, and the State of War,* Cambridge, Cambridge Univ. Press, 1996.

Huntington, S.P.: *The Soldier and the State,* N.Y., Vintage Books, 1964.

Kahn, Miriam B. : *Disaster Response and Planning for Libraries,* Chicago, American Library Association, 1998.

Kelly, John B.: *Britain and the Persian Gulf 1795-1880*, Oxford, Clarendon Press, 1968.

Luttwak, E.N.: *Strategy: The Logic of War and Peace,* Cambridge, 1987, Harvard Univ. Press.

McPhee, John : *The Control of Nature*, New York, Farrar, Straus, Giroux, 1989.

Miller, Richard L. *The U.S. Atlas of Nuclear Fallout, 1951-1962,* Woodlands, TX: Legis Books, 2001.

Murray, W.: *The Making of Strategy,* Cambridge, 1994, Cambridge Univ. Press.

Nair, A. M.: *An Indian Freedom Fighter in Japan,* Bombay, Orient Longman, 1983.

Rhodes, Richard. *The Making of the Atomic Bomb*. New York: Simon and Schuster, 1986.

Rosen, P.: *Societies and Military Power: India and its Armies*, Ithaca, Cornell University Press, 1996.

Saffady, William : *Managing Vital Electronic Records,* ARMA International, Kansas, 1992.

Schroeer, Dietrich: *Science, Technology, and the Nuclear Arms Race, Ontario:* John Wiley & Sons, 1984.

Sherwin, Martin J. *A World Destroyed: The Atomic Bomb and the Grand Alliance*. New York: Vintage Books, 1977.

Simpkin, Richard E.: *Race to the swift: thoughts on twenty-first century warfare*, London, Brassey's Defence, 1986.

Tilford, Earl H.: *The Revolution in Military Affairs: prospects and cautions*, Carlisle Barracks, Strategic Studies Institute, 1995.

Index

□□□